First Print Edition [1.0] -1433 h. (2012 c.e.

Copyright © 1433 H./2012 C.E.
Taalib al-Ilm Educational Resources

http://taalib.com
Learn Islaam, Live Islaam.^{SM}

Requests to the Publisher for permission should be addressed to the Permissions Department, Taalib al-Ilm Educational Resources by e-mail: **service@taalib.com**.

Taalib al-Ilm Education Resources products are made available through distributors worldwide. To view a list of current distributors in your region, or information about our distributor/referral program please visit our website. Discounts on bulk quantities of our products are available to community groups, religious institutions, and other not-for-profit entities, inshAllaah. For details and discount information, contact the special sales department by e-mail: **servicc@taalib.com**.

The publisher requests that any corrections regarding translations or knowledge based issues, be sent to us at: **service@taalib.com.** Readers should note that internet web sites offered as citations and/or sources for further information may have changed or no longer be available between the time this was written and when it is read.

We publish a variety of full text and free preview edition electronic ebook formats. Some content that appears in print may not be available in electronic book versions.

ISBN EAN-13:   978-1-938117-13-8   [Soft cover Print Edition]
Library of Congress Control Number: 2012939879

GOLDEN WORDS UPON GOLDEN WORDS…FOR EVERY MUSLIM.

"Imaam al-Barbahaaree, may Allaah have mercy upon him said:

May Allaah have mercy upon you! Examine carefully the speech of everyone you hear from in your time particularly. So do not act in haste and do not enter into anything from it until you ask and see: Did any of the Companions of the Prophet, may Allaah's praise and salutations be upon him, speak about it, or did any of the scholars? So if you find a narration from them about it, cling to it, do not go beyond it for anything and do not give precedence to anything over it and thus fall into the Fire.

Explanation by Sheikh Saaleh al-Fauzaan, may Allaah preserve him:

'Do not be hasty in accepting as correct what you may hear from the people especially in these later times. As now there are many who speak about so many various matters, issuing rulings and ascribing to themselves both knowledge and the right to speak. This is especially the case after the emergence and spread of new modern day media technologies. Such that everyone now can speak and bring forth that which is in truth worthless; by this meaning words of no true value - speaking about whatever they wish in the name of knowledge and in the name of the religion of Islaam. It has even reached the point that you find the people of misguidance and the members of the various groups of misguidance and deviance from the religion speaking as well. Such individuals have now become those who speak in the name of the religion of Islaam through means such as the various satellite television channels. Therefore be very cautious!

It is upon you oh Muslim, and upon you oh student of knowledge individually, to verify matters and not rush to embrace everything and anything you may hear. It is upon you to verify the truth of what you hear, asking, 'Who else also makes this same statement or claim?', 'Where did this thought or concept originate or come from?', 'Who is its reference or source authority?'. Asking what are the evidences which support it from within the Book and the Sunnah? And inquiring where has the individual who is putting this forth studied and taken his knowledge from? From who has he studied the knowledge of Islaam?

Each of these matters requires verification through inquiry and investigation, especially in the present age and time. As it is not every speaker who should rightly be considered a source of knowledge, even if he is well spoken and eloquent, and can manipulate words captivating his listeners. Do not be taken in and accept him until you are aware of the degree and scope of what he possesses of knowledge and understanding. As perhaps someone's words may be few, but possess true understanding, and perhaps another will have a great deal of speech yet he is actually ignorant to such a degree that he doesn't actually posses anything of true understanding. Rather he only has the ability to enchant with his speech so that the people are deceived. Yet he puts forth the perception that he is a scholar, that he is someone of true understanding and comprehension, that he is a capable thinker, and so forth. Through such means and ways he is able to deceive and beguile the people, taking them away from the way of truth.

Therefore what is to be given true consideration is not the amount of the speech put forth or that one can extensively discuss a subject. Rather the criterion that is to be given consideration is what that speech contains within it of sound authentic knowledge, what it contains of the established and transmitted principles of Islaam. As perhaps a short or brief statement which is connected to or has a foundation in the established principles can be of greater benefit than a great deal of speech which simply rambles on, and through hearing you don't actually receive very much benefit from.

This is the reality which is present in our time; one sees a tremendous amount of speech which only possesses within it a small amount of actual knowledge. We see the presence of many speakers yet few people of true understanding and comprehension.' "

[The eminent major scholar Sheikh Saaleh al-Fauzaan, may Allaah preserve him- 'A Valued Gift for the Reader Of Comments Upon the Book Sharh as-Sunnah', page 102-103]

❦ *Is not He better than your so-called gods, He Who originates creation and shall then repeat it, and Who provides for you from heaven and earth? Is there any god with Allaah? Say: 'Bring forth your proofs, if you are truthful.'* ❧-(Surah an-Naml: 64)

Explanation: ❦ **Say: "Bring forth your proofs.."** ❧ This is a command for the Prophet, may Allaah praise and salutation be upon him, to rebuke them immediately after they had put forward their own rebuke. Meaning: '*Say to them: bring your proof, whether it is an intellectual proof or a proof from transmitted knowledge, that would stand as evidence that there is another with Allaah, the Most Glorified and the Most Exalted*'. Additionally, it has been said that it means: '*Bring your proof that there is anyone other than Allaah, the Most High, who is capable of doing that which has been mentioned from His actions, the Most Glorified and the Most Exalted.*' ❦**...if you are truthful.**❧ meaning, in this claim. From this it is derived that a claim is not accepted unless clearly indicated by evidences."
[*Tafseer al-'Aloosee: vol. 15, page 14*]

Sheikh Rabee'a Ibn Hadee Umair al-Madkhalee, may Allaah preserve him said,

'It is possible for someone to simply say, "*So and so said such and such.*" However we should say, "*Produce your proof.*" So why did you not ask them for their proof by saying to them: "*Where was this said?*" Ask them questions such as this, as from your weapons are such questions as: "*Where is this from? From which book? From which cassette?...*" '
[*The Overwhelming Falsehoods of 'Abdul-Lateef Bashmeel' page 14*]

The guiding scholar Imaam Sheikh 'Abdul-'Azeez Ibn Abdullah Ibn Baaz, may Allaah have mercy upon him, said,

'It is not proper that any intelligent individual be mislead or deceived by the great numbers from among people from the various countries who engage in such a practice. As the truth is not determined by the numerous people who engage in a matter, rather the truth is known by the Sharee'ah evidences. Just as Allaah the Most High says in Surah al-Baqarah, ❦ **And they say, "None shall enter Paradise unless he be a Jew or a Christian." These are only their own desires. Say "Produce your proof if you are truthful."**❧-(Surah al-Baqarah: 111) And Allaah the Most High says ❦ **And if you obey most of those on the earth, they will mislead you far away from Allaah's path. They follow nothing but conjectures, and they do nothing but lie.**❧-(Surah al-'Ana'an: 116)'
[*Collection of Rulings and Various Statements of Sheikh Ibn Baaz -Vol. 1 page 85*]

Sheikh Muhammad Ibn 'Abdul-Wahaab, may Allaah have mercy upon him, said,

'Additionally verify that knowledge held regarding your beliefs, distinguishing between what is correct and false within it, coming to understand the various areas of knowledge of faith in Allaah alone and the required disbelief in all other objects of worship. You will certainly see various different matters which are called towards and enjoined; so if you see that a matter is in fact one coming from Allaah and His Messenger, then this is what is intended and is desired that you possess. Otherwise, Allaah has certainly given you that which enables you to distinguish between truth and falsehood, if Allaah so wills.

Moreover, this writing of mine- do not conceal it from the author of that work; rather present it to him. He may repent and affirm its truthfulness and then return to the guidance of Allaah, or perhaps if he says that he has a proof for his claims, even if that is only a single statement or if he claims that within my statements there is something unsupported, then request his evidence for that assertion. After this if there is something which continues to cause uncertainty or is a problem for you, then refer it back to me, so that then you are aware of both his statement and mine in that issue. We ask Allaah to guide us, you, and all the Muslims to that which He loves and is pleased with.'

[Personal Letters of Sheikh Muhammad Ibn 'Abdul Wahaab- Conclusion to Letter 20]

Sheikh 'Abdullah Ibn 'Abdur-Rahman Abu Bateen, may Allaah have mercy upon him, said,

'And for an individual, if it becomes clear to him that something is the truth, he should not turn away from it and or be discouraged simply due to the few people who agree with him and the many who oppose him in that, especially in these latter days of this present age.

If the ignorant one says: "*If this was the truth so and so and so and so would have been aware of it!*" However this is the very claim of the disbelievers, in their statement found in the Qur'aan ﴾ *If it had truly been good, they would not have preceded us to it!*"﴿-(Surah al-Ahqaaf: 11) and in their statement ﴾ *Is it these whom Allaah has favored from amongst us?*﴿-(Surah al-Ana'am: 53). Yet certainly as Alee Ibn Abee Taalib, may Allaah be pleased with him, stated "*Know the truth and then you will know it's people.*" But for the one who generally stands upon confusion and uncertainty, then every doubt swirls around him. And if the majority of the people were in fact upon the truth today, then Islaam would not be considered strange, yet by Allaah it is today seen as the most strange of affairs!"

[Durar As-Sanneeyyah -vol. 10, page 400]

Fasting from Alif to Yaa:
A Day by Day Guide to Making the Most of
Ramadhaan

Translated & Compiled by:
By Umm Mujaahid Khadijah Bint Lacina al-Amreekiyyah as-Salafiyyah
With Abu Hamzah Hudhaifah Ibn-Khalil and
Umm Usaamah Sukhailah Bint-Khalil

Table of Contents

CONTENTS

Compiler's Introduction

In the name of Allaah, The Most Gracious, The Most Merciful

All praise is due to Allaah Alone. We praise Him, seek His help, and ask His forgiveness. We seek refuge in Allaah from the evil of our souls, and the adverse consequences of our deeds. Whomsoever Allaah guides, there is none who can misguide him, and whoever He misguides, there is none who can guide him.

I bear witness that there is nothing worthy of worship except for Allaah; He is alone and has no partners. I bear witness and testify that Muhammad, may Allaah's praise and salutations be upon him and his family, is His perfect worshipper, and messenger.

❧ *Oh you who believe, fear Allaah as He ought to be feared and do not die except while you are Muslims.* ❧–(Surah Aal-'Imraan:102)

❧ *Oh mankind, fear Allaah who created you from a single soul and from that, He created its mate. And from them He brought forth many men and women. And fear Allaah to whom you demand your mutual rights. Verily, Allaah is an ever All-Watcher over you.* ❧–(Surah an-Nisaa:1)

❧ *Oh you who believe, fear Allaah and speak a word that is truthful (and to the point) - He will rectify your deeds and forgive you your sins. And whoever obeys Allaah and His Messenger has achieved a great success.* ❧–(Surah al-Ahzaab:70-71)

As to what follows: then the best of speech is the speech of Allaah, and the best guidance is the guidance of Muhammad, may Allaah's praise and salutations be upon him and his family. And the worst of affairs are newly invented matters (in the religion), and every newly invented matter is a misguidance, and every misguidance is in the Hellfire.

To Proceed:

Alhamdulillah, a few years ago my son, Mujaahid ibn Lacina, translated the book, "Fasting from Alif to Yaa" for some Muslim women's internet groups I was then a member of. Alhamdulillah, it received a very positive response, and I believe it has been sent out more than once in the years since it was first posted. Mash'Allaah, this original translation was lost to us with a computer crash. So, when we decided to use this very beneficial book again in this compilation, we had to translate it again. Two of my other children, Abu Hamzah, Hudhaifah ibn Khalil and Umm Usaama, Sukhailah bint Khalil, assisted me in this endeavor, may Allaah reward them.

As we were translating I began to think of ways that perhaps we could add to the benefit of this small treatise. First and foremost, it seemed important to stress the importance of knowledge and beneficial action- and to give people clear examples of how to implement what they were learning in their everyday lives. Insh'Allaah this could assist them not only in the blessed month of Ramadhaan, but year round, in every aspect of their lives. To accomplish this, I added additional points of benefit under each letter in a section titled "Further Points of Benefit." This is based upon the theme of the letter of the day, and draws largely upon rulings and talks given by Sheikh Muhammad ibn Saalih al-'Utheimeen and Sheikh Saalih ibn Fauzaan ibn 'Abdullah ibn Fauzaan, alhamdulillah.

Secondly, I wanted to help parents get their children involved in Ramadhaan as well. As sister Murfat mentions in her booklet, "You have an excellent example in the salaf, the righteous predecessors; for the Companions, may Allaah be pleased with them, would have their small children fast and they would give them toys of wool- then if they asked for food, or one of them cried from hunger, they gave him those toys to distract them until they finished their fast."

We want to encourage our little ones to fast as they are able to, and to reward them for this; and if we can do this through educating and entertaining them with that which is beneficial, then that is ideal, mash'Allaah. So in the "Family Time" section of each chapter we have chosen to tell the story of one of the Prophets, whose examples we should strive to follow, and to add activities related to his story. The stories are not in order, mash'Allaah, and all of the prophets and messengers are not included, as this would be beyond the scope of this work. All of the stories of the prophets and messengers are based upon an authenticated and checked version of "Tafseer ibn Katheer," and so, insh'Allaah should be the true and authentic stories. On the few days in which we did not choose to do this, we have made special iftaar menus that highlight different Muslim countries, along with recipes- so that our children begin to understand the universality of Islaam and our connection to Muslims all over the world, insh'Allaah. This section is not so much a step-by-step guide to each activity; rather it is meant to give us and our children ideas and get started on making something beneficial that will help in remembering the story of the prophet or messenger just learned about, insh'Allaah.

I pray that this compilation benefits the Muslims, and that Allaah accept it from us as a good deed done seeking His face alone. I ask that he guide the Muslims and give us success in both this life and the next, and that He assist us in taking full advantage of this blessed month of Ramadhaan.

Umm Mujaahid Khadijah Bint Lacina
Ash-Shihr, Yemen
14 Sha'ban 1432

[Corresponding to the May 13th of 2006 C.E.]

Introduction from Original book "Fasting from Alif to Yaa"
By Murfat bint Kaamal ibn 'Abdullaah Usrah

All praise is due to Allaah Alone. We praise Him, seek His help, and ask His forgiveness. We seek refuge in Allaah from the evil of our souls, and the adverse consequences of our deeds. Whomsoever Allaah guides, there is none who can misguide him, and whoever He misguides, there is none who can guide him. I bear witness that there is nothing worthy of worship except for Allaah; He is alone and has no partners. I bear witness and testify that Muhammad, may Allaah's praise and good mention be upon him and his family, is His perfect worshipper, and messenger.

To Proceed:
Indeed, the blessed month of Ramadhaan is from the greatest times for good for the Muslim Ummah.Allaah, the Most High, says, "The month of Ramadhaan in which was revealed the Qur'aan, a guidance for mankind and clear proofs for the guidance and the Criterion (between right and wrong). So, whoever of you sights (the crescent on the first night of) the month (of Ramadan, i.e. is present at his home), he must observe saum (the fast) that month." (Surat al-Baqarah, From Ayat 185)In this summarized guide it pleases me, my Muslim sister, to set before you some of the rulings and benefits related to the fast arranged in alphabetical order, and that which I adhered to in this was utilizing a small amount of information and presenting it in a summarized manner.
And it is a small endeavor. I ask Allaah, Mighty and Majestic, to benefit me and you through it, and to make it a righteous action performed solely for the face of The Most Generous, following the Sunnah of His Prophet, may Allaah's praise and salutations be upon him. So if I fulfill this goal, then it is from Allaah and all praise is due to Him Alone, and if I am in error, then it is from myself and the Shaytaan, and I ask for Allaah's forgiveness.
Lastly, do not forget, oh sister, the author of these lines, making du'a for her good.

End of Sister Murfat's Introduction

Day 1:
The Letter أ: اللإحتساب (al-Ihtisaab)
(consciously seeking the reward of Allaah with good deeds)

What is meant by this is being conscious of seeking the reward from Allaah, the Most High, with acts of obedience, seeking the Face of The Most Generous, as in the fast of Ramadhaan.

The Prophet, may Allaah's praise and salutations be upon him, said, *{The one who fasts Ramadhaan with faith and seeking the reward with Allaah, all of his previous sins will be forgiven.}* (Agreed Upon)

So take care, my noble sister, that your fast is performed desiring the reward of Allaah, and seeking Allaah's Face, Mighty and Majestic is He, without anything other than that, in order to earn the great reward.

And remember that seeking the reward of Allaah when performing good deeds has comprehensive rewards. From the most important of them are:

1. The fulfillment or actualization of purity of intention (الإخلاص) *al-ikhlaas*

2. Staying away from showing off

3. Strengthening one's faith

4. Achieving happiness in both worlds

Also, seeking the reward of Allaah changes commonplace activities (such as sleeping and eating) into worship.

So seek the reward of Allaah when you are making the food for your family and guests to break their fast with, keeping your eyes on the Prophet's, may Allaah's praise and salutations be upon him, saying,

{The one who feeds the one who is breaking his fast has a reward like that of the fasting person, except that it does not take away any reward from the one who is fasting.} (Ahmad, and Sheikh al-Albaani has declared it to be authentic)

Further Points of Benefit

Mash'Allaah, the matter of intention is one that can change our lives, for the better or for the worse. At best, when we consciously strive to make every act we do in every moment of every day intended for Allaah alone, we truly begin to realize the meaning of the verse, *I did not create the Jinn nor the men except to worship me.* Thus we strive to worship Him in all that we do, from the most mundane acts of cooking or cleaning, to our prayer, charity and fasting.

In Islaam, all actions can be broken down into five categories: waajib, mustahab, mubah, makrooh, and haraam. [make 3x5 cards]

Waajib: if an act is waajib, it is obligatory that the Muslim carry it out. He will be punished if he does not perform it, and rewarded for performing it. For example, the five daily prayers, the obligatory charity, and the fast of Ramadhaan.

Mustahab: These acts are recommended. They are pleasing to Allaah, and the doer will be rewarded if he does them. He will not, however, be punished if he does

17

not do them. An example of this is would be the night prayers, and fasting outside of Ramadhaan.

Mubah: These are neutral acts…the doer is neither rewarded nor punished for doing them; for example, choosing to eat from that which is halal for us, such as to choose either chicken or beef for a meal.

Makrooh: These acts are disliked. It is something that does not please Allaah, but there is no specific punishment set aside for it. For example, drinking while standing up, wearing one shoe, or unnecessary movement in the salaat.

Haraam: These are the forbidden acts. If one does them, he is punished by Allaah, and if he leaves them, he is rewarded for obedience to Allaah. An example would be to drink alcohol, to tell a lie, or to associate others with Allaah in worship.

A very good habit to get into, insh'Allaah, is to examine whatever action we are about to perform, and contemplate what its ruling is from the above list. Then, see how we can raise it in rank, so that we get more reward for it.

So today, this first day of Ramadhaan, when you sit down to read and recite Qur'aan in the morning with your children, look into your heart and see why you are doing it. Is it to show your husband what a good mom you are? Is it because it takes your mind off eating? See if you can make your intention solely to please Allaah in this- through doing it for Him alone. When you are cooking *iftaar* for your friends- think about if you are making a certain dish to show off what a good cook you are. If so, try to rectify your intention by making it to please them and honor your guests, and to get the rewards of helping them break their fast- thus doing it to please Allaah.

And this works for common everyday actions as well. You are trying to decide whether to make lasagna or cheeseburgers for supper, and you remember that your husband loves lasagna- so you make this to please him, and thus to please Allaah. You keep the house clean and tidy because it makes your husband happy- thus pleasing Allaah. You give some old clothes to a needy person instead of throwing them out, even though it is a bit more difficult- doing it to help them and please Allaah. The possibilities are endless, alhamdulillah, for us to live consciously, striving always to worship Allaah.

And remember, my sisters, that making our intentions to other than Allaah can constitute either minor or major shirk. Sheikh 'Abdul Lateef ibn 'Abdur Rahman, may Allaah have mercy upon him, says, "As for *shirk* of purpose and intention, then that is the sea which has no shore, and few are those who escape from it. As the one who desires by his actions other than the face of Allaah, the Most High, or intends something for a reason other than drawing nearer to Allaah, and seeks a portion from it, then he has committed *shirk* in purpose and intention" (as quoted in "al-Waajibaat, the Obligatory Matters")

Family Time

Islaam is a complete way of life for us, alhamdulillah. If we truly believe in Allaah and all that He revealed, and all that the Prophet Muhammad, may Allaah's praise and salutations be upon him, taught us, and act upon what we know and believe, then our whole lives are colored by the paintbrush of our Islaam.

Eemaan is an Arabic word that means, simply, faith. If we have *eemaan* in something, then we believe in it, and trust in it. A Muslim is commanded by Allaah to have *eemaan* in six things. These are:

1. Allaah. We know and understand Allaah through what He has taught us about Himself in the Qur'aan and from the sayings of the Prophet Muhammad, may Allaah's praise and salutations be upon him.

2. His angels. We believe that Allaah created angels from light, and that they are real, true, beings, created to worship Allaah. We don't know how many of them there are, but they perform many duties for Allaah, such as writing down our good and bad deeds. There is one angel, Jibreel, who is responsible for carrying Allaah's message to His chosen prophets and messengers.

3. His books. Allaah has sent books down to the people on earth in order to guide them to that which is right, and to keep them away from that which is evil. We know the names of some of these books, such as the Injeel and the Tawrah, but there are some we do not know the names of. We believe in all of them, whether we know their names or not. Allaah sent the Qur'aan to all of the mankind and the jinn, to guide them for the rest of time, alhamdulillah.

4. His Messengers. Allaah has chosen some men to be His prophets and messengers here on earth. The prophets are chosen to carry the message of the book that has come before them to the people, while the messengers are chosen to bring and teach a new book. The Prophet Muhammad, may Allaah's praise and salutations be upon him, is the last and final prophet and messenger, sent with the Qur'aan for all of mankind and the jinn to follow.

5. The Day of Judgment. Allaah has created a set time for the earth to exist, and for us all to live upon it. At the end of this time there will come a day when every creature will stand up and be asked about how they believed and acted during their time on earth, and they will be rewarded or punished for this. There are signs which we have been given to know when that day is near. After this day, the people will be sent either to a beautiful, wonderful Paradise as a reward for their goodness, or to the Hellfire to be punished for their evil deeds.

6. Divine Destiny. We believe that everything that happens, only happens because Allaah willed it. If we get sick, it is because Allaah willed this for us, and when we become well, it is because Allaah willed this for us. We must always keep faith in Allaah, and know that He only wants good for us, and try very hard to please Him in all that we do- everything happens for a

19

reason, whether we know the reason right away or not.

These are called the pillars of *eemaan*, or faith. Think of your eemaan as a building. If it is built upon these six pillars, and you understand them, and believe in them, and act upon them, then your building will be strong and upright. If, however, you do not believe in any one of them, or you do not act upon them, then the building of your faith will be weak and perhaps fall down. We must work very hard to be sure that our pillars are strong, and our building upright and good.

The Prophets and Messengers

Ramadhaan is a special time for Muslims. We are told that in this month we should increase in good deeds. One of the ways we can do this it to learn about some of our prophets and messengers. They were very righteous people- they really lived, and we know how they lived and believed and acted because Allaah has told us about this in the Qur'aan, and Prophet Muhammad, may Allaah's praise and salutations be upon him, has told us about them as well. They are very good examples for us to follow, as Allaah guided them to that which was best and most pleasing to Him.

They were people like us- they were happy sometimes, and sad sometimes, and they got angry. They were children, grew up to be grown-ups, many of them married, some of them had children, and when Allaah willed it, they died. They were people like us, but they were special, as well. Allaah taught them and guided them, and sent them as teachers, warners, and examples for all of mankind.

Allaah does not talk directly to us. Instead, He teaches and guides us through His prophets and messengers. Angel Jibreel is a very special angel that Allaah sends with His message to His messengers. One very special messenger you will learn about in this blessed month is Moosa- one of the things that made him special was that Allaah spoke directly to him!!!

Allaah sent different prophets and messengers to different people at different times, but the main message that they brought was all the same- and this was to worship Allaah alone. We have to know that Allaah is the One who created us and who gives us what we need to live. We have to know that Allaah is the only One worthy of our worship. We have to know that Allaah has beautiful names and attributes that are only for Him. Attributes is a big word, but basically what it means is that these are things that Allaah tells us about Himself. For example, He tells us that He is merciful. Our mothers are merciful too- but their mercy is nothing like Allaah's. Allaah's mercy is perfect and complete. Allaah tells us some of His names, like al-Khaaliq, the Creator. You can create pictures with paints and houses out of sticks, but Allaah is the Creator of everything. He made it so that you are able to build those things and make those things that you make, and He makes everything out of nothing!!! So His creation is perfect and complete. We learn about Allaah through the Qur'aan, and the Prophet Muhammad, may Allaah's praise and salutations be upon him, and Allaah has told us to learn about Him by looking around us and seeing the amazing things that He has created. Nothing is perfect except Allaah, and everything He does is perfect.

This month, we are going to tell you about some of Allaah's prophets and messengers. We aren't going to tell you about ALL of them, though. Also, some of them, like Prophet Muhammad, may Allaah's praise and salutations be upon him, have very long stories, and they did many interesting and amazing things- we can't tell you everything about them in our short stories. So after this month is done, you should keep on trying to learn about Allaah's prophets and messengers, and you should do your best to be like them in your everyday life, insh'Allaah.

Hands On Learning

1. Play a game to see how many prophets and messengers you know about. Do you know who they were sent to? Remember that though all of them were sent at different times to different people, their basic message was the same- the oneness of Allaah, and worshipping Him alone. You should know at least one of them already- Muhammad, may Allaah's praise and salutations be upon him, who was sent with the Qur'aan. He is the final prophet and messenger, and the Qur'aan is the final Book sent by Allaah until the Day of Judgment. Also remember that some of them were prophets, and some of them were prophets and messengers both.

    Some of the prophets and messengers are: Aadam, Nuh, Ibraaheem, Ishaaq, Ismaa'il, Yusuf, Ya'qub, Yunus, Ayoob, Daawud, Suleimaan, Idrees, Zakkariyyah, Yahya, 'Isa, Saalih, Hud, Shu'ayb, Lut, Moosa, Haarun, and Muhammad, may Allaah's praise and salutations be upon them all.

2. We are going to make a book of prophets and messengers this month. You will fill in a page every time you finish reading a prophet or messenger's story. Having this book will make it easy for you to review what you learned this month throughout the rest of the year, insh'Allaah. There are many ways to make a booklet like this. Here is one way, but you can use a different way if you like.

    First of all, you need heavy paper, like construction paper or cardstock. You will also need a paper punch, and some yarn or clips that you put through the holes, and then spread the tails out to either side to hold the book together. Decide how big you want your book to be. You can use a whole piece of paper for each prophet, or you can cut it in half and use a half for each. Count out 22 pieces of paper. Measure with your ruler down the left hand side of each paper to mark where you want to use your paper punch to make a hole for the binding. The holes should be about an inch apart. After you have marked them, punch them out with the paper punch. Place your papers in a neat pile, making sure all the edges are straight and your holes line up. Use your special paper tacks or yarn to hold the papers together. For the yarn, you simply weave through the holes a few times to make the binding. The top page is for you to decorate however you like- it is the cover of your book. The bottom page is the back of your book. Each page inside will be for one of the prophets, as you learn about him this month, insh'Allaah. Use your imagination! You can use markers, crayons, glitter glue, construction paper- whatever you like- to make each page different and fun to look at, insh'Allaah!

Day 2:
The Letter ب: البشارة
(*al-Bishaarah*) (glad tidings)

Praise Allaah alone, oh my sister, that this blessed month has reached you, and have glad tidings of much good if you turn to Allaah during it, with the correct intention.

The Prophet, may Allaah's praise and salutations be upon him, said, *{On the first night of Ramadhaan the Shayaateen and disobedient jinn are shackled, and the doors of the Fire are closed, and none of them are open, and the doors of Jennah (Paradise) are open, and none of them are shut. Also, a caller calls every night, "Oh seeker of good come forward, and oh seeker of evil, stay back". And Allaah frees people from the Hellfire- and this happens every night.}* (Ibn Maajah, and Sheikh al-Albaani declared it to be hasan)

He, may Allaah's praise and salutations be upon him, also said, *{Verily, in Jennah there is a door called ar-Rayyan through which those who fast will enter on the Day of Resurrection, and none other than them in will enter it. It will be said, "Where are those who fast?" and they will enter from this door. After the last one of them enters, then it will be shut so no one else can enter.}* (Agreed upon)

And our righteous predecessors used to say, when it became Ramadhaan, "Oh Allaah, the month of Ramadhaan has come and cast its shadow over us; so send it upon us with peace, and make us submit to it, and bestow upon us fasting and praying at night during it, and grant us sincerity and help us to strive during it, and give us strength and energy and protect us from trials during it."

Further Points of Benefit

Alhamdulillah, many of the people today seem to look on Ramadhaan as merely a time to gather with family and friends, eat rich foods, stay up late, and sleep half the day away. It is almost thought of as a holiday, mash'Allaah, rather than as the blessed month it truly is. When the glad tidings of the month of Ramadhaan beginning reach us, we should not start planning parties and feasts; rather, we should remind ourselves of the blessedness and uniqueness of this blessed month.

Look more closely at some of the characteristics of Ramadhaan mentioned in the hadeeth above:

1. The Shayaateen and disobedient jinn are shackled

2. The doors of the Fire are closed, and none of them are open

3. The doors of Jennah are open, and none of them are shut

4. A caller calls every night, "Oh seeker of good come forward, and oh seeker of evil, stay back".

5. Allaah frees people from the Hellfire

In what other month do all of these things happen? The answer is clear- only in Ramadhaan. How can we spend the whole month in sleep, gluttony and heedlessness when Allaah has granted us so many blessings unique to it?!? We should be striving to increase ourselves in good deeds- and this is through action of the heart, tongue and limbs. We should increase in reading and reciting Qur'aan. Now is a good time to review the hadeeth concerning the beginning revelation of the Qur'aan to the Prophet Muhammad, may Allaah's praise and salutations be upon him- truly a beautiful and amazing occurrence, alhamdulillah. We should strive to correct our intentions, to grow in certainty and love of Allaah and our religion. We should pray the prayers in a conscious, mindful manner, striving to make our hearts incline and our limbs prostrate as perfectly as we are able. We should be extra generous and kind to others, and remind them of the blessedness of this month and encourage them to righteous action as well.

1. Look at the supplication of the Pious Predecessors: Oh Allaah...

2. Send the month of Ramadhaan upon us with peace

3. Make us submit to it- to perform that which is obligatory for us to do in this month

4. Bestow upon us fasting – think of the people who use any and all excuses for not fasting, not even truly considering if their excuse is valid or not, or asking a person of knowledge concerning it, may Allaah protect us from that. We should be eager to fast, not running away from it. We should look at it as a trial, one with rewards beyond measure.

5. Bestow upon us praying at night- and this is a voluntary act that brings immense rewards, and the taraaweeh prayer specifically is only for this blessed month. We should strive to perform it to the best of our abilities.

6. Grant us sincerity in it- let our intentions be for Allaah alone so that we get the true reward for our fasting, and not just hunger and thirst

7. Help us to strive during it- in the obligatory actions as well as performing extra acts of worship

8. Give us strength and energy- as fasting is truly a trial for our hearts, minds and bodies. If one of these is not strong, then it weakens the others.

9. Protect us from trials during it

Alhamdulillah, this is truly a beautiful and comprehensive supplication. May Allaah grant us understanding, comprehension, and strength during this beautiful and blessed month.

Family Time

The Story of the Prophet Aadam

Allaah, the Most High, wished to make a new creation so He said to the angels,

❝*Verily I am going to place (mankind) generation after generation on earth.*❞– (Surah al-Baqarah, Ayat 30)

The angels are a creation of Allaah, which He chose to worship Him, and guided to His Obedience. They never tire of praising him and praise and glorify Him day and night. They do everything that they are commanded with.

The angels asked Allaah, ❝*Will you place therein those who will make mischief therein and shed blood, while we glorify you with praises and thanks and sanctify you?*❞–(Surah al-Baqarah, Ayat 30)

Allaah answered them with an answer that would bring peace to their hearts, saying: ❝*I know that which you do not know.*❞–(Surah al-Baqarah, Ayat 30)

Then Allaah created Aadam, the father of all people, from clay. He made him in the best way, and then He blew his soul into him.

Allaah ordered all of the angels to prostrate to Aadam, to honor him. All of the angels obeyed Allaah's command and prostrated to Aadam, May Allaah's praise be upon him. Only Iblees, or Shaytaan, who was from the Jinn, refused to obey the command of his Lord, because he was too proud and arrogant. He would not prostrate and remained stubborn in his disobedience and disbelief in Allaah.

Allaah said to Iblees, ❝*Oh Iblees! What prevents you from prostrating to one whom I have created with Both My Hands? Are you too proud(to fall prostrate to Aadam) or are you one of the high and exalted*❞–(Surah Saad, Ayat 75)

Iblees said, ❝*I am better than him, You created me from fire and You created him from clay."*❞–(Surah Saad, Ayat 76)

Allaah replied, ❝*Then get out of here, for verily you are outcast. And verily My Curse is on you until the Day of Judgment.*❞–(Surah Saad, Ayat 77-78)

Iblees wanted his Lord to leave him until the Day of Judgment, and to allow him to live until the Resurrection, so he said, ❝*My Lord! Give me respite until the day the dead are resurrected.*❞–(Surah Saad, Ayat 79)

Allaah gave him what he asked, saying, ❝*Verily! You are of those who allowed respite until the Day of the time appointed.*❞–(Surah Saad, Ayat 80-81)

However, even though Allaah gave Iblees what he wanted, and made his wish come true, Iblees did not thank Allaah for what He did for him. Instead, he returned ungratefulness and disbelief for the good that Allaah granted him. He said, ❝*Because You have sent me astray, surely I will sit in wait for them on Your Straight Path. Then I will come to them from in front of them, and behind them, from their right and from their left, and You will not find most of them to be thankful. (They will not be dutiful to You.)*❞–(Surah al-A'raaf, Ayat 16-17)

And the Shaytaan still does this- he tries to find ways to make us do things that Allaah does not like, or that will make Him angry. We must always be on our guard against him. One way to keep the Shaytaan from bothering us is to say, *"Audhubillaah"* or, "I seek refuge with Allaah" when we become angry, or frightened, or when we are thinking of doing something that Allaah would not like.

Allaah disgraced Iblees and expelled him, and told him that he would not be able to deceive the faithful servants of Allaah. He told him that whoever followed him from among the deceived and weak people then he would be his companion in the Fire. He said to Iblees, *Get out from here, disgraced and expelled. Whoever follows you, then surely I will fill Hell with you all.* -(Surah al-A'raaf, Ayat 18)

Allaah created Aadam's wife, Hawwa, from Aadam's rib, and bestowed His blessings upon them, and entered them into Paradise. He told Aadam not to forget that Iblees was his enemy, and his wife's enemy, and that he would try to deceive them and get them out of Paradise. Allaah said to him, *Oh Aadam! Dwell you and your wife in the Paradise and eat both of you freely with pleasure and delight of things therein, wherever you wish, but do not come near this tree, or you will be of the wrongdoers.* -(Surah al-Baqarah, Ayat 35) So Allaah gave them the freedom to eat whatever they wished in Paradise, except from one tree, which they were not to eat the fruit of.

Iblees began to plot how he could deceive them and expel them from the blessings and beauty that they were in. He wanted to trick them into eating from the tree that Allaah forbade them to eat from. He came to Aadam and whispered to him, trying to trick him into eating from the tree, *Your Lord did not forbid you from this tree except that you should become angels or become of the immortals.* -(Surah al-A'raaf, Ayat 20)

He swore by Allaah, in order to make them think that he was telling the truth, and he said, *Verily I am one of the sincere well-wishers for you both.* -(Surah al-A'raaf, Ayat 21)

Think of this the next time one of your so-called friends tries to get you to do something that you know is bad, or that your parents wouldn't like for you to do- this is why Allaah warns us that there are *Shayaateen* from the people as well as the Jinn. When a person tries to get you to do something that you think might be wrong, don't listen to him, and be strong, knowing that by not doing this bad thing you will please Allaah, and be rewarded.

Shaytaan succeeded in making Aadam and Hawwa forget the warning that Allaah had given them concerning Iblees, and they obeyed him and ate from the tree. When they disobeyed Allaah, that which was covering and beautifying their bodies came away, and they were left naked. They were ashamed and felt the seriousness of the sin that they committed. They began to cover themselves with the leaves of the Paradise, and Allaah called out to them, *Did I not forbid you that tree and tell that the Shaytaan is an open enemy to you?* -(Surah al-A'raaf, Ayat 22)

When Aadam and Hawwa heard this from their Lord, they turned to Him in repentance, and asked Him to forgive them and have mercy upon them.

Allaah placed them on the earth, and forgave them , saying, ❧*Get down, all of you, from this place. Then whenever there comes to you guidance from me, whoever follows my guidance will have no fear on them, nor shall they grieve.*❧–(Surah al-Baqarah, Ayat 38)

Thus, for humankind there are two paths, with no others: the path of faith and guidance, and the path of disbelief and misguidance. Whoever follows the path of faith and guidance, the straight path that Allaah has made clear to us, then he need not fear, and Allaah will reward him with good in this world and the Hereafter. However, the one who follows the path of disbelief, and follows the *Shaytaan,* then this life will be a punishment for him, and in the next life he will be thrown into the Fire forever, and he will taste the worst of punishments.

Points of Benefit:

1. The Shaytaan is the enemy of the children of Aadam, so we must disobey his commands.

2. Obedience causes Allaah to have mercy on us, and disobedience causes Him to become angry with us.

3. Arrogance and deception are a cause for evil, as because of them Iblees was expelled from Paradise, and was cursed.

4. The Shaytaan is a creation that we cannot see; he whispers to us, and tries to make us commit evil and sins.

5. Shayateen can be from the people too- you have to be careful of people who try to get you to do bad things, or who talk about evil things or say bad things about other people, or things like this. It is better for you to make sure that your friends are all good people who help you to do good things too.

6. Repentance and asking for Allaah's forgiveness wipe away all sins, like what happened to Aadam and Hawwa when they asked for His forgiveness after they ate from the tree.

Hands On Learning

1. Make the page for Aadam in your prophet book. Write his name with hollow letters and color them in as you like. Draw a little halal picture or write a verse from the Qur'aan from the story to remind you of who Aadam was and what he did.

2. Show your page to someone in your family, or to a friend, and tell them all that you can remember about the story of Aadam.

3. We do not know what the garden looked like when Aadam and Hawwa lived in it, and we do not know what the gardens of Paradise will look like when all the Believers live in them after the Day of Judgment. But this does not mean that you can't use your imagination to think of the most beautiful garden you can. Close your eyes and think about what you would like in a garden-trees with all different kinds of fruits, cool steams of water, beautiful flowers-whatever you like can be in your garden. Now decide on how you want to show us your garden. You can use watercolor or tempura paints, or crayons, or construction paper and glue- whatever you like. Just let your imagination lead you, and show us the beautiful garden that you have imagined in your head.

Day 3:
The Letter ت: التراويح
(*at-Taraaweeh*)
(the night prayer specific to Ramadhaan)

And from those things which are specific to the month of Ramadhaan is the *taraaweeh* prayer. al-Haafidh ibn Haajir, may Allaah have mercy upon him, said, "The meaning of *taraaweeh* is the plural of *tarweeha*, and it is the single instance of resting, in the same way as *tasleemah* is from *salam*. And the congregational prayer in the nights of Ramadhaan was named *taraaweeh* because when they first began to pray in congregation they would rest between every two *tasleem*s (the saying of Assalamu Aleikum or one of the other legislated sayings at the end)."

In the two saheehs, those of al-Bukhaari and Muslim, it is narrated that the Prophet, may Allaah's praise and salutations be upon him, said, *{Whoever prays the night prayer during Ramadhaan, having faith in Allaah and awaiting His reward, Allaah forgives him all of his previous sins.}*

And Imaam an-Nawaawi, may Allaah have mercy upon him, said that the meaning of praying the night prayer during Ramadhaan was *taraaweeh*.

And al-Haafidh ibn Haajir, may Allaah have mercy upon him, was of the opinion that the *taraaweeh* is that which was meant by praying the night prayer, because they do not pray any other prayer in the night during Ramadhaan except for it.

As for its description in the Sunnah, it is, as the Mother of the Believers, 'Aishah, may Allaah be pleased with her, said when she was asked about the Prophet's prayer during Ramadhaan. She said, *{He never exceeded eleven raka'at during Ramadhaan or at other times. He would pray four- but do not ask me about their beauty and their length (as she would be unable to describe this). And then he would pray four more, but do not ask me about their beauty and their length. Then he would pray three...}* (This hadeeth was narrated by al-Bukhaari)

It is recommended for the person who is praying *taraaweeh* to follow the Imaam in his prayer until the Imaam leaves. The Prophet, may Allaah's praise and salutations be upon him, said, *{Verily if a man prays with the Imaam until he leaves, it is written for him as if he has prayed the whole night.}* (This is narrated in the four (books of hadeeth), and al-Albaani declared it to be authentic)

Further Points of Benefit

Alhamdulillah, the night prayer throughout the year has many benefits- and the *taraaweeh* prayer is the night prayer which is specific to the month of Ramadhaan. At no other time during the year can we reap the benefits of this beautiful salaat. From them are:

1. In general, all of the previous sins of the one who prays it with faith and seeking Allaah's Face are forgiven

2. If one prays behind the Imaam until the Imaam finished the prayer, then the reward written for him is as if he prayed the whole night, alhamdulillah

3. Another benefit which may come along with praying it is that we accustom ourselves to praying during the night, and then, insh'Allah we can make

this a part of our lives year round.

Sheikh Saalih ibn Fauzaan ibn 'Abdullah al-Fauzaan, may Allaah preserve him, says, concerning taraaweeh:

"All praise is due to Allaah, alone, and may His praise and salutations be upon the Messenger of Allaah. To Proceed:

The *taraaweeh* prayer is from those things which are specific to Ramadhaan, and it is confirmed and established in the Sunnah- indeed, it is the most confirmed of the acts of the Sunnah. The Prophet, may Allaah's praise and salutations be upon him, performed it with his Companions for a few nights successively during Ramadhaan- he prayed, and they prayed behind them- and then he removed himself from them for the rest of the nights, fearing that the prayer would become obligatory upon them. This is because if he were to persist and adhere to this and not leave it, it would become obligatory- so he separated from them in order that they know that it was not an obligation but was, rather, a confirmed Sunnah.

And it is specific to the month or Ramadhaan, and salaat at-taraaweeh takes place in the first part of the night. And when the last ten days of the month arrive, then they would increase, praying into the latter part of the night in order that the commemoration of the night (of Qadr) be complete and perfect for them. As the Prophet, may Allaah's praise and salutations be upon him, prayed and slept during the first twenty days- and when the last ten nights came, he would apply himself more diligently and tighten his waist wrap and waken his family. And in a narration, *{...and observe worship the entire night...}* (al-Bukhaari (450) and Muslim (533)) And in another narration, *{...he did not experience sleep...}*

So briefly, the *taraaweeh* prayer is a confirmed and established Sunnah which is performed in congregation in the masaajid. It is not necessary for a Muslim to stay away from it or leave it (as the Prophet, may Allaah's praise and salutations be upon him did) as in doing so many benefits would pass him by, as he, may Allaah's praise and salutations be upon him, said, *{{The one who fasts Ramadhaan with faith and seeking the reward with Allaah, all of his previous sins will be forgiven.}* (al-Bukhaari (660) and Muslim (1031))…

…and many of the Pious Predecessors- with their striving in performance of righteous actions- would not leave off praying the taraaweeh prayer and the night prayer (*at-tahajjud*) with the Imaam, because they knew and understood the reward that went along with these things. So they would pray the *taraaweeh* (in the first part of the night) and then in the latter part of the night they would pray the *tahajjud,* and they would lengthen their standing, so much so that it was narrated that they had to resort to leaning on sticks due to the length of their standing (in prayer). And they tied ropes between the pillars and held onto them due to the length of their standing. And they would not depart until Fajr came, so that it was feared that they would miss their pre-fasting meal. This is all from their desire to attain the many blessings and the goodness of this month…" ("Majaalis Shahr Ramadhaan al-

Mubaarak wa Itihaaf ahl Eemaan bi Duroos Shahr Ramadhaan" Pages 72-73)

So, my sister, compare how you spend your nights in this blessed month with the manner in which the Messenger of Allaah, his Companions, and the Pious Predecessors spent their nights in Ramadhaan- when we see how they strove to attain success, and they were better than us, how can we not put forth every effort to strive to be like them, and to do all we can to seek Allaah's pleasure and blessings? They did not waste these precious nights in idle talk, eating, drinking, watching television, or playing useless games. Rather, they devoted their nights, as well as their days, to the worship of Allaah. May Allaah grand us steadfastness and strength, and turn our hearts to that which will bring success in this life as well as the Hereafter.

Family Time

Yusuf and Ya'qub- Part One

The children of prophet Ibraaheem, May Allaah's praise be upon him, were divided into two branches: The children of his elder son, Ismaa'il, may Allaah's Praise be upon him- and the last of the messengers, Muhammad, may Allaah's praise and salutations be upon him- was from these; and the children of his younger son, Ishaaq.

Ishaaq, May Allaah's praise be upon him, had a son named Ya'qub. Ya'qub's story is found in the Qur'aan with the story of his sons. Ya'qub had twelve sons, the youngest of whom were Yusuf and Benyamin. When Yusuf's brothers saw that their father loved Yusuf and Benyamin more than he loved them, they were filled with envy towards Yusuf.

One day, Yusuf saw a surprising dream. He told his father about it, saying, ❴*Oh my father! Verily, I saw (in a dream) eleven stars and the sun and the moon-I saw them prostrating themselves to me.* ❵-(Surah Yusuf, Ayat 4)

When his father heard this, he knew that it meant that Yusuf was going to have an important future, so he cautioned him not to tell his brothers, as they might become jealous and do harm to him.

Yusuf's brothers were envious, because their father loved him more than them, even though they were a group of strong young men. They said, ❴*Truly, Yusuf and his brother are dearer to our father than we are, while we are a strong group. Really, our father is in plain error.*❵-(Surah Yusuf, 8)

They began to plot against Yusuf, in order to get him out of the way so that their father would love them more. They said, ❴ *Kill Yusuf or cast him out to some other land, so that the favor of your father will be given to you alone, and after that you will be righteous people* ❵-(Surah Yusuf, 9)

However, the eldest of them did not like these cruel ideas. He said to them, ❴*Do not kill Yusuf, but if you must do something, then throw him to the bottom of a (dry) well, where he will be picked up by some caravan of travelers."*❵-(Surah Yusuf, 10)

You can see here in the story of Yusuf and his brothers how bad it is to be jealous of other people. When you are jealous, it means that you feel bad that someone else has something you don't have- you think that you should have it instead of them, or along with them. Even good people get jealous, it is just the way people are. So you might want your brother's toy car, or think that he doesn't deserve to have it. This doesn't make you a bad person, but it does mean that you have to work hard to make yourself not feel this way so that you do not do something wrong, like Yusuf's brothers did. They were so upset because they thought that their father loved Yusuf more, that some of them wanted to kill him! Alhamdulillah, the oldest brother knew that this was wrong, and stopped them from it- but he still wanted to harm Yusuf, so he was still not trying to get rid of his jealousy all the way. When you are jealous, take time to seek protection with Allaah from your jealousy and anger. Think of all the good things that Allaah has blessed you with, and be thankful for them. And whatever you do, don't be mean to someone just because you are jealous of them, insh'Allaah.

Once they had all agreed on this course of action, they went to their father and asked him to let Yusuf go with them the next day to play and enjoy himself. They promised that they would take good care of him. Ya'qub was afraid that they would be careless of Yusuf and allow him to be eaten by a wolf, so he did not want to let him go. But they reassured him saying, *If a wolf devours him while we are a strong group (to guard him) then surely we are the losers.*-(Surah Yusuf, 14)

When Ya'qub finally allowed them to take Yusuf, they took him and threw him in a well. However Allaah revealed something to Yusuf when they threw him in the well, and told him that one day he would tell his brothers of the evil they had done, and they would not recognize him or know who he was.

Meanwhile Yusuf's brothers stained his shirt with false blood, and brought it to their father that night weeping. They told him, *Oh Father! We went racing with one another and left Yusuf by our belongings and a wolf ate him; but you will never believe us even when we speak the truth.*

Ya'qub knew that they were lying, so he said, *Nay, but you have made up a tale.* Even though he was filled with grief at the loss of his son, he remained patient, and made a beautiful response to the misfortune that befell him, saying, *So (for me) patience is most fitting. And it is Allaah's help (alone) that can be sought against that which you describe.*-(Surah Yusuf, 18)

While Yusuf was in the well, a caravan of travelers came along and sent their water drawer to get them water. However, when he drew up the bucket there was no water in it, but only a small boy! They were happy to find him because they knew that they could make a good profit by selling him as a slave. They took him with them to Egypt, where they sold him cheaply to Al-Aziz, who was a government advisor. He brought Yusuf home with him and told his wife, *Make his stay comfortable, as maybe he will benefit us, or we can adopt him as a son.*-(Surah Yusuf, Ayat 21)

We see here how Yusuf was already patient, though he was a child- just as his father, Ya'qub, was patient, even though he knew his sons must have done something bad to Yusuf. Allaah comforted him when he was in the well, and he was patient with his situation, and the person who bought him was a good man, who wanted him to be comfortable.

Yusuf lived with Al-Aziz until he grew into a strong young man whom Allaah had blessed with great beauty and handsomeness.

The wife of Al-Aziz fell in love with Yusuf, and she attempted to make him do an evil act and disobey Allaah. However, Allaah kept evil away from him, and Yusuf refused and turned away from her. He would not disobey his Lord and betray his master. He said to her, *I seek refuge in Allaah! Truly, he (your husband) is my master! He made me live in great comfort. Verily, the wrong doers will never be successful.* (Surah Yusuf, Ayat, 23)

However, she would not accept his refusal. He ran away from her, trying to get out the door, and she chased him, pulling on his shirt from behind until it ripped. When they reached the door of the palace, Yusuf's master was at the door. She hurried to blame Yusuf, in order to free herself, saying to Al-Aziz, *What is the punishment for one who intended evil against your wife, except that he be imprisoned or made to taste a painful torment?*-(Surah Yusuf, Ayat, 25)

Yusuf denied her false accusations and told him, *It was she that sought to seduce me,"*-(Surah Yusuf, Ayat 26)

Al-Aziz did not know which one of them was lying and which one was telling the truth. Then, a wise person from her relatives bore witness saying, *If it be that his shirt is torn from the front then her tale is true and he is a liar! But if it be that his shirt is torn from the back, then she has told a lie, and he is speaking the truth."* When Al-Aziz saw that his shirt was torn from the back, he knew that Yusuf was telling the truth, because if Yusuf was running away, and she was trying to pull him back, then his shirt would be ripped in the back. He said to Yusuf, "Oh Yusuf, turn away from this" He said to his wife, "Ask forgiveness for your sin. Verily, you were of the sinful*-(Surah Yusuf, Ayat, 29)

Soon, the news spread throughout the city, and the women began to talk about the wife of Al-Aziz, and make fun of her. They said, *The wife of Al-Aziz is seeking to seduce her slave, indeed she loves him violently, verily we see her in plain error."*-(Surah Yusuf, Ayat 30)

When she heard of their accusations, she invited them to the palace and prepared a feast for them. She gave each one of them a knife to cut their food with. Then she ordered Yusuf to come out before them. When they saw Yusuf's great beauty, they were so surprised that they cut their own hands instead of the food. They said, *How perfect is Allaah! This is no man! This can be none other than a noble angel."*-(Surah Yusuf, Ayat, 31)

Al-Aziz's wife said, ❨*This is the young man whom you blamed me about, and I did seek to seduce him, but he refused. Now, if he refuses to obey my order then he will certainly be cast into prison, and he will be disgraced.*❩–(Surah Yusuf, Ayat, 32)

All the women began calling Yusuf to do evil, but he turned away from them and remained firm. He supplicated his Lord, saying, ❨*Oh my Lord! Prison is dearer to me than that to which they invite me. Unless you turn your plot away from me, I will feel inclined to them, and be one of the ignorant.*❩–(Surah Yusuf, Ayat, 33)

Allaah answered Yusuf's supplication, and turned their plot away from him, and granted him strength and patience.

See what a good example Yusuf is for all of us, alhamdulillah. The evil wife of his owner tried again and again to make him do evil- and when that didn't work, she got her friends to come and try to get him to do evil as well. But Yusuf simply asked Allaah for strength and patience, and Allaah granted him this. This can be very hard- sometimes when people we think of as friends try to get us to do something we know is bad, it is difficult for us to refuse, and turn away from doing this bad thing. But if we ask Allaah for help in this, He will help us- and every time we say no to evil and yes to good, it will become easier for us, insh'Allaah. It is not smart or strong to give in to what other people want when we know that they are wrong, and what they are calling to is something that displeases Allaah. It takes real strength and intelligence and goodness to refuse to do evil and to remain strong in our faith and commitment to Allaah!

Soon, the news spread throughout the city, and everyone talked about what had happened with Yusuf and the wife of Al-Aziz. Finally, Al-Aziz decided to throw Yusuf in jail, even though he knew that he was innocent, so that the people would stop speaking about the matter.

This was not fair of Al-Aziz to do to Yusuf, was it? He knew that Yusuf was innocent, but he cared so much about what the people would say about him and his wife that he had Yusuf put into prison. He had always treated him well, and now he was causing him harm, mash'Allaah. This shows you again how important it is to stand up for what is right, even if other people pick on you or talk badly about you.

While Yusuf was in jail, two young men were put into jail with him. They were impressed by his good manners and they trusted him. One night, they each saw a dream, and they decided to ask Yusuf to interpret the dreams for them. One of them told Yusuf, ❨*Verily, I saw myself in a dream pressing wine."* The other one said, *"Verily, I saw myself in a dream, carrying bread on my head, and the birds were eating from it."* They said to Yusuf, *"Inform us of the interpretation of this. Verily, we think that you are one of those who do good.*❩–(Surah Yusuf, Ayat, 36)

Yusuf was steadfast in calling to Allaah even though he was in prison. He told them that he would tell them what the dreams meant before any food was brought to them to eat, as Allaah had taught him how to interpret dreams. He called them to worship Allaah alone, and to leave the worship of many different gods. He asked them, *Are many different gods better, or Allaah, The One, The Irresistible?*-(Surah Yusuf, Ayat, 39) He reminded them that the gods they worshipped were nothing other than names that they and their fathers had made up, for which Allaah had sent down no authority. He told them that Allaah had commanded that they worship none except Him, alone, with no partners.

Look how strong and good Yusuf was, even in prison! He took the time and effort to call the people with him to Islaam- to worship Allaah alone!

Then Yusuf told them what their dreams meant, saying to them, *Oh two companions of the prison! As for one of you, then he will pour out wine for his master to drink, and as for the other, then he will be crucified and the birds will eat from his head. Thus the case is judged concerning that which you asked about.*-(Surah Yusuf, Ayat, 41)

It was from Yusuf's wisdom and mercy that he did not tell them which one would live and which one would be killed, so as not to cause harm and worry to the one who would be crucified.

Yusuf said to the one whom he knew would be saved, "Mention me to your lord." He wanted the young man to tell his master about Yusuf when he got out of prison, so that they would take him out. But when the man was freed from prison, he forgot all about Yusuf, so Yusuf stayed in prison for some years.

Hands On Learning

1. Dreams can be very funny things. Sometimes they make sense to us, and sometimes they don't. Sometimes they make us happy, and sometimes they scare us. We shouldn't worry when we have a bad dream. What we should do is not talk about it, and ask Allaah for protection from the Shaytaan ("*Audhubillahi min ash-shaytaan ir-rajeem*"). We do this three times, and each time we do it, we spit over our left shoulder, as this is the Sunnah of Prophet Muhammad, may Allaah's praise and salutations be upon him. Insh'Allaah Allaah will protect you from having any more bad dreams that night.

Some dreams, though, are good, and some even have meaning that we won't understand. Some people have knowledge and are able to tell what a dream means. Most people, though, don't have this ability. Just for fun, keep a notebook and pen by your bed, and write down any funny or interesting dreams you have. Maybe someday you will meet someone who will be able to tell you what they mean, just like Yusuf told the people what their dreams meant in the story.

2. Make a dream pillow to help you sleep and have good dreams. All you need is a small piece of soft cotton fabric, maybe as big as a handkerchief- dream pillows are not as big as the pillow you lay your head on at night. You also need some nice smelling herbs. Most sleep or dream pillows use lavender, chamomile, and hops, or herbs similar to these, but really you can try whatever is in your kitchen that your mom will let you use. Chamomile is very good, and many people have this tasty tea herb in their cupboards. You don't want to use herbs that would keep you awake, like mint or rosemary- you want to go to sleep and dream good dreams, insh'Allaah! Fold your little piece of fabric in half. Sew (or have your mom or big sister help you) three of the sides shut, leaving one of the shorter sides open. Put your herb mixture in the little bag you have just made. Turn under a small hem, and sew the fourth side shut. If you like decorate your little pillow with ribbons or lace. Place the little pillow under your big pillow, and when you go to bed give it a little squeeze to let out the pretty smell of the herbs. See if this helps you sleep, or helps you have good dreams, insh'Allaah!

3. The prophet Yusuf, *aleihi salaam,* had a dream. He described it to Ya'qub, saying, ❧*Oh my father! Verily, I saw (in a dream) eleven stars and the sun and the moon-I saw them prostrating themselves to me.*❧-(Surat Yusuf, Ayat, 4)

    The sun, the moon, and the stars are mentioned by Allaah in the Qur'aan many times- He tells us that He has placed them in the Heavens for different reasons. One of these reasons is simply to be a sign to us of His greatness, and His blessings upon us. Wouldn't you like to go to sleep under the stars, moons and planets? Well, of course you do this every night, but usually your ceiling is between you and them, so you can't see them. Why not make a mobile of the amazing things that Allaah placed in the sky for us? You can use a coat hanger for the top part, the part that you will hang from your ceiling. You will need some light cardboard on which to draw the shapes of the sun, moon, stars and planets- you can look in a book to see how neat some of the planets look, and color yours like them if you like! Use a paper punch to make a hole in the top of each of your stars, suns, moons, or planets. Cut white thread into various lengths, and thread it through these holes. Then tie each one to the hanger. Hang it above your bed, and when you see it, let it remind you of the amazing things which Allaah placed in the Heavens, and remember how Great and All-Powerful Allaah is, and be thankful that He has created you and made you a Muslim, and given you the chance to experience all of the amazing things He has created.

Day 4:

The Letter ث: ثبوت الشهر
(*Thaboot ash-shahr*)
(to establish that the month has begun)

The beginning and end of the month are established by the sighting of the crescent moon. The Prophet, may Allaah's praise and salutations be upon him, said, *{Do not fast until you sight the crescent moon, and do not break your fast until you see the crescent moon. But if it is obscured from your view by clouds, then reckon for it.}* and in a narration, *{...then finish thirty days.}* (Agreed upon)

Imaam an-Nawaawi, may Allaah have mercy upon him, mentioned that the meaning of his saying *{...if it is obscured from your view by clouds...}* is that clouds came between you and it (so you cannot see it). And to prove this he mentioned that it is not permissible to fast the day of doubt, or the thirtieth of Sha'baan if the night of the thirtieth is cloudy (and the night of the thirtieth refers to the night before the day of the thirtieth). And this proves that calculations cannot be utilized for this purpose (meaning you can't rely upon computed calculations or predictions to determine the establishment of the month). And Sheikh al-Islaam ibn Taymiyyah, may Allaah have mercy upon him, mentioned the consensus of the scholars that it is not allowed to depend on calculations to determine the month.

The Muslim must fast with the people of the country in which he resides at that time, and break his fast with them. The Prophet, may Allaah's praise and salutations be upon him, said, *{The fast is the day you all fast, and breaking the fast is on the day that you all break your fast. And the slaughtering of the animals (for the Eid) is the day you all slaughter your animals.}* (Narrated by at-Tirmidhi, and al-Albaani has declared it to be authentic)

There is much confusion today regarding establishing the coming of the month of Ramadhaan, mash'Allaah. New technology for predicting its appearance, as well as spreading the news of its coming, has caused many people to rely upon these electronic wonders to verify both its beginning and its end, no matter where they are in the world.

Sheikh Saalih ibn Fauzaan ibn 'Abdullah al-Fauzaan, may Allaah preserve him, says concerning this issue:

"All praise is due to Allaah, who has made the crescent moon as a method of telling time for the people, and may His praise and salutations be upon our Prophet Muhammad, his family, his Companions, and those who follow him in righteousness. To Proceed:

Allaah, the Most High, says, *So, whoever of you sights (the crescent on the first night of) the month (of Ramadhaan) he must observe the fast that month.* In this verse Allaah, Glorified and Exalted is He, made obligatory the fasting of the month of Ramadhaan from its beginning to its end. And its beginning can be determined by either of two ways:

The First Method: The actual sighting of the crescent moon. As al-Bukhaari, Muslim, and other than them have related from Ibn 'Umar, may Allaah be pleased with them both, that the Prophet, may Allaah's praise and salutations be upon him, said, *{When you see the crescent moon then fast; and when you see the crescent moon (a* month later) break your fast. But if it is obscured by clouds then complete the month (as thirty days).} (al-Bukhaari (1900) and Muslim (1080))

Imaam Ahmad and an-Nasaa'i narrated from Ibn 'Umar, may Allaah be pleased with them both, that the Prophet, may Allaah's praise and salutations be upon him, said, {Do not fast until you sight the crescent moon, and do not break your fast until you see the crescent moon. But if it is obscured from your view by clouds, then reckon for it.}

And at-Tabaraani narrated from Talq ibn 'Ali, may Allaah be pleased with him, {Verily Allaah made the crescent moon as a method of telling time. So when you see it, fast, and when you see it (again at the end of the month), break your fast.} (at-Tabaraani in "al-Mu'jam al-Kabeer" 8237)

And in these noble ahaadeeth is the obligation of fasting Ramadhaan upon sighting the crescent moon, and the prohibition of fasting without sighting the crescent moon, and that Allaah, Mighty and Majestic, made the crescent moon as a way to tell time for the people so that they could know the times of their worship and work. As Allaah, the Most High, said, ❖They ask you (Oh Muhammad) about the crescent moons. Say: "They are signs to mark fixed periods of time for mankind and for the pilgrimage.❖-(Surat al-Baqarah, From Ayat 189)

This is from the mercy of Allaah towards His servants in that He connected the obligation of the fast to a clear and obvious sign which can be seen with the eyes. It is not obligatory that all of the people see the crescent moon; rather, if anyone sees it, even one person, then they must all fast. Ibn 'Abbaas, may Allaah be pleased with him, said, {A Bedouin came to the Prophet, may Allaah's praise and salutations be upon him, and said, "I have seen the crescent moon (meaning the crescent moon signaling the beginning of Ramadhaan)." The Prophet, may Allaah's praise and salutations be upon him, said, {Do you testify that there is none worthy of worship except for Allaah?} The Bedouin replied, "Yes." The Prophet said, {Do you testify that Muhammad is the Messenger of Allaah?} He replied, "Yes." Then the Prophet, may Allaah's praise and salutations be upon him, said, {Oh Bilaal, announce to the people that they should fast tomorrow.}} (Abu Daawud, 2340, 2341)

And ibn 'Umar, may Allaah be pleased with them both, narrated, {The people looked for the crescent moon, and I mentioned to the Prophet, may Allaah's praise and salutations be upon him, that I had seen it. So he fasted and told the people to fast.} (Abu Daawud, 2342)

The Second Method: The second method of determining the entrance of Ramadhaan, which is used when the crescent moon is not seen, is finishing Sha'baan as thirty days, as the Prophet, may Allaah's praise and salutations be upon him, said, {if it is obscured from your view by clouds then finish thirty days.} And the meaning of "Obscured from your vision" is that if the crescent moon is obscured by something so it is not seen on the night before the thirtieth of Sha'baan- due to clouds or rain- then finish the thirty days of Sha'baan in their entirety. And the meaning of this is that it is forbidden to fast the day of doubt. And 'Ammar ibn Yaasir, may Allaah be pleased with him, said, "Whoever fasted the day of doubt has disobeyed Abu Qaasim *(the Messenger of Allaah, may Allaah's praise and salutations be upon him)."*

And what is obligatory upon the Muslim is following that which the Messenger of Allaah brought in his fasting and all other acts of worship. And Allaah and His Messenger, may Allaah's praise and salutations be upon him, made clear the entrance of the month with two obvious, well-known signs, known by both the common person and the educated one- either seeing the crescent moon or finishing the thirty days of Sha'baan. So whoever brought something claiming that it makes fasting obligatory which is not in the Islamic legislation has disobeyed Allaah and His Messenger, may Allaah's praise and salutations be upon him. As those who study astronomy and predict the beginning of the month with mathematical calculations- they do this despite the fact that they can make a mistake in their calculations, and that it is a mysterious method, unknown to the majority of the people…

And I have heard that some of the judges will reject the testimony of several honest people for the opinion of an ignorant astronomer that it will be seen or not! So he is of those who reject the truth after it has come to them…

And in this is hardship and annoyance for the Ummah. As Allaah, the Most High, says, ❧*…and (Allaah) has not laid upon you in religion any hardship.*❧-(Surat al-Hajj, From Ayat 78) So what is obligatory upon the Muslims is staying with that which Allaah and His Messenger, may Allaah's praise and salutations be upon him, obligated, in this matter as well as in others; and to help each other in good deeds and piety. And Allaah is the Owner of All Success." ("Majaalis Shahr Ramadhaan al-Mubaarak wa Itihaaf ahl Eemaan bi Duroos Shahr Ramadhaan" Pages 131-134)

So follow the Sunnah in this, as in all other things, Oh Sister, in order to reap the benefits and please Allaah, the Most High, who sent His Messenger as a mercy and guide for all of mankind.

Family Time

Yusuf and Ya'qub Part Two

Then one day, the King of the land saw a strange dream. He saw seven thin cows eating seven fat cows, and seven green ears of corn, and seven dry ones. He called all the notables to him and asked them to tell him what it meant, but none of them could. When the young man who had been in prison with Yusuf heard about it, he remembered how wisely and truthfully Yusuf interpreted dreams, so he sought permission from the King to go to Yusuf. He went to Yusuf and asked him what the dream meant. Yusuf told him that for seven years the crop would as abundant as usual, and that they should save all that they did not need to eat for later. After that there would be seven hard years, in which they would need eat that which they had stored away from the other years. Then would come a year in which there would be much rain, and the people would once again press oil and wine.

The young man went back to the king, and told him of Yusuf's interpretation of the dream, and of what Yusuf advised them to do. The king realized how knowledgeable and wise Yusuf must be, and so he commanded that he be brought. But when they went to Yusuf, he refused to come with them without his innocence being proven. He sent the king's messenger back, and told him that they must look into that with which he was accused, and see his innocence before he would come with them.

The King called for the women, and asked them, *What was your affair when you sought to seduce Yusuf?*-(Surat Yusuf, Ayat 51) The women answered, "Allaah forbid! We know of no evil against him!"-(Surat Yusuf, Ayat 51) The wife of Al-Aziz admitted her guilt, saying, *Now the truth is clear to all. It was I who sought to seduce him, and surely he is truthful.*-(Surat Yusuf, Ayat 51)

Yusuf said, *I asked for this enquiry in order that Al-Aziz should know that I did not betray him in his absence."*

The King said, *Bring him to me so that I may attach him to me.* Yusuf was brought to the king, and when he spoke to him, the king knew what good manners and wisdom Yusuf possessed, and so he said to him, *Verily from this day you are high in rank and fully trusted with us.* -(Surat Yusuf, Ayat 54)

Alhamdulillah, see how Yusuf's patience and his willingness to help others helped him? The man who had been in prison with him remembered the good he had done by interpreting his dream for him, and told the King about him. Yusuf then helped the King by explaining the King's dream to him, and this made the King want to help him. The King saw how wise and knowledgeable Yusuf was, and so he sent for him.

Now we see how brave Yusuf was, and how honest, alhamdulillah. He didn't just come running when the King called for him- instead, he wanted it to be very clear that he was imprisoned unjustly. So he refused the offer of freedom until his good name was cleared! Alhamdulillah, he was very brave to do this- what if it hadn't been proven that he was innocent? He would have had to stay in jail, mash'Allaah. But Yusuf trusted Allaah- he knew that Allaah would make every matter clear and free him of his accusations, alhamdulillah. See how important it was to Yusuf that Al-Aziz knew that he had been an honest, faithful servant to him, so that he would not think badly of Yusuf, alhamdulillah. We should try to be this way as well- we should always be honest and good to people, so that Allaah will be pleased with us, and so that the people will know that we are worthy of their trust, insh'Allaah.

Yusuf wished to help the people get through the times of drought and hardship that he knew were coming, and so he said, *Set me over the storehouses of the land, as I will indeed guard them with full knowledge.*-(Surat Yusuf, Ayat 55) Thus, Yusuf was raised in position in the land, and he was given full authority over it.

When the seven hard years came, the people in Egypt still had food because Yusuf had guarded over and saved grain from the years before. Soon people from many other places began to come to buy grain and provisions from Egypt. In Kan'aan, where Yusuf was from, Ya'qub and his sons needed food. They decided to go to Egypt in order to buy food from the Egyptians. When they entered upon Yusuf, they did not recognize him, but he immediately recognized them. He gave them all the provisions they needed, and then he told them, *Bring me a brother of yours from your father. Do you not see that I give full measure, and that I am the best of hosts?*-(Surat Yusuf, Ayat 59)

He wanted them to bring Benyamin to him, in order that he might see him. He told them that if they did not bring Benyamin, then he would not give them any more food or provisions. They promised that they would try to get their father to give them permission to bring Benyamin, even though they did not think that he would trust them with him. Then Yusuf told his servants to put his brother's money with which they had bought the food back in their bags, so that they would think well of him and wish to return, and bring their brother, Benyamin with them.

When Yusuf's brothers went back to Kan'aan, they told their father how generous the minister of Egypt was, and they said to him, *Oh Father! We will get no more measures of grain unless we take our brother. So send him with us, and we shall get our measure, and truly we will guard him.*-(Surat Yusuf, Ayat 63)

Ya'qub refused, saying, *Can I entrust him to you when I already entrusted his brother to you before?*

See how the wickedness and lying that the brothers fell into before affected them now?! Their own father knew that he could not trust them, due to the fact that they lied to him and did evil to Yusuf so many years before. This is what usually happens-if we do something to make people not trust us, it is very hard to overcome this and have them trust us again. Isn't it better just to be honest, so that everyone knows that we are truthful and worthy of their trust?

When Yusuf's brothers opened their bags, they were surprised to see that their money had been returned to them. They said to their father, *Oh Father! What more could we desire? Our money has been returned to us, so we shall get more food for our family, and we shall guard our brother, and add one more camel's load of grain. This measure is easy for the king to give.*-(Surat Yusuf, Ayat 65)

Ya'qub said that he would not send Benyamin with them unless they swore a solemn oath that they would bring him back unless they themselves were surrounded by enemies. They swore the oath, and then they got ready to set off to Egypt with Benyamin. Ya'qub said, *Oh my sons! Do not enter from one gate, but enter from different gates, and I cannot avail you against Allaah at all.*-(Surat Yusuf, Ayat 67) Ya'qub feared the evil eye for them, as they were handsome and looked beautiful and graceful.

See how important it is to be truthful when you make an oath? Ya'qub knew that his sons would not lie when they were swearing by Allaah to do something, and so he entrusted Benyamin to them, alhamdulillah. So if you ever take an oath, remember that you can only swear by Allaah- and make sure that you are telling the truth when you do it!! Do not take this lightly, it is very important.

And look how he still loved his sons, even though they had previously wronged him- alhamdulillah, this is how it usually is with parents, they will be patient and willing to always expect the good from you, and keep loving you, even when you do something wrong. So you should take care to do your best always to be honest and obedient to them, and when you do something wrong, it is always better to admit it then to make things worse by lying to them. And if your parents are forgiving and loving, you must remember that Allaah is the All-Forgiving- He is always ready to forgive you if you ask Him to, and you really mean it. And Allaah loves you more than anyone on earth can ever love you, and He wants what is good for you, alhamdulillah.

When Yusuf's brothers went in he before him along with Benyamin, he gave them a place of honor as privileged guests. He met Benyamin in private and told him the story of what happened and that he was in fact his brother. He ordered him to hide this news from the others, and told him not to be sad because of what Yusuf's brothers did to him.

After Yusuf supplied them with provisions, he ordered his servants to place the king's silver bowl in Benyamin's bag. Then he told someone to shout, ❖*Oh you in the caravan! Surely you are thieves!*❖-(Surat Yusuf, Ayat 70)

They turned back and asked him what had been lost. He told them that the king's silver goblet, or cup, was missing, and that whoever found it would get a camel load of provisions as a reward.

They said to him, ❖*By Allaah! Indeed, you know that we did not come to make mischief in the land, and that we are not thieves!*❖-(Surat Yusuf, Ayat 73)

Yusuf's men asked what the punishment should be for whoever was found with it. They replied that according to the law of Prophet Ibraaheem, he should be given as a slave to the one from whom he stole. So when the cup was found in Benyamin's bag, they took him as a slave. When Yusuf's brothers saw this they started to try to get Yusuf to release Benyamin. They tried to raise compassion in his heart by telling about his old father who loved him so dearly, but to no avail.

When they went back and told their father what had happened, He repeated the same words he said when he saw them bringing Yusuf's shirt stained with false blood. He did not believe them, because he thought that they had done the same thing to him as they had done to Yusuf. This was a just judgment upon them for their lies before.

Again, see how their previous lies affected them now, years later- Ya'qub still could not trust them to tell the truth. He feared that they had done evil to Benyamin, just as they had done evil to Yusuf so long ago.

Ya'qub sent his sons out to inquire about Yusuf and his brother, in a good manner, not as spies. So they went back to Egypt and entered upon Yusuf. They said to him, *Oh Aziz! A hard time has hit us and our family, and we have brought only poor capital, so pay us in full measure.* They had only been able to bring a little money in exchange for the food, so they asked Yusuf to give them the full amount even though they had less money. When they told him about the afflictions and hardship that they were going through, he remembered his father's grief on losing two of his children, and he felt pity and compassion towards them.

Yusuf was truly a forgiving person, wasn't he? His brothers had separated him from his family years ago, yet now he felt sorry for them!!

Yusuf cried and revealed his true identity to them, saying, *Do you know what you did with Yusuf and his brother, while you were ignorant?* -(Surat Yusuf, Ayat 89) By this he meant, "when you separated them?" They were astonished, and said, *Are you indeed Yusuf ?* -(Surat Yusuf, Ayat 90) He replied, *I am Yusuf, and this is my brother.* -(Surat Yusuf, Ayat 90) He was referring to Benyamin when he said this.

They admitted their error and acknowledged that they had made a mistake against him and wronged him. He said, *There is no reproach for you on this day, may Allaah forgive you, and He is the most merciful of forgivers.* -(Surat Yusuf, Ayat 92)

Look how Yusuf forgave his brothers! Perhaps we should try to more forgiving of others who we think have done wrong to us…as most likely no one could have wronged us as much as Yusuf was wronged by his brothers!

He then sent them to his father with his shirt, and told them to throw it over his face, and he would once again be able to see. Ya'qub had lost his sight from excessive weeping. He also told them to bring the entire family to Egypt. When the caravan left Egypt, a wind blew the scent of Yusuf's shirt to Ya'qub. He said, *I do indeed find the smell of Yusuf, except that you might think me senile."* -(Surat Yusuf, Ayat 94) His children that were left behind with him answered him harshly and said, *Certainly you are in your old error.* -(Surat Yusuf, Ayat 95)

This was a mercy from Allaah to His prophet, Ya'qub- he allowed the fragrance of Yusuf's shirt to come to him even though it was not there with him. This gave him hope, even though his children that were there spoke to him harshly. Mash'Allaah, look how he was right, and they were wrong!

Then, the son of Ya'qub who had carried in Yusuf's shirt stained with false blood brought the good news and Yusuf's shirt in order to erase the error he had committed before. He threw it on his father's face and his sight was restored to him. His sons asked him humbly to ask forgiveness for them, which he did immediately.

All of Yusuf's family then came to Egypt and entered it safely. He took his parents to himself, and raised them up on the bedstead upon which he sat. Then Yusuf's parents and brothers fell down before him prostrate, and he said, *◆Oh my father! This is the interpretation of my dream before.◆*-(Surat Yusuf, Ayat 100) Meaning, the dream in which he saw eleven stars, the sun, and the moon prostrating to him. Then Yusuf begged and invoked Allaah, that he might continue the bounty and favor he had bestowed upon him in this life in the Hereafter, and that when death came to him that he might die as a Muslim.

Points of Benefit

1. You should always bear with patience anything that Allaah decrees, and not despair of His mercy.

2. Allaah helps His righteous servants and brings good to them, both in this world and the next.

3. You should hold tight to the obedience of Allaah, and be careful not to fall into doing anything that He forbids.

4. You must call to Allaah at all times and in all places.

5. If you believe in Allaah then that is a cause for Him to send His mercy down upon you.

6. Forgiveness and pardoning are from the attributes of the believers.

7. If you do anything wrong, then you must repent to Allaah, and ask His forgiveness.

8. You should always be humble, and not be proud because of what you have or can do.

Hands on Learning

1. Make the page for Ya'qub, and a page for Yusuf in your prophet book. Write the prophet's name with hollow letters and color them in as you like. Draw a little picture or write a verse from the Qur'aan from the story to remind you of who they were and what they did.

2. Show your pages to someone in your family, or to a friend, and tell them all that you can remember about the story of Yusuf and his father Ya'qub.

3. In this part of the story of the prophets Yusuf and Ya'qub, Ya'qub, Yusuf's father, is blind, until Yusuf's shirt is thrown over him- then he can see again- and this is a miracle that Allaah granted to them, alhamdulillah. Most of us can see pretty well, though some of us need glasses. It is hard for us to imagine what it would be like to be blind. Try being blind today, just for a little while- half an hour, or maybe an hour, insh'Allaah. Have someone tie

a piece of fabric over your eyes, and see what it is like for those people who cannot see at all, mash'Allaah. You will find that you will need more help with things than you did before, mash'Allaah, so make sure that someone is helping you with this- maybe take turns with your brother, sister, or friend to try this. Try to do things that you always do that are easy for you, like reading, eating, or drawing. Have someone put five or ten things into a bag or box, and you pick each one up and try to tell what it is just by feeling it. Try to tell who you are talking to, not by their voice, or seeing them, but by touching their faces. And when you take off your blindfold, be thankful for the gift of sight that Allaah has given you, and make du'a for all of those people that have not been blessed with this.

4. Yusuf put a goblet into his brother Benyamin's bag, so that his brother would be found with it, and he would have an excuse to keep Benyamin with him while his other brothers returned to their father. A goblet is a fancy drinking glass. Try to imagine what this goblet might have looked like. Would it have jewels on it? Would it be glass, or gold or silver? We don't know what it really looked like, but use your imagination to picture it. Try to show other people what you are imagining, using whatever tools you want to use- crayons, construction paper and glue, tissue paper, paper mache, markers- whatever you like. Make it look like you think a king's drinking glass would look.

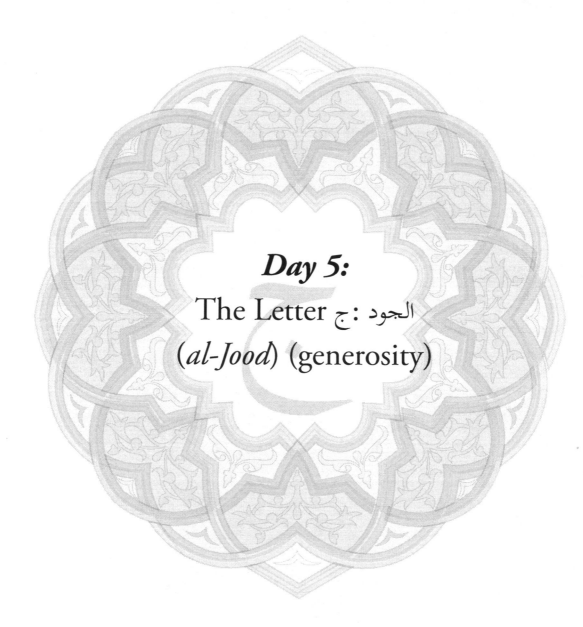

Day 5:

The Letter ج : الجود
(*al-Jood*) (generosity)

In this noble month, remember, my Sister in Allaah, that you have brothers and sisters in Islaam who are suffering from hunger, poverty and illness throughout the year. So this month should be a starting point or foundation for you in being generous and giving.

You have a great example in the Messenger of Allaah, may Allaah's praise and salutations be upon him, as it is narrated from 'Abdullaah ibn 'Abbaas, may Allaah be pleased with him, that he said, *{The Messenger of Allaah, may Allaah's praise and salutations be upon him, was the most generous of the people, and he used to be more generous in the month of Ramadhaan when Jibreel visited him- and Jibreel used to meet him on every night of Ramadhaan till the end of the month. The Prophet used to recite the Qur'aan to Jibreel, and when Jibreel met him, he used to be more generous than a fast wind (which causes rain and brings good).}* ("Saheeh al-Bukhaari", in the Book of Fasting)

al-Haafidh Ibn Haajir, may Allaah have mercy upon him, mentioned in his explanation of the hadeeth the similarity between his, may Allaah's praise and salutations be upon him, generosity, and the generosity of the fast wind. He said that what is meant by the wind is the wind of mercy which Allaah, the Most High, sends to bring down the rain which is a cause of the rain striking both the barren and fertile earth. So its good and its benefit are general, encompassing he who is in a state of poverty and need, as well as one who is in a state of prosperity and whose needs are fulfilled. And this (the generosity of the Prophet) is greater than that which comes from this rain which comes from a fast wind.

Further Points of Benefit

Allaah, the Most High, says in His Noble Book,

◊Worship Allaah and join none with Him (in worship); and do good to parents, kinsfolk, orphans, al-masaakeen (the needy), the neighbor who is near of kin, the neighbor who is a stranger, the companion by your side, the wayfarer (you meet), and those (slaves) whom your right hands possess.◊-(Surat an-Nisaa, From Ayat 36) In a more general verse, He, Glorified and Exalted is He, says,

◊Help you one another in al-birr and at-taqwa (virtue, righteousness and piety); but do not help one another in sin and transgression.◊-(Surat al-Maa'idah, From Ayat 2)

Alhamdulillah, these verses are general, to be used as guidelines for the entire year- but how much more so should we strive to make them a reality in this blessed month of Ramadhaan- the month in which the Messenger of Allaah, may Allaah's praise and salutations be upon him, who was the most generous of men, made a special effort to increase his generous acts?

And remember that generosity is not something which is only for the rich, those who can afford to give of their wealth without feeling any straitening of their own circumstances. Rather, this generosity is for all of us, rich and poor, young and old, male and female- we should give whatever it is within our capability to give, and we should do so gladly with a light heart, doing it for the sake of Allaah alone, not for the praise of the people, mash'Allaah.

It has been related from Abi Hurairah, may Allaah be pleased with him, that a man came to the Prophet, may Allaah's praise and salutations be upon him, and he (the Prophet, may Allaah's praise and salutations be upon him) sent to his wives (to see about giving the man food). They said, "We do not have anything except for water." So the Messenger of Allaah, may Allaah's praise and salutations be upon him, said (to the people), *{Who will take care of him?}* or, *{Who will entertain this man as a guest?}* A man from the Ansaar said, "I will!" He then went with him to his wife, and said, "Honor the guest of the Messenger of Allaah, may Allaah's praise and salutations be upon him." She replied, "We do not have anything except food for our children." He said, "Prepare your food and turn down the lamp, and put the children to bed if they want supper." She acted as if she were fixing the lamp, and then put it out completely. Then they pretended as if they were eating (while the guest actually ate) and they went to sleep hungry. So when morning came he (the host) went to the Messenger of Allaah, may Allaah's praise and salutations be upon him, and he (the Prophet) said, *{Allaah laughed last night.}* or, *{Allaah marveled at what the two of you did.}* And so Allah revealed, *❊…and give them (emigrants) preference over themselves even though they were in need of that. And whosoever is saved from his own covetousness, such are they who will be the successful.❊*-(Surat al-Hashr, From Ayat 9) (al-Bukhaari, No. 3798, and Muslim No. 2054)

There are many manners and forms of generosity and charity. From them are greeting your fellow Muslim with a smile, giving them the salaam, being kind, giving good advice, commanding the good and forbidding the evil, assisting them in any way we are able- and this includes physical assistance, monetary assistance, advice, supplication, and more-giving them gifts, teaching them from the religion…the list could go on and on, alhamdulillah. Allaah has made it easy for us to be generous with ourselves, our time, and our resources in one way or another- we simply have to seek out the opportunities to bestow what we have upon others, and then proceed to do so solely to please Allaah alone.

Perhaps we should also mention that the one who is the receiver of generosity or charity should accept with good character as well, even if what is received is not what one hoped for. For example if one were to ask for one hundred dollars and be given fifty, he should not then feel cheated or shortchanged or angry with the one who gave. Rather, he should be thankful for whatever is given, and should supplicate for the one who bestowed the gift upon him. And Allaah knows best.

Family Time

The Story of the Prophet Ibraaheem Part 1

When Ibraaheem, may Allaah's praise be upon him, was born, the people worshipped many made up lords other than Allaah. Some worshipped the sun and the planets, while some worshipped idols and statues. Ibraaheem's father was named Aazar, and he carved idols and sold them to his people, while worshipping them as well. But Allaah wished for good for Ibraaheem, so he protected him from worshipping the idols of his people, and filled his heart with the glow of tawheed. This means that he worshipped Allaah, alone, and he knew that Allaah was the only One who created him and gave him what he needed to stay alive. When Ibraaheem grew into a young man, Allaah sent him to his people, to call them to the worship of Allaah alone, and to warn them to leave off worshipping idols, or the sun and planets.

The first person who Ibraaheem turned to was his own father, Aazar. He said to him, *Oh my father! Why do you worship that which hears not, sees not, and cannot avail you in anything? Oh my father! Verily there has come to me knowledge that has not come to you. So follow me, I will guide you to the straight path. Oh my father! Do not worship the Shaytaan! Verily, Shaytaan has been a rebel against the most gracious. Oh my father! Verily I fear lest a punishment from the Most Gracious should overtake you, so that you become a companion of Shaytaan.*-(Surat Maryam, Ayats 41-45)

His father replied, *Do you revile my gods, Oh Ibraaheem!*-(Surat Maryam, Ayat 46) He told Ibraaheem that if he did not stop, he would punish him and curse him. He told Ibraaheem to leave and get away from him.

But Ibraaheem only replied with patience and forbearance, saying, *Peace be with you! I will ask forgiveness of my lord for you.*-(Surat Maryam, Ayat 47) He did not reply to his father's threats and evil promises with the like; rather, he answered him with good, patient words.

An idol is something like a stone, or a statue, that people worship instead of Allaah. Sometimes they think that their god is the idol itself, or that their god is in the idol, and sometimes they think that the idol just represents their gods- but either way this is forbidden- we must only worship Allaah, alone, in the ways in which Allaah has told us to worship in the Qur'aan and from Prophet Muhammad, may Allaah's praise and salutations be upon him.

We see here how much Ibraaheem must have loved his father, as he went to him first, to call him to worship Allaah alone and to leave off worshipping the idols. He wanted to save his father first, and to turn him to the worship of Allaah alone. We should always want good for our parents, and Islaam is the best thing that we could possibly wish for them, as it will give them success in this life and the next, if Allaah wills this.

Also, look at how kind and patient Ibraaheem was with his father when his father scorned and threatened him. It can be awfully hard sometimes to be patient and good to people who are being mean or impolite to us, but we should try to be this way anyway. Sometimes people will see your kindness and goodness, and this could lead them to listen to what is correct, or to want to be kind and good in return.

Then Ibraaheem spoke to his father and his people saying, ❧*What are these images to which you are devoted?*❧-(Surat Al-Anbiyaa', Ayat 52)

They could find no proofs or good answer except to say, ❧*We found our fathers worshipping them.*❧-(Surat Al-Anbiyaa', Ayat 53)

Ibraaheem said to them, ❧*Indeed, you and your fathers have been in clear error.*❧-(Surat Al-Anbiyaa', Ayat 54) Meaning, "Both you and your fathers are misguided and are not following any straight path."

Doesn't the answer of the people sound silly? They were only worshipping those images and idols because they saw their fathers and their people worshipping them. They didn't have any other reason than that! In Islaam, we are told that we have to learn about our religion. Learning about our religion means that we learn about Allaah, His Messenger Muhammad, may Allaah's praise and salutations be upon him, and about the religion of Islaam. And we don't do this just by listening to what everybody says. Instead, we should learn about our religion from the Qur'aan, and the Sunnah of the Messenger of Allaah, and we should look to the good scholars to explain things to us that we might not understand at first. In other words, we learn about our religion with its proofs. If your mother teaches you that Allaah is merciful, then she can show you in the Qur'aan where Allaah tells us that He is merciful. If your dad tells you to be generous because the Prophet, may Allaah's praise and salutations be upon him, was generous, then he can show you in hadeeths how generous he was, insh'Allaah. Islaam is not a made-up religion- it is real, and true, and we can refer to the sources of Islaam- the Qur'aan and the Sunnah- to see the proofs for our beliefs, alhamdulillah.

So then Ibraaheem began to think how he could change their ideas and beliefs, and get them to understand the weakness and inability of their gods. He waited until a festival day came in which they would all leave to go outside of the town. When all the people were leaving to celebrate the festival, they passed by Ibraaheem and asked him, "Oh Ibraaheem! Are you not coming out with us?" He said to them, "I am sick."

When everyone had left, Ibraaheem went to the temple in which the idols were kept. He saw the idols standing there dumb, unmoving, with heaps of food spread before them as offerings to them. He said mockingly to them, "Why do you not eat and drink?" But the idols did not answer a word, for they were only rocks which could not hear or see or speak. Ibraaheem said to them, "What is the matter with you that you do not speak?!?" Then Ibraaheem took an axe and broke all the idols up, except the biggest one. Then he put the axe in the hand of the largest one, so that it looked like it had broken the other idols.

Soon, the people returned, and saw that which had been done to their gods. They said, *Who has done this to our gods? He must indeed be one of the wrongdoers.*-(Surat Al-Anbiyaa', Ayat 59) Some of the people said, *We heard a young man talking against him, who is called Ibraaheem.*-(Surat Al-Anbiyaa', Ayat 60)

They then brought Ibraaheem in front of a large gathering of many people, and asked him, *Are you the one who has done this to our gods, Oh Ibraaheem?*-(Surat Al-Anbiyaa', Ayat 62)

He said, *Nay, this one, the biggest of them, did it. Ask them, if they can speak!*-(Surat Al-Anbiyaa', Ayat 63)

His people had to admit that their gods could not speak, and they were filled with confusion and guilt. He then asked them why they were worshipping that which could not hear nor speak, and could not benefit them nor harm them. He defeated them in argument and left them with no way to get out of it.

We see how ignorant the people were, just worshipping stones or wood that could do nothing for them! When Ibraaheem went in and spoke to these idols, he knew they couldn't answer him. He understood that they were not gods, nor did they represent anything that could answer him or help him or do anything at all. If you were to go out and talk to a rock, would you expect it to answer back? No. If you asked it to help you pass a test in school, would you expect it to help you? No! Allaah is the only One who can help you, and He always listens to your prayers and answers them- you can't hear His answer, but you can be sure that He heard you and will answer your prayer, either by giving you what you asked for, or keeping something bad away from you in the same amount of what you asked for, or by giving you something better than what you asked for- and sometimes this could be in the Hereafter- we just have to know and trust that Allaah will listen to us and answer our prayers, and that He wants what is best for us, alhamdulillah.

Look how Ibraaheem showed the people how foolish they were! He put the axe in the hand of the biggest idol, and teased them, telling them that this idol, that can't move or speak, had broken the others- even the people had to admit that this could not have happened- they saw how silly their beliefs were when he did this to them.

Then the people had to resort to using their power and strength, as they could not argue with the truth that Ibraaheem had showed them. They decided to burn Ibraaheem. They gathered together a huge amount of wood, and dug a hole in the ground and set it aflame. Then they took Ibraaheem and threw him into the fire. But Allaah sent down His command to the fire and said to it, *Oh fire! Be coolness and safety for Ibraaheem.*-(Surat Al-Anbiyaa', Ayat 69) Thus Allaah saved Ibraaheem from the fire, and ruined the plan of the disbelievers, and humiliated and defeated them.

You may have been burned by a candle or match at some time- think how much it would hurt to have your whole body burned, mash'Allaah. And yet Ibraaheem trusted in Allaah, as he knew that Allaah would protect him- and Allaah made a miracle for Ibraaheem! He told the fire to be cool and to not harm Ibraaheem, and Ibraaheem was not burned, alhamdulillah!! The people's idols could not have done that, that's for sure- no person could do such a thing, only Allaah!

In the country of Babylon there was an evil king named Nimrod. The people were oppressed by him, and he claimed that he was their god, and made them worship him. When he heard about Ibraaheem, he called for him and asked him about the lord that he called people to worship. He said, *Who is your lord, Oh Ibraaheem?* Ibraaheem answered, "My Lord is He who gives life and causes death."-(Surat Al-Baqarah, Ayat 258)

Nimrod said, *I give life and cause death!*-(Surat Al-Baqarah, Ayat 258) He meant by that that whoever he wished to be dead he would order killed, and whoever he wished to live he would leave alone.

When Ibraaheem saw how he twisted the words to give them a different meaning, he said to him, *Verily, Allaah causes the sun to rise from the east, so cause it to rise from the west.*-(Surat Al-Baqarah, Ayat 258) Nimrod knew that he could not do this and so he was utterly and completely defeated.

You should think of Nimrod whenever you hear of someone calling to himself, trying to get people to follow him. Anytime a person tries to put himself in the position of being worshiped or followed, you should know that what he is calling to is not true. The Messenger of Allaah, may Allaah's praise and salutations be upon him, did not call to himself- he called to Allaah, and to worship Allaah alone. This is what Ibraaheem, Moosa, Yusuf, and all of the other prophets and messengers called to as well. This is the only real and true religion, because people will always make mistakes and fall into error- Allaah never does this. People are born, and then they eventually die. Allaah was not born, and He will not die. People can only do that which Allaah allows them to do. But Allaah can do anything and everything that He wishes to do- He even created everything out of nothing! No person can do this, mash'Allaah. So don't listen to people who claim that they should be followed as only Allaah should be followed, insh'Allaah.

Many of Ibraaheem's people worshipped the planets, and took them as gods instead of Allaah. Ibraaheem decided to try to show them the falsehood of their actions. He waited until night fell, and a planet rose shining in the sky. He said to his people, "This is my lord." Then he waited until the planet set, and could no longer be seen. Then he told them, "I do not like those that set." Meaning, how could this be a lord when it disappears and sets in the sky?! Then he waited until the moon came out, and filled the sky with light, and he said, "This is my lord." But it also disappeared and its light was extinguished, so he told them that this could not be a lord either. Soon the sun rose in the sky and filled the earth with light and warmth, so he said, "This is my lord, this is greater." But then, the sun set, and it became clear to the people that it was not fitting for a lord either. Ibraaheem told his people, "I am indeed free from all that you join as partners with Allaah."

However, his people still remained stubbornly upon falsehood, and tried to argue with him. They threatened him with the evil they thought their gods could do to him. Ibraaheem remained steadfast, as he knew that nothing could harm him except by the will of Allaah.

Ibraaheem was certainly a very brave, wise man. Look how he kept showing the people the ignorance and foolishness of their worshipping false gods! First he showed them how silly it was to think that the big idol could have harmed the others. Then he challenged Nimrod to make the sun rise in the west- as certainly Allaah could do this, but no man could do this. Then, he showed the people how silly they were to worship the planets, moon and sun, as these are thing which rise and fall, and Allaah was never created and Allaah will never die or go away, alhamdulillah.

Still, the people were stubborn, wanting to remain on that which their fathers had been upon. They refused to see the truth no matter how much Ibraaheem told them and showed them. Alhamdulillah, we have to remember that only Allaah can guide people- we can do all that we can to help and teach them, but in the end it is still up to Allaah, alhamdulillah.

Hands On Activities

The moon goes through different phases every month. What this means is that we see different amounts of the moon at different times of the month, due to how much sunshine is reaching it. The moon is important in Islaam, because our calendar is based upon it. Do you remember when Ramadhaan began a few days ago? The Muslims knew it had began because they had looked for the hilaal, or crescent moon to appear in the sky, signaling the beginning of the month. And this crescent signals the beginning of every month, not just Ramadhaan. Another way the moon is important to the Muslims is that we are told that it is good to fast the "white days" of the month- the three days in which the moon is full every single month. This is a good thing to do if we are able because it pleases Allaah, and it also makes our fasting during Ramadhaan a bit easier, alhamdulillah, because we are used to fasting somewhat. We just read how some of the people at the time of Ibraaheem used to worship the moon- this was very silly of them, because, as Ibraaheem showed them, the moon comes and goes- it is simply a creation of Allaah, not a god all by itself.

Here are some activities to help you understand the moon and its phases, insh'Allaah.

1. Every few days this month, go outside with a pencil or black crayon and some paper. Sit down and look at the moon. Try to draw what you see as closely as possible. When you look at the moon, you will see that there are darker parts and lighter parts- draw these into your moon pictures. People used to say that there was a man on the moon because of these shapes. Others said that

the moon was made of green cheese! Both of these ideas are silly, of course. The moon is a huge rock that orbits around the Earth. It has high parts, and low parts, and this is what you are seeing when you see the light and dark sections on the moon. At the end of the month you should have some really neat moon pictures that you made all by yourself, insh'Allaah!

2. Make a small flip book of the moon's phases using blank index cards. On each card, draw a picture of a moon phase. Begin with the new moon, then the crescent, then half, then three quarters, then the full moon- then continue backwards, going to three quarters, then half, then crescent then new again. Draw your pictures nearer to the right side of each card than the left side. Staple the left side. Now, hold the book by the stapled side in your left hand and flip through it with your right hand- it should like the moon is going through a whole month of phases, right before your eyes!

Here are some pictures of the moon in its phases to help you, insh'Allaah.

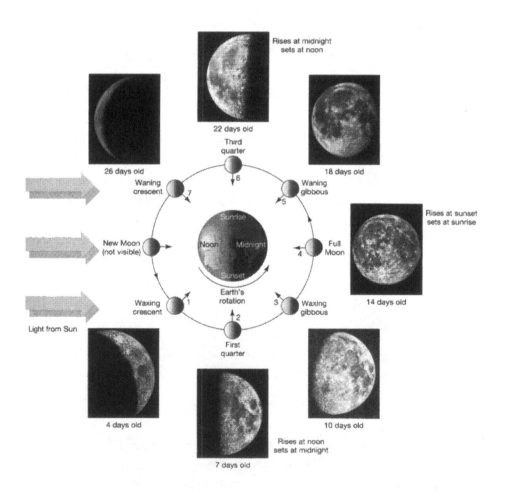

3. Do you know the months of the Islamic calendar? In Islaam, we are told to be different from the non-Muslims as much as we are able- one way that we can be different from them is to learn the months of the Muslim calendar, and use those, and the Muslim days of the week, when we say the date. Remember that the Muslim calendar is based on the moon- so Ramadhaan will not always be during the same season every year, like December or July is for the calendar of disbelievers.

The Muslim months are:

Muharram

Safr

Rabi' al-Awwal

Rabi' ath-Thaani

Jumada al-Awwal

Jumada ath-Thaani

Rajab

Sha'baan

Ramadhaan

Shawwal

Dhul Qa'da

Dhul Hijja

The Muslim days of the week are:

Yawm as-Sabt

Yawm al-Ahad

Yawm al-Ithnain

Yawm ath-Thalaathah

Yawm al-Arba'

Yawm al-Khamees

Yawm al-Jumu'ah

You can make flashcards to help you remember them. Or make two cards for each month and day of the week, and play the memory game with them!

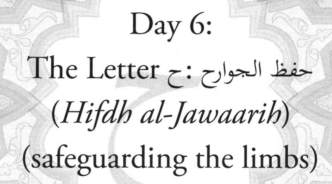

Day 6:
The Letter ح : حفظ الجوارح
(*Hifdh al-Jawaarih*)
(safeguarding the limbs)

Safeguarding the limbs from wrongdoing and sins is affirmed and made obligatory along with the fasting.

The Prophet, may Allaah's praise and salutations be upon him, said, *{Whoever does not leave off evil speech and acting in accordance with such speech, then Allaah has no need for him to leave off his food and drink.}* ("Saheeh al-Bukhaari")

al-Haafidh ibn Haajir, may Allaah have mercy upon him, mentioned that what is meant by this is the rejection of the fasting which is mixed with evil, and the acceptance of the fasting which is free from it. As he mentioned, narrating from al-Baydaawee, that what is intended by the legislation of fasting is not hunger and thirst itself. Rather, what is intended by the fast is that which results from hunger and thirst, such as the cutting off of desires and changing the soul which commands evil to the soul which is confident in the mercy of Allaah.

So, oh dear one, safeguard your limbs from wrongdoing. Do not allow your intellect to contemplate anything except in obedience to Allaah. Do not allow your heart to carry within it anything except good for the male and female Muslims. Do not allow your eyes to fall upon, or your ears to listen to, or your tongue to utter anything except that which Allaah loves and is pleased with- and strive with your soul concerning that.

Allaah, the Most High, says, *As for those who strive hard in Us (Our Cause), We will surely guide them to Our paths (i.e. Allaah's religion). And verily, Allaah is with the muhsinoon (good-doers).*-(Surat al-'Ankaboot, Ayat 69)

Further Points of Benefit

This is incredibly important, mash'Allaah, both within this blessed month and outside of it. We must strive to refrain from any deeds- be those of the heart, tongue or limbs- which are displeasing to Allaah, and turn our hearts and minds and limbs to obedience of Him, as in this is the true happiness and success in this life and the next.

Sheikh Saalih ibn Fauzaan ibn 'Abdullah al-Fauzaan, may Allaah preserve him, says concerning that which is forbidden for the fasting person,

All praise is due to Allaah alone for His favors and beneficence, and may His praise and salutations be upon our Prophet Muhammad, who was the caller to Allaah's pleasure, as well as whoever was guided by his guidance and held tight to his Sunnah until the Day of Judgment. To Proceed:

Know that there are certain etiquettes in regards to fasting which one must take care to manifest in his character so that his fasting will be as outlined in the Islamic legislation, in order that the one who is fasting will receive the full benefit of his fast.

The Prophet, may Allaah's praise and salutations be upon him, said, *{There may be a fasting person who does not benefit from his fast except for in hunger.}* (Ibn Maajah (1690) and an-Nasaa'i in his "Sunan al-Kubra" (3249) and Ahmad (Vol 2, No 373)

and al-Haakim in "al-Mustadrak" and al-Baihaqee in his "Sunan al-Kubra" and al-Haakim said, "It is authentic upon the conditions of al-Bukhaari though they did not narrate it.")

For fasting is not only the leaving off of food and drink; rather it is also abandoning what should not be done from speech and action which are prohibited or disliked. Some of the Pious Predecessors said, "The easiest part of fasting is the leaving off of food and drink; but one is not brought closer to Allaah completely by abandoning usually lawful desires except after being brought closer to Him by leaving off that which is always forbidden to him. And it is always obligatory upon the Muslim to abandon that which is forbidden- but when fasting this is even more strongly the case. So he who performs a prohibited act while not fasting- this is wrongdoing and it deserves punishment. But if he does it while fasting it is wrongdoing and deserves punishment- and it also adversely affects his fast by decreasing its reward or annulling it completely. And the true fasting person is he whose stomach fasts from food and drink, and his limbs fast from wrongdoing, and his tongue fasts from evil and bad talk, and his hearing fasts from music, backbiting and slander, and his eyes fast from looking at that which is forbidden."

The Prophet, may Allaah's praise and salutations be upon him said, *{Whoever does not leave off evil speech and acting in accordance with such speech, then Allaah has no need for him to leave off his food and drink.}* ("Saheeh al-Bukhaari" (1903))

And in the two Saheehs (al-Bukhaari and Muslim) from Abi Hurairah, may Allaah be pleased with him, with a chain of narration connected to the Prophet, may Allaah's praise and salutations be upon him, *{Fasting is a shield; so on the day in which one is fasting he should not speak evilly, nor do evil deeds, or act in an ignorant manner. And if a person fights or abuses him, he should say, "I am fasting."}* *(al-Bukhaari (1894) Muslim (1151)*

And a shield is that which protects its owner and prevents him from being hurt by another person's weapon. So like this, fasting protects the one who is fasting from entering into evil deeds in which the consequence is prompt and everlasting punishment.

And evil speech is immoral and bad speech. Imaam Ahmad and other than him narrated with a chain connected to the Prophet, may Allaah's praise and salutations be upon him, *{Fasting is a shield as long as it is not broken.}* It was asked, "How is it broken?" He, may Allaah's praise and salutations be upon him, replied, *{By lying or backbiting.}* (an-Nasaa'i (2231) Ahmad (195,196) Abu Ya'la in his "Musnad" (878) al-Baihaqi in "ash-Shu'ab" (3294 and 3370))

So this is a proof that backbiting breaks the fast; meaning, it affects it adversely. And as a broken shield does not benefit its owner, so the broken fast will not benefit its owner.

And backbiting, as the Messenger, may Allaah's praise and salutations be upon him said, is {...*speaking about your brother in a way in which he would not like.*} (Muslim (2589) Abu Daawud (4874) at-Tirmidhi (1934))

And it has been said that it breaks the fast due to a narration in Imaam Ahmad's "Musnad": "Two women fasted during the time of the Messenger of Allaah, may Allaah's praise and salutations be upon him, and they were so thirsty that they felt as if they would die. This was mentioned to the Prophet and he turned away from them. And they were once again mentioned to him, so he called them to him and commanded them to vomit. Meaning, to bring up that which was in their stomachs. So they vomited enough to fill a small container with pus, blood with infected matter in it, and meat. So the Prophet, may Allaah's praise and salutations be upon him said, {*These two women fasted from that which Allaah allowed them and did not fast from that which He had prohibited them from; for they sat together and backbit others.*}" (Ahmad Vol. 5, No. 431)

And what happened to these two women from vomiting up these hateful and disgusting matters- it is from the miracles which Allaah performed by the hand of his Messenger to make clear to the people what evil effects came from backbiting.

Allaah, the Most High, says, ❖*And spy not, neither backbite one another. Would one of you like to eat the flesh of his dead brother? You would hate it (so hate backbiting).*❖- (Surat al-Hujuraat, From Ayat 12)

And the hadeeth proves that backbiting breaks the fast of the one who is fasting, and this is figurative; and it annuls the award of the fast, as is agreed to by a majority of the scholars.

And may Allaah's praise and salutations be upon our Prophet, Muhammad, his family, and his Companions. ("Majaalis Shahr Ramadhaan al-Mubaarak wa Itihaaf ahl Eemaan bi Duroos Shahr Ramadhaan" Pages 161-163)

So beware, oh my sisters, of wasting your precious time during this blessed month in idle talk, gossip, backbiting and slander- and this is by speaking it, or through listening to it. Mash'Allaah, the women fall into this easily- look closely at the definition of backbiting given by Sheikh Fauzaan above- it is anything that your sister would not like said about her. So next time you are with your companions, truly contemplate the worth of every word that you speak or hear, and understand how it will weigh in the scale of your deeds on the Day of Judgment. Choose your companions wisely, and guard your tongue from all vain and evil talk.

Family Time

The Story of the Prophet Ibraaheem Part 2

Ibraaheem traveled to Shaam along with his wife, and his nephew, Lut. When Ibraaheem grew old, his wife Saarah had still not given him any children. Saarah felt sorry for Ibraaheem, because she had not been able to have any children, so she gave him her servant, Haajar, to marry. Ibraaheem married Haajar, and soon she had a beautiful baby named Ismaa'eel. When Saarah saw how much Ibraaheem loved his son, Ismaa'eel, she began to feel jealous of Haajar, and she wished that she had been given a child too.

Allaah ordered Ibraaheem to take his wife Haajar, and his baby, Ismaa'eel, and bring them to the land of Makkah to live. Ibraaheem traveled with them through the hot desert until they reached Makkah. At that time, Makkah was a dry, hot place, with no people living there, no plants, and no water. Here Ibraaheem left his wife and child, and returned to Shaam. He supplicated Allaah saying, *❝Oh My Lord! I have made some of my offspring dwell in an uncultivable valley by Your Sacred House, in order, Oh Our Lord, that they might perform Salaah. So fill some hearts among men with love towards them, and provide them with fruits so that they may give thanks.❞*- (Surat Ibraaheem, Ayat 38)

Haajar stayed behind with her little boy, and she was patient and calm, knowing that Allaah would provide for them. Soon the food and water that Ibraaheem had left for them ran out, and her milk dried up so that she could not nurse her baby. The baby began to cry from hunger and thirst, and Haajar was filled with sorrow and pity for him. She left him and began to run here and there, looking for water. She climbed up the mountain of Safaa, and then she ran down and ran until she reached the mountain of Marwah, but she did not see anyone. She ran back and forth between the two mountains seven times, but she did not find any water, and so she returned to the baby. When she came back, she was surprised to see water flowing from under the feet of the baby. She hurried to catch the water and give some to her baby to drink, and drink some herself. This water was the blessed water of Zamzam. It still flows today in Makkah.

Both Saarah and Haajar are good examples for us. Saarah knew that her husband wanted a child, and so she chose not to be selfish, and helped him to marry another wife so that this would be possible. In Islaam, we are told to want for our brother Muslim what we want for ourselves. This means that we want good for ourselves, so we should want good for others as well. And, as we don't like bad things to happen to us, we shouldn't want bad things to happen to others, either. Saarah did get jealous later, but jealousy, as we talked about before, is an emotion everyone feels, like sadness or anger. Insh'Allaah we have to try to deal with it in a good way when it happens, though this is not always easy.

We see Haajar's patience, and her faith in Ibraaheem and in Allaah. She traveled far from the land she was born and raised in, with only her husband and baby. And when Ibraaheem left her in Makkah, she was not angry or upset. She knew he had a reason for doing this, and she knew that Allaah would take care of her and her baby. Look also at her compassion and love for her baby, as she ran back and forth looking for water- this is something that the pilgrims do when they go on Hajj, to remind themselves of Haajar's search. And Allaah provided her and the baby with the water of Zamzam, which is a very pure and blessed water that still flows today, alhamdulillah, and it is still just as pure and good as the day that Haajar found it.

One day, a caravan of people passed by, and they saw birds circling in the valley where Haajar and Ismaa'eel were. They were surprised, because they knew that there had been no water there, and birds will not stay where there is no water. They went to see why they were there, and they found Haajar and her son, Ismaa'eel, and the well of Zamzam. They asked Haajar if they could stay and live there, and she agreed. Their tribe was called Jurhum, and they spoke Arabic. Baby Ismaa'eel was raised among them, and learned to speak Arabic from them. When he grew up, he married one of their daughters. Sometimes Ibraaheem would come to visit his wife and son in Makkah, before returning to Shaam.

One day, when Ibraaheem was in Shaam with his wife Saarah, he was surprised by three young handsome men, who came to him and greeted him, saying, ◈*Salaama," He answered them with: "Salaamun! You are a people unknown to me.*◈-(Surat Adh-Dhaariyaat, Ayat 25)

They were really the angels sent by Allaah, named Jibreel, Mikaa'eel, and Israafeel, but they were in the form of men, so Ibraaheem did not know who they were.

Then Ibraaheem went quickly into his house, and had a fat roasted calf prepared for his guests. He brought it out, and placed it in front of them and said, ◈*Will you not eat?*◈-(Surat Adh-Dhaariyaat, Ayat 27)

The guests did not stretch out their hands to eat from the food. This was because they were really angels. When Ibraaheem saw that they were not eating, he felt afraid of them. If they were people with good will, they would have eaten from the food.

They told him, ◈*Do not be afraid. We are angels who have been sent to destroy the people of Lut for their evil deeds.*◈Saarah was happy to hear that the evil people would be destroyed, so she laughed. Then the angels gave them the good news that they would have a child. Saarah was so surprised that she cried out and hit her face. She did not know how she could have a child. She had never been able to even when she was young, and now she was an old woman!

The angels told her that she would indeed have a child, as Allaah had said so, and He knows everything.

Saarah became pregnant, and soon she had a baby named Ishaaq. Ibraaheem and Saarah were filled with joy, and they thanked Allaah for the amazing blessing that he had given them. Ishaaq was thirteen years younger than his elder brother, Ismaa'eel. He also grew up to be a prophet, and he was the father of Ya'qub, and the grandfather of Yusuf.

Here we see the generosity of Ibraaheem and Saarah, that they prepared a special meal for these people whom they had never even met before. They wanted to honor them and make them feel welcome and special. They felt bad when the angels didn't eat, because they didn't know yet that they were angels. They thought there might be something wrong, because they didn't eat.

Also, we see how Saarah trusted Allaah. Even though she was an old woman, and Ibraaheem was an old man, she believed that He had the power to make it so she would have a baby, alhamdulillah. We have to always remember to turn to Allaah for anything that we want or need, because only Allaah can give us these things. Even if your mother or father actually gives you something, you have to remember that it is Allaah who made this happen, and thank Him as well as your parents, insh'Allaah.

Ismaa'eel grew older, and became big enough to help his father with all the things he had to do. Ibraaheem loved his son very much, and he held him very dear. One time, while he was asleep with Ismaa'eel next to him, he saw in a dream that he was slaughtering Ismaa'eel. The dreams of a prophet are revelation from Allaah, so he knew that this meant that Allaah was telling him to do this thing. He was filled with sorrow, as Ismaa'eel was his first son, and had a special place in his heart that could not be filled by anything else. But Ibraaheem was strong and patient, so he told Ismaa'eel about it, and asked him what he thought. Even though Ismaa'eel was only a young boy, he knew that his duty was to obey Allaah and his father, so he said, ❰*Oh my father! Do that which you are told to do. If Allaah wills, you will find that I am patient.*❱-(Surat As-Saaffaat, Ayat 102)

Ibraaheem got ready to sacrifice his son, and laid him on his forehead, and took the knife in his hand. Then, he heard a voice calling him, saying, ❰*Oh Ibraaheem! You have fulfilled the dream*❱-(Surat As-Saaffaat, Ayat 104-105) Ibraaheem turned, and he saw a fine white ram with horns. Ibraaheem was told to sacrifice the ram instead. This was the way that Allaah rewarded him for his patience and obedience, and ransomed his son for him. Ismaa'eel grew up into a man, and Allaah made him a prophet, and he had many children. These children also had children, and from these children was our Prophet, Muhammad, May Allaah's praise and salutations be upon him.

Ibraaheem and Ismaa'eel were truly brave, faithful, men- look how they simply accepted what Allaah had commanded them with. It is not always easy to be obedient and good when we know that we should be, but we must always try to do what we are told. This has a lot of benefits- in this life and the next life, alhamdulillah. Think about how you like it when you tell your little brother or your friend to do something, and they do it without fighting or complaining. Shouldn't you do this for your parents and teachers- and especially, shouldn't you do this for Allaah? By being obedient, we please Allaah, and He is the One who created us and gives us what we need to live- we owe it to Him to listen and obey.

Soon, another command from Allaah came to Ibraaheem. He told him to build the Ka'bah in Makkah. Ibraaheem and Ismaa'eel began to build the Ka'bah, Ismaa'eel bringing the stones, and Ibraaheem placing them on the walls. Allaah sent down the Black Stone from the heavens, and they placed it in the walls. When the walls began to get too high to reach, Ibraaheem stood on a rock, and his footprints were pressed into it. This rock is called 'Maqaam Ibraaheem' and it is in Makkah today. So many people have touched the stone that it has been worn down, and you cannot see the foot prints anymore. While they were working, they asked Allaah to accept this work from them. They also asked Him to make them submit to His commands, and to teach them how to make Hajj and Umrah at the Ka'bah, and accept their repentance.

Today, every year, millions of Muslims make Hajj and Umrah to the Ka'bah, and they remember the amazing story of Ibraaheem and Ismaa'eel, who built the Ka'bah. When they run between Safaa and Marwaa, they remember the story of Haajar, looking for water, and when they drink from Zamzam water, they think of how it sprung from under Ismaa'eel's feet. In addition, when they sacrifice their animals, they are reminded of Ibraaheem's patience when ordered to sacrifice his son, and of how Allaah ransomed him.

Points of Benefit

1. You must love Allaah and obey Him in whatever He commands, no matter what it is.

2. You must always be dutiful to your parents, and obey them. You must stay away from annoying them, disobeying them, and treating them badly.

3. Allaah took the hardship away from Ibraaheem and Ismaa'eel, because they believed in Him, and were ready to do anything they told them.

4. When you are called to give something up for Allaah, then you should do it.

5. When you are in need of anything, then turn to Allaah and ask Him for it, and trust that He will answer your prayer.

Hands On Activities

1. Make the pages for Ibraaheem and his sons, Ishaaq and Ismaa'eel, in your prophet book. Write the prophet's name with hollow letters and color them in as you like. Draw a little picture or write a verse from the Qur'aan from the story to remind you of who they were and what they did.

2. Show your pages to someone in your family, or to a friend, and tell them all that you can remember about the story of Ibraaheem and his sons.

3. Have you ever seen a picture of the Ka'bah in Makkah? If you haven't, have your parents or teacher show you a photograph of it. When you see it, you will see that it looks like a huge black cube with a thick ring of gold around the top. What you are looking at is not really the surface of the Ka'bah. You are looking at a huge cloth which the people use to cover the Ka'bah, to protect it. Every year a new cover is made and put on the Ka'bah. The gold that you see is fancy stitching- they do it with gold thread!! Also there are times when the King of Saudi Arabia, who is the one who is in charge of the Ka'bah, goes inside and makes sure it is clean. One thing to remember is that the Ka'bah that you see is not the same one that Ibraaheem and Ismaa'eel built. It has been re-built more than once through the years, mash'Allaah. But the stone that Ibraaheem stood on is STILL there- there is a large structure over it. If you ever go there, ask to see where that stone is. Also, if you look at the Ka'bah, you will see one stone that is set apart from the others, surrounded by a special silver frame. This is the Black Stone- Allaah sent this stone from Heaven, and it is from the original building that Ibraaheem and Ismaa'eel built!!

   Why don't you try to make a model of the Ka'bah? You can use a square box for this. If it has words or pictures on it, simply cover it with construction paper. If you like, you can try to make a fabric covering for it like the real Ka'bah, or you can simply paint, color, or use the proper colors of construction paper to make your Ka'bah the right color, insh'Allaah. You could even make a model out of wood, blocks, stone, or clay, if you like. Or, if you want, just draw a picture of it, insh'Allaah.

4. Think of the generosity of Ibraaheem and Saarah. What are some ways that you can be kind and generous to others? Write down some ways to be kind and generous to your brothers and sisters, to your parents, to your neighbors, and to your community. Circle the ones you think you can do this week. Put a check next to the ones you think you can do this month. Put a box around the ones you want to try to do over the next year, after Ramadhaan has finished, insh'Allaah.

Day 7:
The Letter خ: الخروج من المنزل
(*al-Khurooj min al-Manzil*)
(leaving the house)

During the month of Ramadhaan the women going out from their houses increases, whether in order to perform the taraaweeh prayer, or to go to the shops in order to purchase that which is necessary for the Eid celebration, or other than that. So before you embark upon that, dear sister, remember that the foundational principle concerning the woman is that she stays in her house.

Indeed, her prayer in her house is better for her than her prayer in the masjid, along with the fact that it is permissible for her to go to it.

The Prophet, may Allaah's praise and salutations be upon him, said, *{Do not forbid the maidservants of Allaah from going to the masjids; but their houses are better for them.}* (reported in Abu Daawud, and Sheikh al-Albaani has declared it to be authentic)

So what is the matter with you, in regards that which is less than that (i.e. not as important as the prayer) from seeking the worldly things?!? So, oh beloved one, do not go out often without necessity, and do not waste these great nights in the marketplaces.

Also, remember the Prophet's, may Allaah's praise and salutations be upon him, saying, *{The woman is 'aurah (that which must be concealed); so when she goes out, the Shaytaan elevates her (in the sight of others).}* (at-Tirmidhi, and Sheikh al-Albaani has declared it to be authentic)

And if you are compelled to leave the house, then adhere to and comply with the legislated, covering, hijaab, along with its conditions which have been mentioned by the people of knowledge. And they are:

1. That it encompasses the entire body

2. It is not beautiful in and of itself

3. It is thick and is not transparent

4. It is wide and loose- it is not narrow or form-fitting

5. It is not perfumed

6. It does not resemble the clothing of the men

7. It does not resemble the clothing of the disbelieving women

8. It is not from the clothing of fame or notoriety

Further Points of Benefit

Mash'Allaah, this trend of the women going out often, and increasing in this during the blessed month of Ramadhaan, can be seen both in the Western countries as well as the Muslim countries, may Allaah rectify us all. In the West, women go out during the day to "take their minds off fasting," spending precious time shopping for things which are not necessary, or simply going out with others who are shopping to pass the time. Here in the Muslim countries the markets are open until all hours of the night, and women go out to them after 'Isha and waste their time in a similar fashion.

Indeed we know that it is permissible for a woman to go out to meet her needs, as long as she is dressed in the proper hijaab and conducts herself with modestly and good character. But what, oh sister, do you consider a need? Think about this the next time you want to just "get out of the house"- is this a necessity, or is it simply a desire? Especially during this beautiful month of Ramadhaan, when we should be striving to perform any actions that will please Allaah and assist us in reaping the benefits of this blessed month. Besides going out to the markets, one should also consider when they go out to spend time with friends. While this is not forbidden, we must take the time to consider why we are going out, and with whom we will be visiting, and we must make the effort to make sure that the conversation is beneficial, and free of vain or evil talk, insh'Allaah.

Sheikh Muhammad ibn Saalih al-'Utheimeen, may Allaah have mercy upon him, said, discussing the idea that a Muslim woman consider herself a "prisoner" in her own home,

"…A woman within her house is free to go to any area of the house, and take care of any needs within her home, and work for herself- so where is the confinement, and where is the prison? Yes, it could be considered a prison by the one who wishes to needlessly go out and be like men…so it is upon women to fear Allaah and to refer back to whatever was stated by their Lord and Creator, and refer back to whatever was commanded by the Messenger of the Lord of All the Worlds, may Allaah's praise and salutations be upon him, to them and to other women. And that is that they be aware and know that they will meet Allaah, the Most Glorified and the Most Exalted, and that He will ask them what was their response and stance towards the Messenger sent to them and his guidance. And indeed no one knows when an individual will return back to Allaah and be questioned. Certainly a woman may start the morning within her home, her fortress, and when the evening arrives she would have entered her grave. Or she may spend the evening in her house, and when the morning arrives she has entered her grave. Therefore these Muslim women must fear Allaah, and turn away from the corrupt Western callers; as these Western callers are those who, after they consumed that corruption, they threw its remaining bones and gristle to us. And some of us snatched up that remaining bone and gristle after these Western nations have already consumed whatever benefit it had!" (from the radio program *Nur alaa Dhaarb*, as quoted in "My Home, My Path," page 12)

Mash'Allaah, we should strive to make our homes places of beauty, comfort, and benefit, a refuge for ourselves and our families, a place to spend our time in ways which please Allaah, the Most High. Then, when we do go out, we must make sure that our reasons and intentions are good, and that we wear the correct hijaab, and behave in a manner which is proper and pleasing to Allaah. And Allaah knows best.

Family Time

Yesterday, we discussed how generous Ibraaheem and Saarah were to their guests. Tonight, the whole family will, insh'Allaah, take part in making a special meal to share. If possible, invite some guests over to share your food, or take some over to a friend or neighbor who may not have something nice to have, or who you think would appreciate sharing in your meal. Keep in mind the blessings of helping someone else break their fast- your reward is like their fast! And of course the reward for generosity and selflessness, alhamdulillah.

Remember that the Sunnah is to break one's fast with dates and water- so insh'Allaah do this first, then eat the meal below later in the evening. We tried to come up with some foods that would be fun to make, and that wouldn't cost a lot of money or be wasteful, alhamdulillah. Each meal will focus on foods from a different Muslim country or group of people, insh'Allaah. Try to get everyone in the family involved- even your father and little brothers and sisters- the more people, the more fun!

Special Ramadhaan Meal Number One:

These are recipes from Egypt. Remember Egypt is where Yusuf was sold into slavery and put into prison, and where he helped the people get through the years of no rain and widespread hunger, alhamdulillah. Look on a map or globe and find Egypt. What is the river that flows through it? Is it a small country, or a big one? What are some of the main cities in Egypt? See if you can get a book, or go to a website that has photographs from Egypt. If you like, try to decorate the room you eat in to make it look at least a little bit Egyptian!

If you don't make all of these recipes, at least try one or two, insh'Allaah, to see how they taste, so you know how your Egyptian brothers and sisters eat. Also, try to buy or bake some pita bread, as this is the most common bread eaten in Egypt. It is flat, and round, and you can open up to make a nifty little pocket to put your *falafels* or anything else you want to eat inside!

Falafel

These are eaten as a snack food all over the Middle East. They are made in many different ways, depending on where you are and who is doing the cooking!

This makes about 24 falafel

4 cups cooked chickpeas (garbanzo beans) or two 15 oz cans, drained- you can also use fava beans for these, or half and half- each will be different!

5 cloves of garlic, minced

2 tsp cumin

1 tsp turmeric

¼ tsp crushed red pepper (optional)

1 tsp salt

1 medium onion, minced

¼ cup parsley, minced (optional)

¼ cup water

1 tbsp lemon juice

1/3 cup flour

Vegetable oil for frying them in

1. Combine all the ingredients except the flour in a blender and blend into a smooth batter. Or, you can mash them together in a bowl.

2. Add the flour, stirring it in well. The batter should be fairly stiff.

3. Heat a heavy skillet and add 4 tbsp of oil. When it is hot, drop the batter by flattened tablespoonfuls into the oil. Don't overcrowd the skillet! Let them cook for about 10 minutes on each side, so that they are golden and crisp. Don't let them get too brown, or they will be hard. You will probably need to add more oil at some point.

These are great in pita bread, or dipped in tahini, yogurt, hot sauce or, while this is not Egyptian, ketchup!

Fatat Dejaj Gazawah
To make ahead:

Make rice to equal about two or three cups- cover and set aside

Then you need:

1 3lb chicken, with its skin on

2 large onions, cut into quarters

3 cardamom pods, opened

2 medium cinnamon sticks

Salt and pepper to taste

Combine all the ingredients in a large pot and add water to cover by a couple of inches. Cover, bring it to boil, and reduce the heat to medium. Let it cook for an hour and a half, adding water if needed to keep it covered. Skim any foam off the top as it rises. Remove the chicken from the stock and let it cool.

Now you need:

Chicken from above, cut into pieces

Stock from above

Salt and pepper to taste

20 cloves of garlic, mashed

1 ½ cups lemon juice

2 hot peppers, seeded and finely chopped

Pita or other flat bread. Flour tortillas could possibly be substituted, or possibly regular loaf bread, though the result will not be the same.

1. Preheat your broiler

2. Season the chicken pieces with the salt and pepper and place them on a baking sheet. Broil them until the chicken is a nice golden color. This should take about two minutes. Cover with aluminum foil and set aside.

3. Combine the garlic, lemon juice, and hot pepper in a bowl and set aside.

4. Use a large serving platter. Place one piece of the flat bread on the platter. Break the rest of the flat bread up into 3 or 4 inch pieces and arrange them around the edge of the platter. Drizzle about ½ cup of the garlic/lemon juice mixture and ½ cup of chicken stock over the bread. Put the rice over the center piece of bread, mounding it up high, but leaving an edge of bread showing around it. Arrange the chicken pieces over the rice. When you serve it, make sure everyone gets some of each layer. Serve the remaining garlic/lemon juice mixture on the side, for people to add to their servings as they like.

Pasta with Lentils
This is to Egyptians, what macaroni and cheese is to Americans- it is comfort food!

To make ahead (or buy already prepared tomato sauce)

3 tbsp olive oil

Two medium onions, minced

6 or 7 cloves of garlic, mashed

One fifteen ounce can crushed tomatoes

1 tsp vinegar

1 tsp salt

1 tsp black pepper

A dash of red pepper

1. Heat the oil in a heavy pot. Add the onions and sauté for about five minutes, until they are soft and translucent. Add the garlic and tomato sauce, stirring until the onions are well coated. Cover the pot and bring to a boil. Reduce the heat and simmer for about 25 minutes.

2. Add the remaining ingredients and simmer for a couple of minutes more. Cover and set aside.

Now you need:

2 cups dried brown lentils, picked over and rinsed well

2 tsp salt

1 cup uncooked elbow macaroni

2 cups of uncooked rice

½ cup olive oil

3 or 4 large onions, cut in half and then sliced very thinly

2 tsp ground cumin

Black pepper to taste

Tomato sauce (from a jar or from above)

1. Place the lentils in a large pot and cover with water by a couple of inches. Bring it to a boil over high heat, then reduce the heat and simmer them until tender. Add 1 teaspoon of salt, and remove from heat.

2. Cook the macaroni according to package directions. Don't cook it to mush, you want it to be firm. Drain and set aside.

3. Cook the rice according to package directions. Set aside when finished.

4. Heat the olive oil in a large skillet over high heat. Add the onions and fry until crisp, about eight to ten minutes. We don't cook ours as long, as we like them to be a little softer. Transfer the onions to a paper towel covered plate to drain. Reserve the cooking oil.

5. Combine the lentils, rice, macaroni, cumin and black pepper in a large pot and stir well. Add the reserved cooking oil and about a fourth of the onions, and stir until the oil is absorbed. Place the pot over low heat and cook, continuously stirring, for 10 minutes. Season to taste with salt.

6. Spoon the lentil mixture onto a large serving platter and sprinkle the remaining fried onions on top. Serve with the tomato sauce on the side, so people can add as much as they like.

Dessert

You could buy some baklava from a bakery or Middle Eastern store, or just serve lots of fresh fruits and nuts. All over the Middle East, people love to eat fresh fruit, and it is very good for you!!

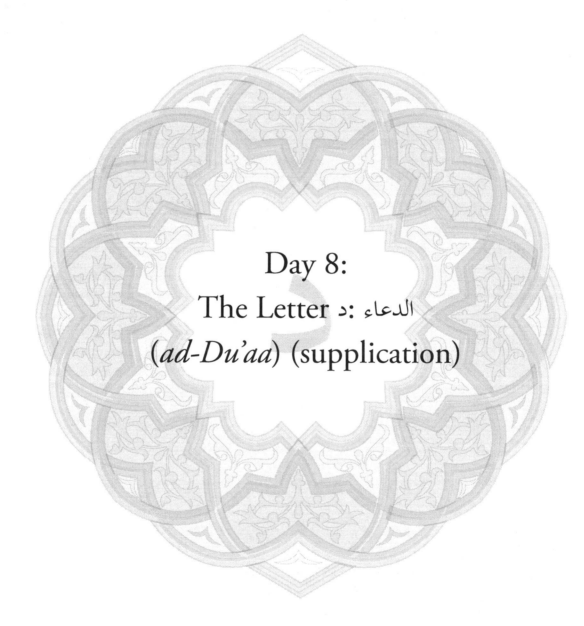

Day 8:
The Letter د: الدعاء
(*ad-Du'aa*) (supplication)

Allaah, the Most High, says, ❨*And your Lord said: "Invoke Me and ask Me for anything, I will respond to your (invocation). Verily, those who scorn My worship [i.e. do not invoke Me, and do not believe in My Oneness,] they will surely enter Hell in humiliation!*❩-(Surat al-Ghaafir, Ayat 60)

It is narrated in a hadeeth that the Prophet, may Allaah's praise and salutations be upon him, said, {*Supplication is worship.*} (Ahmad and other than him, and Sheikh al-Albaani has declared it to be authentic)

So do not let this noble month pass by without striving in relation to supplication and seeking refuge with Allaah, Glorified is He, the Most High, and asking Him for the good in this life and the Hereafter- specifically in the times when the supplications are answered. And from them, by way of example, are:

1. The one who is fasting until he breaks his fast
2. The oppressed one
3. The traveler
4. The parent supplicating for his child
5. The Muslim for his brother Muslim in his absence
6. Between the adhaan and the iqaama
7. In the last third of the night
8. When prostrating in the obligatory prayers
9. When it is raining
10. In the last hour of the day of Juma'ah (Friday)

Do not neglect purity of intention concerning the du'aa, and urgency in it, and avoiding rushing through it, and certainty that it will be answered. Remember the hadeeth of the Prophet, may Allaah's praise and salutations be upon him, {*Indeed your Lord is bashful and generous. He is shy or unwilling concerning His servant, if he (the servant) raises his hands to Him in supplication, that He return them empty, with nothing in them.*} (Abu Daawud, and Sheikh al-Albaani has declared it to be authentic)

So do not be negligent in supplicating and choosing the times when supplication is answered, so that you will not be from those about whom the Prophet, may Allaah's praise and salutations be upon him, said, {*The one who falls short most is the one who falls short in his supplication. And the most stingy of people is the one who is stingy with the salaam (Islamic greeting).*} (Narrated by al-Bayhaqi, and Sheikh al-Albaani has declared it to be authentic.)

Further Points of Benefit

Mash'Allaah, I have heard people say, "The least I can do is make du'a for so and so"…rather, that which one should say is that one of the BEST things one can do is to make du'a, alhamdulillah!! Indeed the One who listens to our du'a and answers them is the only One who has power over all things- there is no better way to get results then to supplicate to our Lord with sincerity, seeking His assistance in any matter. No matter what else we do, whatever course of action we take, its success will only occur by the mercy and permission of Allaah, Mighty and Majestic.

The Conditions for Supplication to be Accepted and the Etiquettes of Supplication:

It is upon the Muslim to adhere to these conditions and etiquettes for this noble act of worship. And all of these conditions and etiquettes are taken from these two verses from Surat al-A'raaf:

❖Invoke your Lord with humility and in secret; for verily He likes not the aggressors. And do not do mischief on the earth, after it has been set in order, and invoke Him with fear and hope. Surely, Allaah's Mercy is (ever) near to the good-doers." (Ayats 55-56)

in which they have been either directly stated, or taken by inference by the noble people of knowledge.

1. That the one who is supplicating have tawheed (belief in the Oneness and Uniqueness of Allaah) in Allaah- in His Lordship, His worship, and His names and attributes- and that his heart be filled with tawheed and the tree of eemaan (faith). As one of the conditions of the acceptance of supplication is that he has obeyed his Lord and left off disobedience to Him. Allaah, the Most High, says,*❖And when My slaves ask you (Oh Muhammad) concerning Me, then (answer them), I am indeed near (to them by My Knowledge). I respond to the invocations of the supplicant when he calls on Me (without any mediator or intercessor). So let them obey Me and believe in Me, so that they may be led aright.❖*-(Surat al-Baqarah, Ayat 186)

2. That it be a legislated supplication, performed in a manner which conforms with the Islamic Legislation.

3. That the one who is supplicating believe that Allaah, Glorified is He, is the only One who is able to answer his du'a by bringing him benefit or protecting him from harm.

4. That the one who is making the du'a fulfills the two pillars of worship: al-ikhlaas, or purity of intention for Allaah alone, and mutaaba', or following the guidance of the Prophet and how he performed the act of worship.

5. Turning to Allaah, alone, with supplication and invocation

6. That his source of food be permissible, and his source of clothing be permissible, and his source of shelter be permissible, and his source of

income be permissible; and that he commands the good and forbids the evil.

7. That he is not transgressing on himself by doing that which is prohibited, and clothing himself in evil deeds such as bad conduct towards his parents or breaking the ties of kinship.

8. That he does not ask in his supplication for something which is evil or which involves breaking the ties of kinship.

9. That he not try to hurry up or slow down the answer of his supplication or lose hope in its being answered, for he is supplicating a generous Lord.

10. That he begin his supplication by praising Allaah with that which is appropriate, and sending the praise and salutations upon His Messenger.

11. That he have certainty that his supplication will be answered.

12. That he send praise and salutations upon the Messenger in the best manner, which is in the beginning of his du'a, in the middle, and in the end. The next best manner is that he do so in the beginning and in the end. Then the next best is that he do so in the beginning.

13. That he begin with himself in his supplication if he is alone, as the Prophet, may Allaah's praise and salutations be upon him, used to do, as did the rest of the Prophets. However, if there were others supplicating with them they would make their du'a in a plural form.

14. That he believes that Allaah, the Most High, will bring him the benefit or stop the harm or change the evil.

15. That he beseeches Allaah by the tawheed of the supplicant and the names and attributes of Allaah and the good deeds of the supplicant before asking for what he needs.

In doing this, there are three levels: The best is to ask Allaah, Glorified and Exalted, by His names and attributes, as some of the scholars interpret the verse *And (all) the Most Beautiful Names belong to Allaah, so call on Him by them, and leave the company of those who belie or deny (or utter impious speech against) His Names.*-(Surat al-A'raaf, From Ayat 180) to mean this. The second is that you ask Him by your need and your good deeds. So you say, for example, "I am your poor, needy, humble servant seeking refuge" and similar things. The third is that you do not mention either of those things, but simply ask for what you need.

16. That he be in a state of purity in a pure place, and well or neatly dressed, if this is possible.

17. That he raises his hands

(Summarized from the book "*Tasheeh ad-Du'a*" by Bakr ibn 'Abdullah Abu Zaid, Pages 21-30)

Family Time

The Story of the Prophet Nuh

Aadam, May Allaah's praise be upon him, died after he had taught his children that they should not worship anyone except Allaah, alone, with no partners. He told them about his story with Iblees, and that Iblees was their enemy. He warned them that Iblees would try to lead them astray, so they must be careful not to fall into his plots and traps. Aadam's children spread throughout the earth, and for a long time they remained true to the right path, and only worshipped Allaah alone.

The Shaytaan hated to see them obeying Allaah, and so he tried his best to turn them away from their religion. He finally found a way to lead them astray. He saw that there were many righteous people among them whom they loved and respected. The most righteous and beloved of these were five men named Wadd, Suwaa', Yaghuth, Ya'uq, and Nasr. When they died, Shaytaan inspired the people to create statues in honor of them, and to name them with their names. They made these statues, and when they saw them, they would remember how righteous the men they were named after used to be, and this would make them want to be more like them. They did not worship these statues, but later, when these people had died, others came after them who were ignorant and worshipped the statues instead of Allaah.

Here we see how people can be lead astray and fall into evil with worshiping the idols. The people thought they were doing good by making the statues of these righteous people, thinking it would help them to remember the goodness of the people themselves. But eventually, the people came to worship the statues themselves, forgetting why they had originally made the statues. This is one of the reasons that Allaah forbids us from making statues and having pictures of things with souls. Not only is this competing with Allaah in creation, but it is also something that could lead us to worship others than Allaah- and that is the greatest sin that one can commit!

Allaah, The Most High, wanted to send a messenger to them, to remind them of the Straight Path. He sent Nuh, may Allaah's praise be upon him, to them. He was a righteous, generous, noble and kind man from among them. He loved good for them, and did his best to make them see the truth. He wanted to warn them of Allaah's punishment, so they could be saved from it. So Nuh went to his people and said to them, *Oh my people! Verily, I am a plain warner to you! You should worship Allaah, and have Taqwa of Him, and obey me. He will forgive your sins and give you respite to an appointed time.* -(Surat Nuh, Ayats 1-4)

He called them to Allaah night and day. He called to them constantly for nine hundred and fifty years. He was patient and kind to them. But all of this did not do them any good. Whenever he tried to call them to the right path, they would stick their fingers in their ears so that they could not hear what he was telling them. Nuh did not lose patience, however, and called to them in public and in private. He tried every way he could think of to make them turn away from their falsehood, but they were too stubborn. Only a few of the poor people answered his call and believed in him.

Look at Nuh- he called to his people for nine hundred and fifty years!! What a patient man he must have been, and he truly must have wanted good for his people to not give up on them. Think of the last time you tried to teach someone something, or get them to do something you wanted to do. Can you imagine doing that for over nine hundred years? This shows what a very good man Nuh was, and how patient, and how much he wanted for the people to turn away from their evil deeds and turn to Allaah and worship Him alone.

Nuh encouraged his people by telling them that if they asked for Allaah's forgiveness, then Allaah would send rain down on them to water their crops, and He would give them money, children, gardens, and cause rivers to flow by them. He also frightened them by asking them why they did not fear Allaah's punishment and torment.

Nuh used many different ways to call his people to Allaah, just as we saw Ibraaheem doing, mash'Allaah. He told them of the rewards of asking for Allaah's forgiveness and worshiping Allaah alone, and he also told them that Allaah would punish them for not doing these things. This is something that affects people, alhamdulillah. They want to be rewarded, and they fear being punished.

However, Nuh's people were too proud and arrogant to believe. They said to each other, *You shall not leave your gods, and you shall not leave Wadd and Suwaa' and Yaghuth and Ya'uq and Nasr.*-(Surat Nuh, Ayat 23) They scoffed at Nuh and said he was a fool. They told him to bring Allaah's punishment down upon them, if he was really telling the truth. Nuh supplicated to Allaah saying, *Leave not one of the disbelievers on the earth.*-(Surat Nuh, Ayat 26)

The people turned away from Nuh's message, and turned away from Allaah. They called him names. You know how hard it is when people call you names. If someone makes fun of you for being Muslim, or for worshiping Allaah, then think of Nuh. His own people called him a fool, and they made fun of him, and he stayed strong in his faith. He knew he was right, and he wasn't going to be turned away from the good just because people teased him and were cruel. Finally, he turned to Allaah alone to help him- and he asked Allaah to destroy all of the disbelievers on the earth. And he only did this when it was clear that they would not accept his message. So when people are mean to you or make fun of you for being Muslim, just stay strong, and be patient, and remember that Allaah supports and loves you.

Allaah ordered him to build a boat for the believers, and told him that the disbelievers would all be drowned. Nuh began to build the boat as Allaah told him to. When his people passed by and saw him building a boat on dry land they laughed at him and scoffed at him. Nuh paid no attention to their jests, and patiently went on building the boat. When the boat was finished, Allaah told him to take one pair of every living thing, one male and one female, on the boat with him. He also told him to take all those who believed. Then Allaah flooded the earth with water. The disbelievers all ran, trying to reach the mountains and hills, but they could never escape from the punishment of Allaah. The waves rose over all the mountains and covered them, drowning all those who disbelieved.

Again, Nuh ignored the people who were making fun of him, and continued to do as Allaah commanded him to do. Then Nuh took all of the believers, and males and females of every living thing, onto his boat. He took males and females so that they could mate and have babies after the waters went away, so that they would continue to live upon the Earth.

Then Allaah flooded the whole Earth with water, and the disbelievers became frightened and tried to hide from His punishment upon them. But they could not- wherever they went, the waters followed them, and they all drowned. This should remind us that we can't hide from Allaah. No matter where we go, Allaah knows where we are, and He knows what we are doing, whether it is good or bad. Think if you stole a cookie from your friend. Where could you go to hide and eat it where he wouldn't know where you are? You could find lots of places to hide where your friend couldn't find you. This is not true of Allaah. Allaah hears everything, and He sees everything, and He is everywhere with His knowledge- no matter where you go, Allaah knows you are there. No matter what you do, or what you think, Allaah knows this. So remember this, and try to only do those things which Allaah loves and is pleased with, and you will be rewarded by Allaah for this.

While Nuh and those who believed in him were floating in the boat, Nuh saw his son who was a disbeliever, struggling against the water. He said to him, *◈Oh my son! Embark with us, and do not be with the disbelievers."◈*-(Surat Hud, Ayat 42) His son replied, *◈I will take myself to some mountain, it will save me from the water,◈*-(Surat Hud, Ayat 43) But then the waves came in between them, and Nuh's son was drowned because he refused to believe in Allaah.

Nuh lost his own son, because his son did not believe in Allaah. Even when he tried one last time to get him to believe, and come in the boat, his son thought he could escape Allaah's punishment. He could not. He drowned with everyone else. Think how Nuh must have felt about that- his own son- not only did he die, but he died not believing in Allaah and worshiping Him alone. Think how much Nuh must have trusted in Allaah, and accepted what Allaah had decreed for him and his son- he did not become sad or angry with Allaah, because he understood that everything happens for a reason, and Allaah is the Most Wise, and He is the Best of Planners.

After all the people on the earth were drowned except for those on the ship, Allaah commanded the earth to swallow all the water that had gathered on it. The ship with Nuh and the believers came to rest on a mountain called al-Judi. Then Allaah commanded them to leave the ship, and He said, "Oh Nuh! Come down (from the ship) with peace from Us and blessings upon you and those people who are with you."-(Surat Hud, Ayat 48) So the people left the boat and once again lived on the earth with peace and blessings from Allaah. They worshipped Allaah alone, and they worshipped nothing along with Him, as the earth was purified from all of the disbelievers.

Points of Benefit

1. If you worship Allaah alone with no partners than you will be successful in this life and the hereafter.

2. Shaytaan is the worst enemy of the children of Aadam, and he is not happy unless they are disobeying Allaah.

3. You must be patient in calling to Allaah, no matter how long it takes to bring the people to the straight path.

4. When you call to Allaah, you must try all the ways you can think of to bring them to the straight path. This includes being a good example for them, and letting them see the goodness of Islaam by seeing what a good person you are.

5. Allaah helps those who believe, and does not allow harm to reach them.

6. You should never make fun of any Muslim, as the result of that is evil for you, and punishment from Allaah.

7. Allaah does not look at someone's money or position; rather, he only looks at their belief and faith in Him. We should do this as well, insh'Allaah, and choose as our friends those who are strong in their faith in Allaah.

Hands on Activities

1. Make the page for Nuh in your prophet book. Write the prophet's name with hollow letters and color them in as you like. Draw a little picture or write a verse from the Qur'aan from the story to remind you of who he was and what he did.

2. Show your pages to someone in your family, or to a friend, and tell them all that you can remember about the story of Nuh.

3. There are many supplications we can use to call on Allaah. We are going to mention a few in English- but try to learn them in Arabic as well, insh'Allaah. Remember that when you are speaking Arabic, you are speaking the language that the Prophet Muhammad, may Allaah's praise and salutations be upon him, spoke, and the language that the Qur'aan was revealed in.

What to say when you wake up:

Alhamdulillah aladhi ahyanaa be'dama amaatana wa ilayhi nashoor

"All praise is to due to Allaah, who brings us to life after we have died (slept) and unto Him is the Resurrection"

What to say when you go to sleep:

Bismika Allahumma amootu wa ahyaa

"In your name, oh Allaah I live and die"

What to say when you leave your house:

Bismillaahi tawakkaltu 'ala Allaah, wa la hawla wa la quwata illa billaah

"In the name of Allaah, I put my trust in Allaah, and there is no power nor might except with Allaah"

What to say when you enter your house:

Bismillaahi walajnaa, wa bismillaahi kharajnaa wa 'ala rabbinaa tawakkalnaa

"In the name of Allaah we enter, and in the name of Allaah we leave, and we put our trust in Allaah." And then one should greet his family with the Islamic greeting

What to say when you go into the bathroom:

Allahumma innee a'udhu bika min al-khubthi wa al-khabaa'ith

"Oh Allaah, I seek refuge in you from the male and female jinn"

And you step in with your left foot.

What to say when you leave the bathroom:

Ghufraanak

(Oh Allaah)" I seek your forgiveness"

And you step out with your right foot

4. Allaah commanded Nuh to build a boat- think of how big the boat must have been to have the believers on it, as well as the pairs of animals!! This was Allaah's mercy upon the believers- they were saved from drowning, along with the animals, so they could continue on the Earth worshiping Allaah, alone. They put their trust in Allaah, knowing that He would watch over them and keep them safe while the waters rose and the rain fell, and the

Earth was covered in water.

We can't know what the ship that Nuh built looked like, but we can use our imaginations to think about it. What do you think the ship would have been made of? At that time, probably wood. How big would it have been? Would there have been places for the animals and people to do down into the ship to get out of the weather? Why not try to make a model of how you imagine Nuh's ship could have looked like? You can use popsicle sticks, Legos, or whatever you want to make it with. Or, you can draw a picture of the boat-think of how the boat may have looked, with water all around it, and the rains pouring down. You can draw one of the boat during the time that the waters were rising and the rain was falling- use dark colors for the clouds, and big bold lines to show the bad weather and the high seas. Then draw one of the ship after the waters went away, when the sun was shining and the world was fresh and new. Use bright, happy colors to show the sky and earth at that time, insh'Allaah. You can also use construction paper, or whatever you like, to make your pictures. Use your imagination and have fun! We can't know what the ship that Nuh built look like, but we can use our imaginations. What do you think the ship would have been made of? At that time, probably wood. How big would it have been? Would there have been places for the animals and people to go down into the ship to get out of the weather? Why not try to make a model of how you imagine Nuh's ship might have looked. You can use popsicle sticks, Legos, or whatever you want to make it. Or, draw a picture of the boat- think of how the boat must have looked, with water all around it, and the rains pouring down. You can draw one of the boat during the time that the waters were rising and the rain was falling- use dark colors for the clouds, and big bold lines to show the bad weather and high seas. Then draw one of the ship after the waters went away, when the sun was shining and the world was fresh and new. Use bright, happy colors to show the sky and earth at that time, insh'Allaah. You can also use construction paper, or whatever you like, to make your pictures. Use your imagination and have fun!

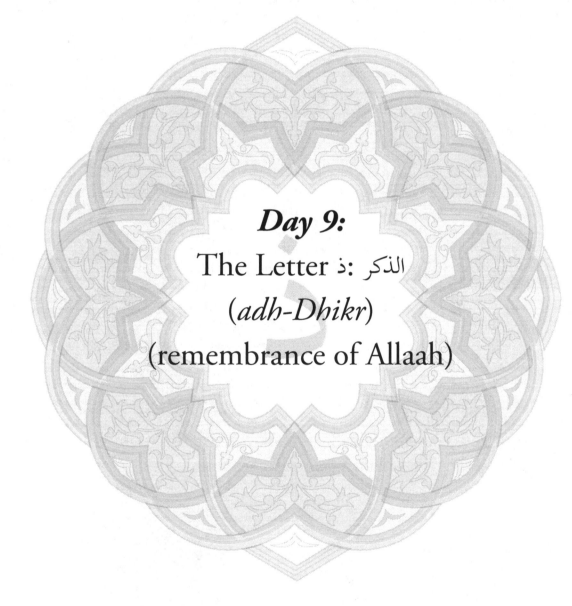

Day 9:
The Letter ذ: الذكر
(*adh-Dhikr*)
(remembrance of Allaah)

In this excellent month hasten, my dear sister, to remember Allaah much; and do not allow your tongue to pause in remembrance in any state or condition you are in- even when you are doing your housework, following in this the example of the Messenger, may Allaah's praise and salutations be upon him.

The Mother of the Believers, 'Aishah, may Allaah be pleased with her, narrated, *{The Prophet, may Allaah's praise and salutations be upon him, would remember Allaah constantly.}* (Muslim)

And have glad tidings from the hadeeth of the Prophet, may Allaah's praise and salutations be upon him, *{There are three people whom Allaah will not reject their supplication: the one who remembers Allaah often, the oppressed, and the just imaam.}* (al-Bayhaqi, and Sheikh al-Albaani declared it to be hasan)

Remember his, may Allaahs' praise and salutations be upon him, saying, *{The best of dhikr (remembrance) is la ilaaha ila Allaah (there is no god worthy of worship except Allaah) and the best of du'a (supplication) is alhamdulillah (all praise is due to Allaah alone).}* (an-Nasaa'ee, and Sheikh al-Albaani has declared it to be hasan)

And his, may Allaah's praise and salutations be upon him, saying *{The best of speech is subhan'Allaah (Glory be to Allaah) and alhamdulillah (all praise is due to Allaah) and la ilaaha ila Allaah (there is no god worthy of worship except Allaah) and Allaahu Akbar (Allaah is the greatest).}* (Ahmad, and Sheikh al-Albaani has declared it to be authentic)

And his, may Allaah's praise and salutations be upon him, saying, *{There are two words which are light on the tongue and heavy on the scales and beloved to the Most Merciful: subhan'Allaah wa bihamdihi (all glory and praise is due to Allaah) and subhan'Allaahu al-'adheem (Glory be to Allaah the Great).}* (al-Bukhaari)

And know that in remembrance of Allaah lies the bringing of the hearts to life. The Prophet, may Allaah's praise and salutations be upon him, said, *{The likeness of he who remembers his Lord and he who does not remember his Lord is like the one who is alive and the one who is dead.}* (al-Bukhaari)

Further Points of Benefit

Alhamdulillah, this is yet another habit which we should strive to make a part of our lives outside of Ramadhaan as well as during this blessed month. We all know how easy it is to form a bad habit- forming a good habit may be a bit more work, but the results are worth it, mash'Allaah, as our faith can increase, our connection to our Lord strengthen, and we come to rely upon and remember the Lord of the Worlds in all that we do. Look at the last hadeeth mentioned above: *{The likeness of he who remembers his Lord and he who does not remember his Lord is like the one who is alive and the one who is dead.}* These are not empty words, my sister; rather, they give us a concrete example of the difference between the one who remembers his Lord often and the one who does not. Contemplate its meaning- think of life, and all that it entails of growth, movement, and feeling. Think of death, its opposite- stagnation, stillness, absence…which state would you rather be in?

These remembrances are short, alhamdulillah, and easy to remember- the best of them is la ilaaha ila Allaah! Which of us can't memorize and remember this? The same for the others mentioned above, mash'Allaah- many of us are already familiar with them, but we have to make them a part of our lives, so that they come to our minds and roll off our tongues with frequency. Also, we must not just say them- we must say them with understanding and belief and certainty in them, and love and purity of intention for Allaah alone.

Ibn Katheer, may Allaah have mercy upon him, said in his "Tafseer" of the verses *Oh you who believe! Remember Allah with much remembrance. And glorify His Praises morning and afternoon.*-(Surat al-Ahzaab, Ayats 41 and 42):

"Allaah commands His believing servants to remember their Lord often, the One Who has bestowed upon them all manner of blessings and favors, because this will bring them a great reward and a magnificent destiny.

Imaam Ahmad narrated that 'Abdullah ibn Busr said, "Two Bedouins came to the Messenger of Allaah, may Allaah's praise and salutations be upon him, and one of them said, "Oh Messenger of Allaah, which of the people is best?" He, may Allaah's praise and salutations be upon him, replied, *{The one whose life is long and whose deeds are good.} The other one asked, "Oh Messenger of Allaah, the laws of Islaam are too much for us. Teach me something which I can hold fast to." He, may Allaah's praise and salutations be upon him, replied, {Keep your tongue moistened with the remembrance of Allaah, the Most High.}* (Ahmad Vol. 4, No. 190)

…Imaam Ahmad recorded that Ibn 'Abdullah ibn 'Umar, may Allaah be pleased with him, said that the Messenger of Allaah, may Allaah's praise and salutations be upon him, said, *{No people sit together without mentioning Allaah, but they will see this as regrettable on the Day of Resurrection.}* (Vol. 2, No. 224)

'Ali ibn Abi Talhah narrated that Ibn 'Abbaas, may Allaah be pleased with him, commented on the verse, *"Remember Allah with much remembrance", saying, "Allaah did not enjoin any duty upon His servants without setting known limits and accepting the excuses of those who have a valid excuse- except for dhikr, as Allaah has not set any limits for it, and no one has any excuse for not remembering Allaah unless he is oppressed and forced to neglect it. Allaah, the Most High, says, "Remember Allaah standing, sitting down, and (reclining) on your sides"-(Surat an- Nisaa, Ayat 103) By night and day, on land and sea, when traveling and remaining home, in abundance and in poverty, in sickness and in health, in secret and openly, in all situations and circumstances. And Allaah, the Most High, says, "And glorify His praises morning and afternoon". If you do this, He and His angels will send blessings upon you."*" (at-Tabari, Vol 20, No. 280) ("Tafseer Ibn Katheer", Vol. 7, Pages 707-709)

So what is your excuse, oh sister, for not implementing this blessed practice of remembering Allaah? Strive in this blessed month to make this a part of your life, woven into the fabric of your very existence, so that you may reap its benefits both now and during the rest of the year.

Family Time

The Story of the Prophet Ayyub

Allaah, The Most High, gives us an example of patience in the story of prophet Ayyub, may Allaah's salutations be upon him. He was afflicted with severe trials, and he gave all of mankind a lesson in patience, faith, certainty, and being pleased with whatever Allaah decrees.

He was a prophet from the offspring of Ibraahim. He was very rich and he and his believing wife lived in prosperity, and they had many children. He had livestock, cattle, crops, and beautiful houses. He used to give generously to all those in need. He helped the orphans and widows and the poor. He was always thankful to Allaah for all the blessings which He had bestowed upon him.

So we see the prophet Ayyub at this stage of his life- he was rich in both money and belongings, and he had a good wife and many children. He was different than many rich people though, who believe that they themselves are responsible for their wealth and good position in life. Ayyub was always thankful to Allaah for his blessings, and worked to help the people who did not have as much as he did. This is because he knew that Allaah was the one who blessed him with all the good that was in his life- whatever wealth he had, and whatever good he could do, it was because of Allaah. This is important to remember. When we are scared or worried, it is easy to remember to think of Allaah and to ask Him to help us. But what about when we are happy, and things are going well for us? We should still remember Allaah, and thank Him, because He is the One who made all the good things possible, alhamdulillah. This is the way of the true believers in Allaah- they remember Him in times of hardship and in times of ease.

Also, think of Ayyub's generosity- he didn't keep all of his wealth to himself- he used his money and his good position to help poor people, and children with no parents, and women whose husbands were dead. Think about yourself, and the last time you had some extra money or candy. Did you keep it all for yourself, or did you use some of it to make someone else happy? If you kept it for yourself, remember Ayyub, and the next time you are able to help someone else give some of what you have to him or her. Alhamdulillah, you are showing your gratefulness to Allaah by sharing His blessings to you with someone else. You will help someone else, and help yourself at the same time!!

Allaah then tested His servant, Ayyub. He took away all the money, children, and livestock which he had owned. He took everything he had away, and then He tested him in his body, by taking away his good health. He got so sick that no part of his body was healthy except for his heart. He was pushed out to the edge of the city. Everyone left him, and there was no one to help him except his wife. She stayed with him through his illness, and served him. When she could not find any food for him, she went to work as a servant, and used her wages to buy the things they needed. Two men who were the closest of his brothers also used to visit him every morning

93

and every evening.

Mash'Allaah, this is often the way things go- when we have lots of things and everything is good for us, then we have many friends- or people who call themselves our friends! And then when we don't have much, or things are going against us, most of those people who said they were our friends desert us. This shows us the importance of relying on Allaah alone, and not the people, as Allaah will never leave us, and always wants what is best for us when we strive to make Him happy and serve Him. We rely on Him when times are good, and we rely on Him when times are bad.

This also shows us the importance of having good companions, mash'Allaah. Ayyub married a good, believing woman, and she stayed with him and took care of him- she even worked to help provide him with the things that they needed! What a good woman his wife must have been- she must have loved him and been thankful to Allaah for him, as she stood by him in his trials. Also, the two men who visited him every evening- they didn't desert him like everyone else did. Think about your friends. You want the people that are closest to you to be good, righteous people, so that they will stick with you no matter what you go through, insh'Allaah. And the faith of Islaam is the strongest glue to hold you together, alhamdulillah.

Throughout this entire affliction, Ayyub was patient. He focused on the remembrance of Allaah, and he used to spend all his time in worship. When the Shaytaan saw how Ayyub remained steadfast in the remembrance of Allaah and was not upset, even though all this hardship and illness had descended upon him, he was filled with anger. He was mad because he saw that he could not lead him astray.

Ayyub did not despair. He did not get angry at Allaah, or blame Him, or hate Allaah. Instead, he was patient when the illnesses fell upon him, and he remained patient and worshiped Allaah all the way through. Shaytaan hated to see this! The Shaytaan doesn't like to see people who are strong in their faith, and who are patient when hardship comes to them. He wants them to complain, become angry and upset, and to become distanced from Allaah, and blame Allaah for their problems instead of turning to Him for help. You have to always be aware of the tricks Shaytaan plays on us, as he can be very sneaky, and he only wants bad for us- he never wants good for us.

Ayyub's suffering went on for eighteen years. Even those who were close to him began to have doubts about why so many afflictions were coming to him. One day, one of the two men who used to visit him said to the other, "By Allaah, Ayyub must have committed some sin which no one else in the world has ever committed." His friend asked him, "Why do you say that?" He replied, "For eighteen years he has been suffering and Allaah does not have mercy on him and relieve his suffering." He did not know that it was a test for Ayyub, and that Allaah would give him an amazing reward for his patience and faith.

After eighteen years of seeing Ayyub suffer, even his two friends started to think that maybe Allaah had turned against Ayyub. They didn't think about it as a test for Ayyub, and they didn't think of the rewards that Ayyub would eventually receive for his patience and his sticking to Allaah and to his faith. When we suffer, or we see someone else suffer, we have to remember that this suffering does not necessarily mean that Allaah is punishing a person. Allaah tests people with hardship so that they can prove themselves to be strong in faith, and then ultimately they are raised up in rank before Allaah and receive great rewards. So when hardship comes, we should immediately be patient, and seek Allaah's forgiveness for anything which we have done, and then we should work extra hard to please Allaah so that we will pass His test, insh'Allaah.

One day Ayyub supplicated his Lord Allaah saying, *Verily, distress has seized me, and you are the Most merciful of all those who show mercy.*-(Surat Al-Anbiyaa', Ayat 83)

What a beautiful supplication! Ayyub did not ask his Lord for anything, he simply called upon him in this manner and praised Him. Then Allaah revealed to him, *Strike the ground with your foot. This is water to wash in and a refreshing drink.*-(Surat Saad, Ayat 42) When Ayyub struck the ground with his foot, a spring of water gushed out of it. He washed himself in it, and all afflictions on the outside of his body disappeared. Then Allaah commanded him to strike the ground in a different place. Again a spring welled up from the ground, and Ayyub was told to drink from it. When he did this, all his internal illnesses fell away as well, and he was as strong and healthy as ever. Then Allaah sent a rain of locusts made of gold down on him. He began to gather them up in his clothes. Allaah said to him, "Haven't I made you rich enough that you don't need this?" Ayyub said, "Yes, Oh Lord! But I cannot do without your blessing." Then Allaah gave him back his family, and gave him others like them as well. He returned to him all that had been taken from him, and much more than that as well. He rewarded him for his amazing patience in both this world and the next.

Even when Ayyub become distressed, or very sad and upset, over his condition, he didn't ask Allaah to give him anything. Instead, he mentioned Allaah's mercy, and trusted in His mercy to help him in his distress. And look how Allaah rewarded him!! He not only got what he had before his illness and test, but he also received more than that, so he had more of everything. And this is only Ayyub's reward in this life- his reward in the next life will be even better, due to his patience and steadfastness.

When Ayyub was ill, he had gotten angry at his wife because of something she did, so he made an oath that he would hit her a hundred times. After Allaah healed him, how could he repay her mercy and compassion towards him, and her faithful service, by fulfilling his oath and hitting her? That would be cruel and unjust towards her. Allaah showed him the way out, and told him to take a bundle of thin grasses with one hundred pieces, and hit her once with it lightly. Thus, he fulfilled his oath and avoided breaking his vow.

Ayyub felt bad that he had wanted to punish his wife, who had been so patient throughout his trial. But he knew that he could not ignore the oath he had taken. Allaah again showed His mercy to Ayyub, by showing him a way to fulfill his vow without hurting his wife.

Allaah praised His servant Ayyub for his patience and strong faith, saying, ❰*Truly We found him patient! What an excellent servant! Verily, he was ever returning in repentance!*❱-(Surat Saad, Ayat 44)

Points of Benefit:

1. You must be pleased with whatever Allaah decrees.

2. The people who are tried and tested the most are the prophets, and then the righteous people.

3. If you are patient while in distress, then it will be removed.

4. Allaah never forgets His righteous servants.

5. Just because bad things are happening to someone does not mean that they are being punished. Often it is to raise their rank by testing them.

6. If you do many good deeds while you are in ease, then Allaah will help you when hardship comes to you.

7. You should not take gving an oath lightly. Many people today say "WaAllaahi" or "By Allaah" easily, not really thinking about or meaning what they say. This is a very dangerous mistake, and we should stay away from it!

Hands on Learning

1. Make the page for Ayyub in your prophet book. Write the prophet's name with hollow letters and color them in as you like. Draw a little picture or write a verse from the Qur'aan from the story to remind you of who he was and what he did.

2. Show your pages to someone in your family, or to a friend, and tell them all that you can remember about the story of Ayyub.

3. Ayyub started out with great riches and lots of land and beautiful houses. He was thankful to Allaah for all of these things. Later, Allaah tested him by making him sick, and taking away his health and his wealth and most of his family and friends. Ayyub did not feel angry or sad about this, because he had faith in Allaah and trusted Him.

Take a large sheet of paper. Divide it in half. On one half, draw your idea of how you would live if Allaah blessed you with a lot of money. On the other half, draw your idea of how you would live if Allaah tested you by taking away your wealth. Really think about this- as people can be rich, but not spend their money on silly or expensive things. And people can be poor, but still keep what little they have clean and orderly and home-like. 'Umar, may Allaah be pleased with him, lived very simply even though he was one of the heads of the Muslims after the Prophet Muhammad, may Allaah's praise and salutations be upon him, died- it didn't matter that he could have lived in palaces with fancy things, mash'Allaah. However, it is also permissible to spend our money on nice things if Allaah blessed us with wealth- we just shouldn't be extravagant or wasteful when we do so, insh'Allaah. Think about how you would want to live in either of these situations, and draw them side by side so you can compare them.

4. Water is a great blessing from Allaah, alhamdulillah. We already saw how Allaah blessed Haajar and Ismaa'eel when they had no water in Makkah- He caused the well of Zamzam to spring up, alhamdulillah, and this helped to create the village that would eventually become the home of the Ka'bah! Another prophet that you will read about later, Moosa, also was commanded by Allaah to strike the ground and twelve springs of water were created from this. Have you ever been in a desert, or very dry place? Are you fasting this Ramadhaan, so you know what it is like to be thirsty? Water is something that is very easy to take for granted, and we should not do this, as it is a great blessing from Allaah- without water, we could not live. Think about this the next time you let water run down the sink for no reason, or pour out a half a glass of water, or let the hose run in the back yard longer than needed- is this showing your gratefulness to Allaah for this blessing of water?

This experiment will help you see the importance of water. Ask your mother for two dried beans. It doesn't matter what kind. Plant each one in a small container, like a yogurt container. Check every day to see if the soil is dry- if it is, water it- don't water it too much, as too much water isn't good for them at all. After they have grown to be an inch or two high and have some leaves, stop watering one of them. Every day watch what happens to the two plants. Write about your observations in a journal or notebook.

Here is an experiment to help you to be thankful for good, fresh water to drink. Fill two glasses about halfway with water. Leave the room while your mother puts a tablespoon of salt into one of the cups of water and stirs it in well. Come back in and look at the two glasses. Compare them- which one looks better to drink? Which one smells better to drink? Taste a little water from each glass- which one would you rather drink? Remember that most of the water on the Earth is salt water! This is an even more amazing blessing from Allaah- that we have enough fresh water to drink and sustain life on the planet, even though so much of it is salt. Do you know about the water cycle? Look it up in a book, or have your mother or father help you find out about it on the internet. See if you can draw a diagram of the water cycle to help you remember how it works.

The next time it rains, or the next time you take a drink of water- let Allaah know how thankful you are to Him for this blessing of water.

Day 10:

The Letter رخصة الفطر :ر
(*Rukhsat al-Fitr*)
(the permission to break one's fast in certain conditions)

From that which makes it easy on the Muslims is that Allaah, Glorified and Exalted, permitted the traveler to break his fast during the day in Ramadhaan whether it (the fast) is difficult upon him, or it is not.

Narrated Hamzah ibn 'Amr al-Aslaami, may Allaah be pleased with him, that he said, *"Oh Messenger of Allaah! I find that I have strength to fast while traveling- so is there any sin (in that)?"* He, may Allaah's praise and salutations be upon him, said, {*It is a permission from Allaah, Glorified and Exalted; so whoever takes it, then that is good, and whoever wants to fast, then there is no sin on him.*} (Muslim)

And taking advantage of this permission is from the matters which Allaah, Glorified and Exalted, linked to love of Him. He, may Allaah's praise and salutations be upon him, said, {*Indeed Allaah, the Most High, loves that one takes the permission in the same way that He hates for one to commit wrongdoing.*} (Ahmad, and Sheikh al-Albaani has declared it to be authentic)

The esteemed scholar 'Abdul 'Aziz ibn Baaz, may Allaah have mercy upon him, mentioned that it is best for the fasting person to break his fast while traveling without exception. And whoever fasts, then there is nothing on him (in regards to sin or wrongdoing) as it was established that the Prophet, may Allaah's praise and salutations be upon him, did both of these things. And there is no difference in that between the one who travels in cars, or on camels, or ships, or steamers, and one who travels in an airplane- for all of them are encompassed in the meaning of "traveling", and they have been granted this permission. (Summarized from Majmoo' al-Fataawa of the Esteemed Sheikh Ibn Baaz, may Allaah have mercy upon him, Vol. 4, Page 187)

Further Points of Benefit

Sheikh 'Utheimeen, may Allaah have mercy upon him, was asked,

"What is the ruling regarding the fast of the traveler- keeping in mind that, due to the availability of modern means of transportation in this present day it is not difficult for the fasting person to fast?"

He, may Allaah have mercy upon him, replied, "The traveler may fast, or he may break his fast, in accordance with the words of Allaah, the Most High, *"and whoever is ill or on a journey, the same number [of days which one did not observe fasts] must be made up from other days.'*-(Surat al-Baqarah, From Ayat 185)

The Companions, may Allaah be pleased with all of them, went accompanied the Prophet, may Allaah's praise and salutations be upon him, on a journey, and some of them were fasting and some of them were not- and neither group rebuked the other (for what they were doing).

The Prophet, may Allaah's praise and salutations be upon him, used to fast when he was traveling. Abu Darda', may Allaah be pleased with him, said, {*We were with the Prophet, may Allaah's praise and salutations be upon him, on a journey, and the weather was extremely hot. None of us were fasting except for the Messenger of Allaah, may Allaah's praise and salutations be upon him, and 'Abdullah ibn Rawahah.}* (al-Bukhaari (1945) and Muslim (1122)

The ruling in regards to the one who is traveling is that he may choose between fasting and breaking his fast. If the fasting is not too difficult for him, then it is better to fast. There are three benefits in this:

1. He is following the example of the Messenger of Allaah, may Allaah's praise and salutations be upon him.

2. Ease- the fast is made easier for the person; as when a person is fasting with other people then it is easier for him (to fast).

3. Prompt fulfillment of one's obligations

If it is difficult for a person to fast, then he should not fast; and it is not from righteousness to fast on a journey under these circumstances. The Messenger of Allaah, may Allaah's praise and salutations be upon him, saw a man being shaded while people were crowding about him, and he said, *{What is this?}* They answered, "He is fasting." He replied, *{It is not from righteousness to fast on a journey.}* (al-Bukhaari (1946) and Muslim (1115)

This is a general principle which is applied to anyone in a situation which is similar to that of the man who found it difficult to fast.

Based upon this, we say that travel in the present day is easy, as the questioner mentioned, and so in most cases it is not difficult (to fast) on a journey- so if it is not too difficult to fast, then it is better to fast." ("Fataawa Arkaan al-Islaam")

In this we see the mercy of Allaah upon His worshipers, alhamdulillah, as we are given the choice based upon our own situations as to whether or not to fast while on a journey. Insh'Allaah we see the balance in Islaam in this as well.

And remember that it is best that one make up the missing days in a timely manner. 'Aishah, may Allaah be pleased with her, said, *{I had days to make up from Ramadhaan, and I was unable to make them up until Sha'ban (the month before the next Ramadhaan}* (al-Bukhaari (1950)

Sheikh 'Utheimeen, in the above book, says, "But if he delayed it until after the following Ramadhaan, then he should seek forgiveness from Allaah and turn to Him in repentance, and feel remorse for what he has done, and make up for these days. The obligation to make them up is not removed simply because it has been put off; so he must make up these days even if it is after the next Ramadhaan. And Allaah is the One Who Grants Success."

Family Time

The Story of the Prophet Yunus

Yunus Ibn Mattaa, May Allaah's salutations be upon him, was sent by Allaah to the people of Nineveh, which was a town in Mawsil, in northern Iraq. He called them to Allaah for a long time, but they were persistent in their disbelief. Finally, Yunus lost patience with them. He told them that Allaah's punishment would come to them. Then he angrily left the town of Nineveh.

When the people of Nineveh saw him leaving, and thought about the punishment that he had warned them about, they realized that he was telling the truth. They were filled with fright and felt bad for how they had treated their prophet and refused to believe in Allaah.

They all went out to the desert with their children and their flocks. They separated all the mothers from their children. They took the babies away from their mothers, the calves away from the cows, the lambs away from the sheep, and the camels' young away from them. All the babies and their mothers cried, and the people beseeched Allaah and pleaded with him to keep the punishment from them. Allaah spared them the punishment, and they all went back, and worshipped Allaah, and believed in Him.

The people of Nineveh must have been very, very happy when Allaah listened to their prayers asking Him to forgive them for not believing in that which Yunus was telling them about! Think about some time when you did something bad, and later realized that what you did was wrong. Were you able to correct the bad that you did? Sometimes we can't do this very easily, or at all. Maybe the person we treated badly has left, or maybe we ate the candy we took, or whatever. But this does not mean that we should not try to make things right no matter what. If we have done something wrong, we should try to correct the wrong we did if it is at all possible. If something has happened so that we can't do this, like the person we treated badly no longer lives near us, then we should make du'aa for him or her, and ask Allaah to forgive us for what we have done.

Also, look how the people of Nineveh knew that the punishment of Allaah was a true, real thing. They did not think it was an empty warning from prophet Yunus- they knew that Allaah would truly punish them. We should remember this as well. Allaah does punish people for sinning and going against His commands, and this should make us do our best to stay away from doing things that will bring His punishment down upon us. But we are human beings, and Allaah knows that we will sin and fall into mistakes- so He reminds us again and again that He is All-Forgiving, and that He is Most Merciful. If we turn to Allaah with all of our hearts, truly wanting His forgiveness and mercy, and we promise to do our best not to fall into that sin or wrongdoing again, then insh'Allaah He will forgive us and shower us with His mercy. Remember, Allaah's forgiveness and mercy are incredible- we can't even imagine how forgiving and merciful He is, mash'Allaah, but we know it is much more than anyone on earth could ever have, because He alone is Allaah, nothing and no one is like Him. Turning to Allaah in this way, with all of our hearts, truly meaning it, and turning away from the evil that we did and promising to try our best never to do it again, is called tawbah, or repentance.

Meanwhile, Yunus travelled until he came to the sea. He went with some people on a cargo ship. Then, a storm came up while they were at sea. The waves pounded the boat on all sides, and they were at the risk of drowning, because the ship was too heavy. They decided to cast lots to choose someone to throw overboard to lighten the ship.

Casting lots is a way to decide which person has to do something or which person's idea will be accepted, and it is done in different ways. Perhaps someone holds some sticks that are all the same length, except for one which is shorter.. The one who draws the short stick is the one who has to do something or not do that thing. There are ways to do this with stones, and perhaps other ways as well. In this way it is not left to the people to decide something- it is totally left up to Allaah's decree. The Prophet Muhammad, may Allaah's praise and salutations be upon him, used to have his wives draw lots to see which one would travel with him, so that they would not feel that he had chosen unfairly, or was favoring one of them over another one.

The Prophet Yunus was the one decided by the lots for three times in a row, but they did not want to throw him overboard. The people protested violently when they saw Yunus getting ready to throw himself overboard. They wanted him to stay with them, because they had seen how righteous he was, and how he worshipped Allaah. Yunus was patient, and resigned himself to the will of Allaah. He took off his clothes so he could throw himself in the sea. The people on the boat rushed and tried to stop him, but he would not let them. He stood up and cast himself over the side of the boat and into the wild, crashing waves.

Yunus must have been a very righteous, good person. First of all, of course, Allaah chose him to be a prophet. But look at how he won the hearts of the people on the ship so that they loved him and wanted him to stay with them on the ship, even though the lots said that he had to be the one to go overboard. Then look- they told him to stay on the ship and not jump overboard, but he accepted Allaah's will, as seen by the casting of the lots, and trusted in Allaah, and jumped into the stormy sea! He must have been very brave as well. Bravery is only one thing that comes from having faith and trust in Allaah. If we know that He loves us and has decreed everything that will happen to us already, then we don't need to be afraid to do something- like Yunus. He put his trust in Allaah and dove into the crashing waves.

Allaah sent a large fish to come and swallow Yunus. It did not cut him or break his bones. He was swallowed into the fish's stomach, and he was not hurt at all. At first, Yunus thought that he must have died, but he moved his legs, arms and head, and saw that he could not be dead. He prostrated to Allaah, and he said, "Oh Lord! I have taken a place of worship to you which no other person has reached." This was because no one else had ever worshipped Allaah from the belly of a fish before. He also called out to Allaah, through the darkness of the fish's stomach, saying, *❨There is no god but you, Glorified be you! Truly, I have been of the wrongdoers.❩*-(Surat Al-Anbiyaa', Ayat 87)

Think about this- Yunus was swallowed up by a large fish- the fish did not chew him up or harm him, he simply swallowed him whole- so he was in the fish's stomach! It must have been a very big fish, because Yunus was able to move his legs, arms and head, and then was able to prostrate to Allaah. Do you know how to prostrate, or make sujood, to Allaah? We Muslims do this whenever we pray our five obligatory prayers to Allaah every day, and when we make the voluntary ones as well. It is a position of submission, showing how humble we are before Allaah, and showing that we understand how Mighty He is. Did you know you can make sujood at other times than when you are praying? You can only make sujood, or prostrate, to Allaah, but you can do it whenever you feel gratefulness to Him, as well. This is called "sujood ash-shukr" or the prostration of gratefulness. Remember that any good that comes to you comes because Allaah wanted it to come to you- so you must be thankful to Allaah for any and all good that comes to you, large or small. So the next time you do well on a test, or you get a toy or pair of shoes that you have wanted for a long time, or your mother cooks your favorite food, or you get a new baby brother- whatever good happens to you, prostrate to Allaah and thank him for this good, just as Yunus did. Once he realized that he was alive he prostrated and gave thanks to Allaah- and he even said that he was the first person to ever worship Allaah from the inside of a fish! And then He praised Allaah and asked Allaah for forgiveness.

When we ask Allaah for help, we should always glorify Him first, and then call on Him by one of His beautiful names. So if we are asking for Allaah's mercy, we can ask calling Him by His name, ar-Rahmaan, or ar-Raheem. Or if we are asking Him to cure us, or someone we know, we can call Him by His name, ash-Shaafi' or the One who Heals. Or if we are asking Allaah to forgive us, we can call on Him by His name, al-Ghafoor, the All-Forgiving. And always begin with glorifying and praising Him, insh'Allaah.

Because Yunus glorified and worshipped Allaah even while he was inside the fish, Allaah delivered him from his distress. Allaah ordered the fish to cast him out on a shore were there were no buildings and no plants. The fish cast him out on the shore very gently and carefully. Yunus was very sick from having been in the fish's stomach, so Allaah caused a squash plant to grow over him, for him to eat and to heal him.

Here are two MORE miracles that Allaah granted to Yunus. The first was that he was saved from the ship by being swallowed by a fish. Now, because of Yunus' faith and supplication in the stomach of the fish, He made the fish gently expel him from its stomach on a safe shore. However there were no people there, or things for him to eat, and he was sick and so could not go looking for these things- so then Allaah blessed him with a squash plant, which grew over him, providing him with protection, food, and healing, alhamdulillah!

Then Allaah sent him back to his people, who had now believed in the message that he had brought them. There were more than one hundred thousand of his people, and they all believed in Allaah and followed him. Allaah tells us that if Yunus had not called out to Him and glorified Him, he would have stayed in the fish's stomach all the way until the Day of Judgment. This shows how good deeds benefit you, and that if you fear Allaah, He will make things easy for you.

Yunus went back to his people that he had left so long before- the people of Nineveh. Remember how they had all asked Allaah's forgiveness and begun to worship Allaah alone? And there were many, many of them, alhamdulillah. Yunus was rewarded for supplicating to Allaah in the belly of the fish- he was rescued and Allaah returned him to his people. This is the way it is for us as well- this is not something special to Yunus. If you perform good deeds, and fear Allaah's punishment, and call on Him, then He will make things easy for you, insh'Allaah.

May Allaah's praise and salutations be upon Yunus, and all the rest of the prophets and messengers.

Points of Benefit

1. You must always be patient while fulfilling Allaah's commands.
2. Repentance will take away the punishment and Anger of Allaah.
3. If you do good deeds and worship Allaah, the people will love you.
4. Supplication and asking for Allaah's forgiveness are from the things that cause trial and afflictions to be lifted.

Hands on Learning

1. Make the page for Yunus in your prophet book. Write the prophet's name with hollow letters and color them in as you like. Draw a little picture or write a verse from the Qur'aan from the story to remind you of who he was and what he did.
2. Show your pages to someone in your family, or to a friend, and tell them all that you can remember about the story of Yunus.
3. Some of the scholars of Islaam have mentioned that the reason that squash was given to Yunus is that it grows quickly, its leaves offer shade because of their large size and smooth texture, and flies do not like to come near it. Its fruits offer good nourishment, and often they may be eaten raw or cooked, and both the pulp and the peel may be eaten on some types of squash. It is reported in Al-Bukhaari that the Messenger of Allaah used to like squash, and would look for it wherever it was on the plate.

4. We don't know for sure the type of squash that was mentioned in the story. It could be a summer type of squash, like zucchini, or a winter squash like acorn squash. It could also be cucumber, as sometimes the word is translated in this way as well. Do you like any of these types of squash? How about pumpkin? Do you like pumpkin? It is a type of squash too.

Squash plants are very easy to grow- you can even plant them in a large container and let them climb up a trellis on a wall- so they can take up a lot of space on the ground, or they leave the ground pretty empty by training them to go up a wall. It depends on the type of squash, and how much room you have to grow it. If you are able, you should try to grow a squash plant- they are beautiful and very beneficial in many ways, alhamdulillah. They are a good reminder of Allaah's blessings upon us, as we remember how Allaah sent a squash plant to grow to benefit Yunus by giving him shade and protection, as well as food. The leaves of some squash plants can also be used if you get scraped while you are out playing. Wash the area with soap and water, and then mash or blend the leaves from your squash plant and put them on your scrape. Wrap a piece of cotton cloth around it, and let it be for a half an hour or so. Most of the time you can also sauté the young leaves in a little oil and eat them, if you like. Again, this depends on the type of squash you grow, you have to find out about it before you use it.

For this activity ask your mother and father to buy some squash at the grocery store- whichever kind you think you will like. Make sure you have enough for everyone to eat- remember that the Prophet, may Allaah's praise and salutations be upon him, liked squash so much that he would look for the pieces to eat whenever it was served to him! You don't eat the hard stem, and you don't eat the rind of the winter squashes. You can eat the skin of a zucchini but not the stem. Wash it thoroughly beforehand, and if it has been waxed, just peel it off entirely, because the wax is not good for you, mash'Allaah. Have you ever eaten pumpkin seeds? They are very good for you, alhamdulillah. You can roast the seeds of other squashes as well, and some, like zucchini, you just eat with the squash if you like.

Here are three recipes for you to try. One uses summer squash, and one uses winter squash. Try one of these for dinner tonight, and think of Yunus living under his squash plant, insh'Allaah.

Green Squash Bake
3-4 summer squash, such as zucchini

1 medium onion

1 small hot pepper if you like spicy food!

Cut all of these into small pieces, then mix them in a bowl with:

3 tbsp flour

½ tsp baking powder

Salt and pepper to taste

Put this mixture into a small, greased baking dish and top with:

3 beaten eggs

1 cup cheddar cheese, grated

Bake at 350 degrees until the squash is thoroughly cooked. This should take about 30 minutes.

Harvest Stew

In a large saucepan, sauté in 3 tbsp oil:

1 cup chopped onion

2 cloves of garlic, finely chopped

1 tsp chili powder

2 hot peppers, finely chopped, if you like hot food!

Salt, pepper, and oregano to taste

Sauté for ten minutes or so, until the onion is translucent and soft. Add:

2 cups fresh or canned tomatoes, chopped

2 cups pumpkin or other winter squash, peeled and cubed

2 cups fresh, frozen or canned corn

Cook until the squash is tender. Add:

2 cups cooked or canned white or red beans

Simmer for another twenty minutes or so. This is a good, thick stew, mash'Allaah. It goes well with homemade bread!

Salata (Middle Eastern Cucumber Salad)

2 small cucumbers

1 green pepper

¼ cup minced onion

4 medium tomatoes

Mince all of them finely, then add and toss:

2 tbsp olive oil

3 tbsp lemon juice

Salt and pepper to taste

Refrigerate before serving

5. Near the beginning of the story, Yunus was in the boat in a terrible storm. Later, Allaah delivered him to the shore and grew the squash plant for him. Draw either one of these places, and use your crayons, paints, or whatever you like to help us to see what each must have been like. Make your stormy seas look VERY stormy. Or make your squash plant VERY lush and sheltering.

6. Ibn Abi Haatim recorded that Sa'd said that the Messenger of Allaah, may Allaah's praise and salutations be upon him, said, *{Whoever offers supplication in the words of the supplication of Yunus will be answered.}* And the like is narrated by Imaam Ahmad, At-Tirmidhi, and An-Nisaa'i

Learn the du'aa of Yunus in the whale. In Arabic, it sounds something like this:

"La ilaaha ilaa anta subhaanaka innee kuntu min adh-dhaalimeen"

In English, it means,

"There is no god but you, Glorified be you! Truly, I have been of the wrongdoers."

It is found in Surat al-Anbiyyaa, in the Qur'aan. Al-Anbiyyaa means "prophets". Why is this a fitting place for this du'aa?

Teach this du'aa to someone else, and tell them who said it, and what an amazing du'aa it is, alhamdulillah!

Day 11:
The Letter ز: زكاة الفطر
(*zakaat al-fitr*)
(the obligatory charity paid
at the end of Ramadhaan)

Allaah, Glorified and Exalted, legislated the zakaat al-fitr before the Eid prayer. The Prophet, may Allaah's praise and salutations be upon him, said, *{Zakaat al-fitr is a purification for the fasting person from vain and obscene speech, and it (the zakaat) is food for the poor. Whoever gives it before the (Eid) prayer, then it is accepted zakaat. And whoever gives it after the (Eid) prayer, then it is a charity from the different types of charity.}* (al-Bayhaaqi, and al-Albaani has declared it to be authentic)

From the Rulings Pertaining to Zakaat:

1. It is obligatory upon the Muslim to give it for himself and his household, including his children, his wives, and his slaves.

2. The hired servant must pay his own zakaat, unless his employer gives it for him or it was a condition of his service (that the employer pay it for him).

3. The amount is one saa' from the food of the land- dates, or barley, or wheat, or corn or rice; and the saa' equals approximately three kilograms (for each person).

4. It is not obligatory to give the zakaat for the child in the womb, but it is recommended.

5. It is not permissible to give it in the form of money; rather, it is obligatory to give it as food from the food of the land.

6. It is the Sunnah to distribute it to the poor in the land of the one who is paying the zakaat, and not to send or take it to another place.

7. It is permissible to give it before the day of the Eid, by one or two days. The earliest you can give it is the night of the 28th of Ramadhaan. (For more, see Majmoo al-Fataawa of Sheikh Ibn Baaz, may Allaah have mercy upon him, Volume 4, Pages 91-104)

Further Points of Benefit

Az-zakaat is from the pillars of Islaam, and is linked to Allaah's mercy in several places in the Qur'aan. Allaah, the Most High, says,

◈And perform as-salaat, and give az-zakaat and obey the Messenger (Muhammad) that you may receive mercy (from Allaah).◈-(Surat an-Noor, Ayat 56)

◈That (Mercy) I shall ordain for those who are the muttaqoon (the pious) and give zakaat and those who believe in Our ayaat."◈-(Surat al-A'raaf, From Ayat 156)

◈And that which you give in gift (to others), in order that it may increase (your wealth by expecting to get a better one in return) from other people's property, has no increase with Allaah; but that which you give in zakaat seeking Allaah's Countenance, then those they shall have manifold increase.◈-(Surat ar-Room, Ayat 39)

And Allaah makes clear the punishment of the one who refrains from paying the obligatory charity when He, the Most High, says,

◈And let not those who covetously withhold of that which Allaah has bestowed on

them of His bounty (wealth) think that it is good for them (and so they do not pay the obligatory zakaat). Nay, it will be worse for them; the things which they covetously withheld, shall be tied to their necks like a collar on the Day of Resurrection.-(Surat aal-'Imraan, From Ayat 180)

So we should never be stingy in the giving of the zakaat, especially not in this blessed month of Ramadhaan. And it has become commonplace for certain masaajid and organizations to ask for the zakaat in the form of monetary donations- and, as is mentioned above, this is not permissible.

Sheikh Muhammad ibn Saalih al-'Utheimeen, may Allaah have mercy upon him, was asked, "Some scholars say that it is impermissible to give the zakaat al-fitr in the form of rice, since the types of food reported (in the hadeeth) are available (to give instead of it). What is your opinion on this, Esteemed Sheikh?"

He, may Allaah have mercy upon him, answered, "Some scholars say that if the five types of food, which are wheat, dates, barley, raisins and pot cheese, are available, then the zakaat al-fitr will not be fulfilled by giving something other than these. This view totally contradicts the view of those who say it is permissible to pay zakaat al-fitr with any of these things and others, even with money. So these are two very conflicting opinions.

The correct opinion is that it is acceptable to pay with any sort of food for people, because Abu Sa'eed al-Khudree, may Allaah be pleased with him, said, as confirmed in "Saheeh al-Bukhaari", *{We used to pay it during the time of the Prophet, may Allaah's praise and salutations be upon him, with a sa'a of food; and our food consisted of dates, barley, raisins and pot cheese.}* (al-Bukhaari, 1506)

He did not mention wheat, either, and I do not know of any clear, authentic hadeeth in which wheat is mentioned as being given as zakaat al-fitr; however there is no doubt that wheat is permissible (to give as zakaat).

Then there is the hadeeth of Ibn 'Abbaas, may Allaah be pleased with him, in which he said, *{The Messenger of Allaah, may Allaah's praise and salutations be upon him, enjoined the paying of the zakaat al-fitr as a purification for the one who fasted from vain, idle and obscene talk, and for the purpose of feeding those who are destitute.}* (Agreed upon)

Therefore the most correct view is that any food for people is permissible to use as the payment for the zakaat al-fitr, even if it is not one of the five types which have been reported from the scholars of Islamic jurisprudence, because four of these types were simply the common food of the people during the time of the Prophet, may Allaah's praise and salutations be upon him.

Based upon this, it is permissible to pay the zakaat al-fitr in the form of rice; indeed, I am of the opinion that rice is better than anything else in our present time because it is the least trouble and it is what the people desire the most. But having said this, situations differ; so it could be that in the country, a group of people might offer it (the zakaat) as dates, while in another place, raisins are preferred by them, and so a person might offer it as raisins. Likewise, pot cheese or something else (might be that which is most desired). The best thing for each people is that which is most beneficial to them." ("Fataawa Arkaan al-Islaam")

So the zakaat al-fitr must be paid before the Eid prayer, and it must be paid in the form of the food of the people of the land. The scholars also agree that is also best to give it to the needy people in one's own land, rather than to send it off to another place.

We have found, alhamdulillah, that the children enjoy assisting in this giving of the zakaat, helping to choose that which is given and measure it out, and then to deliver it to the needy people who will be receiving it. This causes them to love the giving of the zakaat, and to share in its benefit, and, insh'Allaah, teaches them from a young age about the zakaat and its principles and rulings. And Allaah knows best.

Family Time

The Story of Prophet Hud

The people of Aad lived in Yemen, in the area of Ahqaaf, between Oman and Hadramaut. They were from the descendents of the people of Nuh whom Allaah saved in the ship. For a long time the people of Nuh remained on the guidance that they had been given, but eventually they went astray.

They did not thank Allaah for all that he had given them. Allaah had given them wealth and gardens and children. He had given them great strength, and made them taller than all the other people around them. But they still did not thank Him for all He had done for them. They grew arrogant, and said, *Who is mightier than us in strength?*-(Surat Fussilat, Ayat 15) Allaah says, *Did they not see that Allaah who created them was mightier in strength than them?*-(Surat Fussilat, Ayat 15)

Here are two ways that people go astray and displease Allaah. First of all, is by not being thankful to Allaah for all that He has given us. We have to remember that everything we have, from our parents, to our house, to the cookies we had last night only came to us because Allaah willed that we have it. Without Allaah, we would have nothing- we cannot live without Allaah, Glorified is He. Secondly, being arrogant. Do you remember who else was arrogant from the stories we have already read? Do you remember who wouldn't bow down before Aadam when Allaah commanded him to? Yes- it was Iblees, and he did not bow down because he was arrogant and thought that he was better than Aadam because Aadam was made from clay, while Iblees was a jinn and made from fire. Arrogance often leads to not being thankful. If we think that we are better than other people, or that we are responsible for all the good we have in our lives, then we are arrogant, and we are likely to not listen to the commands of Allaah. Besides displeasing Allaah, arrogance and lack of gratitude also make people not like us. Do you know anyone who acts as if he is better than other people? Do you like this person? And how would you feel if you gave someone a gift and they didn't thank you? You would probably feel hurt or angry. So we must remember to be thankful to Allaah first, and then to people. And we should remember that we are not better than anyone else just because we think we are smarter, or faster, or we have better clothes or more money than they do. We do not know what is in their hearts- and Allaah knows what is in everyone's hearts, and that is what matters- that is what we will be judged for- our belief in Allaah and how we lived it.

These descendents of Nuh began to worship idols that they had made of stone with their own hands. They did not worship Allaah alone, who created them and granted them so many blessings. They began to use the strength that Allaah had given them to do evil to other people. They spread throughout the land and conquered the people who lived there, and then treated them with injustice. They built high palaces on every high place, even though they did not need them or live in them. They only wanted to show off their strength and money.

Allaah gave them wealth and great strength, and they used it to do evil. Insh'Allaah we must always remember to use our gifts for good, in any way we can, and not for evil or to be unjust to others. And look how misguided they were- they worshiped idols that they had made with their own hands!! Think how silly this is. If you made a tree out of clay, would you worship it? No, alhamdulillah. You know that you can squeeze your hand and smash that clay tree- it has no power or ability to do anything for itself, and we know that Allaah has the power and ability to do anything He wants to.

Finally, when the people were following the path of Shaytaan, and the land was filled with evil and injustice, Allaah sent them a messenger to bring them back to path of light and guidance. He sent Hud, may Allaah's salutations be upon him. He was from the most noble men and chiefs among them. Allaah always chooses the Messengers from the best, most honorable people and tribes.

Prophet Hud called to his people and told them to worship Allaah alone, without partners, and to obey and fear him. His people could not believe that he was calling them to leave the worship of their Idols, and worship Allaah alone. They answered, ❖*Verily, we see you in foolishness, and verily, we think you are of the liars.*❖-(Surat Al-A'raaf, Ayat 66) Hud said, ❖*Oh my people! There is no foolishness in me, but I am a Messenger from the Lord of all that exists. I convey to you the messages of my Lord, and I am a trustworthy advisor for you*❖-(Surat Al-A'raaf, Ayat 66)

He advised them to stop building palaces of which they had no need. He told what a waste this was, and it was only to show off to the people. Did they think they could live in great palaces forever? Didn't they know they were going to die and be brought before Allaah? He told them to stop being tyrants, seizing the people unfairly.

Hud told them that they should thank Allaah for His bounty and generosity in sending a messenger to warn them of His torment and to remind them of the right path. Hud reminded them of Allaah's favors, saying, *And remember that he made you successors after the people of Nuh, and increased you amply in stature? So remember the graces bestowed upon you from Allaah, so that you may be successful.*-(Surat Al-A'raaf, Ayat 69) He told them that they could never be successful unless they gave thanks to Allaah for all of His bounty, and worshipped Him alone.

Only a very few people believed in him, and they had to hide their faith so that the people would not do evil to them. Most of the people refused to believe in Prophet Hud's message. They rejected his call and said, *Bring us that with which you have threatened us, if you are of the truthful.*-(Surat Al-A'raaf, Ayat 70)

Hud asked them why they were arguing with him over worshipping idols, when they knew that they and their fathers had made them gods, and given them their names. They knew that Allaah had given them no authority to worship them.

He told them that their punishment would come to them. He said, *Then wait, I am with you among those who wait.*-(Surat Al-A'raaf, Ayat 71)

Look how wise Hud was when dealing with his people. He warned them against using their wealth wastefully, building palaces and such that they did not need. He warned them against oppressing or hurting other people. He told them to be thankful to Allaah, and to stop worshiping useless idols that they made themselves and which had no power. He told them to worship Allaah, and he warned them of Allaah's punishment. And look how evil and blind those people were- they said, in a way which showed that they didn't think it would happen, "Bring us that with which you have threatened us, if you are of the truthful." They didn't believe in Hud's message, and they didn't think Allaah could harm them and punish them for their evil. They were very wrong, mash'Allaah. Remember what Allaah did to the people of Nuh who didn't believe in Him and worship Him alone? Well, read on and hear what He did to the people of Aad.

Allaah saved Hud, and those who believed with him, and then he seized the disbelievers with a dreadful torment. Allaah tells us about the punishment he sent to them in Surat Al-Haaqqah, when he says, *And as for Aad, they were destroyed by a furious violent wind! They were subjected to it for seven nights and eight days in succession, so you could see men lying overthrown, as if they were the hollow trunks of date palms! Do you see any remnants of them?*-(Surat Al-Haaqqah, Ayat 6-8) The wind that Allaah sent to them carried them up, one by one, into the air, and then threw each of them down on his head, crushing his head and pulling it off his body. That was the punishment given to Aad, because of their disbelief and stubbornness.

Points of Benefit

1. You must always be thankful to Allaah for all the good things He gives to you. He gives you your food, your water, your home, and your family. He gave you everything, even your own life.

2. Arrogance or pride is a cause of destruction. This is what brought Iblees into disbelief, when he was too proud to prostrate to Aadam. This is also what happened to Aad, when they thought that no one could be stronger and bigger than them.

3. You must never treat anyone else unfairly, even if they are smaller than you are.

4. You should not be extravagant, and show off to others. You should only have those things which you need. If you have anything that you do not need to use, you should give to someone else who needs it.

5. Allaah saves and assists those who believe in Him.

6. Allaah punishes those who worship others along with him in worship, both in this world and the hereafter.

7. When you hear a strong wind, you should ask Allaah to send good in this wind, not evil.

Hands on Activities

1. Make the page for prophet Hud in your prophet book. Write the prophet's name with hollow letters and color them in as you like. Draw a little picture or write a verse from the Qur'aan from the story to remind you of who he was and what he did.

2. Show your pages to someone in your family, or to a friend, and tell them all that you can remember about the story of Hud and the people of Aad.

3. Look for Yemen on a map. Yemen is a beautiful and diverse country. There are mountains and valleys filled with green plants, and there are deserts where all you see is sand for miles and miles. There is a lot of coastal land, which is usually dry and hot. There are many scholars in Yemen, alhamdulillah, and places to go to learn about Islaam. If you are able, check out the library, an encyclopedia, or the internet and read some more about Yemen and see photographs of this beautiful land.

4. Make a list of all the things that you should thank Allaah for. No matter how many things you think of, and how long your list is, remember that Allaah has given you much more than you could ever write down. Take five minutes after you write your list to thank Allaah for all the good things He has done for you and given you. Thank Him from your heart, and ask Him to make you always remember to be thankful to Him.

5. Aad people felt proud and arrogant and built tall palaces in high places- and then they didn't even live in them. They wanted to show off. Why not build some palaces yourself, out of clay, dirt, sand or stones? Try to make them as fancy and nice as you are able. Then, when you are done, break them down. It's easy, isn't it? And it is even easier for Allaah!!

6. Wind can bring good and wind can bring bad. A good wind brings rain, by the mercy of Allaah, to dry land and plants that need water, for example. A bad wind is like the one that Allaah sent to the people of Aad, which destroyed them. Remember the people of Nineveh, who the prophet Yunus was sent to? They repented of their evil and made du'aa and Allaah forgave them and did not punish them. How is this different from the people of Aad? They did NOT repent, mash'Allaah, or ask Allaah for help, and they were destroyed.

7. We should always make du'aa when we hear a strong wind. This is the du'aa; memorize it and remember to say it the next time you hear the wind blowing hard outside:

Allaahumma innee as'aluka khairahaa wa a'udhu bika min sharrihaa

Oh Allaah, I ask You for its goodness, and I seek protection from You from its evil.

Day 12:
The Letter السحور :س
(*as-Sahoor*)
(the pre-dawn meal eaten before fasting)

The Prophet, may Allaah's praise and salutations be upon him, said, *{The difference between our fast and the fast of the people of the book is eating the pre-dawn meal.}* (Muslim)

And he, may Allaah's praise and salutations be upon him, said, *{Eat the sahoor, for indeed in the sahoor is blessing.}* (al-Bukhaari and Muslim)

And he, may Allaah's praise and salutations be upon him, said, *{In the partaking of the sahoor is blessing; so do not leave it even if one of you takes only a gulp of water. For Allaah and His angels praise the ones who eat the sahoor.}* (Ahmad, and Sheikh al-Albaani has declared it to be hasan)

al-Haafidh ibn Haajar, may Allaah have mercy upon him, has clarified the meaning of the blessing in sahoor as that:

1. It is following the Sunnah

2. Differing from the people of the book

3. Taking strength from it for worshiping

4. Increasing one's energy

5. It guards against the bad manners which result from hunger

6. It is a cause for charity to be given to whomever asks (for charity) at that time or eats along with him

7. It is a cause for the remembrance of Allaah and supplication at a time when it is likely to be answered

8. The intention of fasting can be made at that time for the one who forgot it before he slept.

The Sunnah regarding the sahoor is that it should be eaten late (close to the time of the Fajr adhaan). As he, may Allaah's praise and salutations be upon him, said, { Three things are from the manners of prophethood: eating the iftaar (breaking the fast) early, eating the sahoor late, and placing the right hand over the left in prayer.} (at-Tabarani, and al-Albaani has declared it to be authentic)

It is narrated on Zaid ibn Thaabit, may Allaah be pleased with him, that he said, *{We ate the sahoor with the Messenger of Allaah, may Allaah's praise and salutations be upon him, then we stood up to pray.}* I (the person narrating from Zaid) said, "How much time was between the two?" He said, *{The time it takes to recite fifty verses of Qur'aan.}* (Muslim)

And with your sahoor, oh my dear sister, remember the hadeeth of the Prophet, may Allaah's praise and salutations be upon him, *{What a good sahoor are dates.}* (Ibn Hibban, and al-Albaani has declared it to authentic.

Further Points of Benefit

It has become common amongst the Muslims of today that they break their fast, then stay up late into the night, eating what they call sahoor around one or two o'clock in the morning. They then go to bed and sleep, often missing the Fajr prayer and praying it later, or with their Dhuhr prayer. Mash'Allaah, this is wrong on a number of levels, including the delaying of the Fajr prayer and the eating of the sahoor very early.

Insh'Allaah review the benefits of taking the sahoor our sister mentioned above. They are many, and they are far-reaching, alhamdulillah. Perhaps two of the greatest of them are the ones she lists first: following the example of the Messenger of Allaah, may Allaah's praise and salutations be upon him, and differing from the people of the Book.

Following the Sunnah of the Messenger of Allaah

There are many proofs that it is obligatory upon us to follow not only the Qur'aan, but the Sunnah of His Prophet, may Allaah's praise and salutations be upon him, as well.

First, from the book of Allaah; al-Haafidh ibn Katheer mentions in his tafseer of the Qur'aan the explanation of the verse regarding the one who leaves the way of the first believers, which is found in Surat an-Nisaa:

And whoever contradicts and opposes the Messenger after the right path has been shown clearly to him, and follows other than the believers' way, We shall keep him in the path he has chosen, and burn him in Hell what an evil destination! (Surah an-Nisaa, Ayat 115)

And whoever contradicts and opposes the Messenger after the right path has been shown clearly to him. This refers to whoever intentionally takes a path other than the path of the Law revealed to the Messenger, after the truth has been made clear, apparent and plain to him.

Allaah's statement, *...and follows other than the believers' way...* refers to a type of conduct that is closely related to contradicting the Messenger. This contradiction could be in the form of contradicting a text (from the Qur'aan or Sunnah) or contradicting what the Ummah of Muhammad has agreed on. The Ummah of Muhammad is immune from error when they all agree on something, a miracle that serves to increase their honor, due to the greatness of their Prophet. There are many authentic ahaadeeth on this subject.

Allaah warned against the evil of contradicting the Prophet and his ummah, when He said, *We shall keep him in the path he has chosen, and burn him in Hell-what an evil destination!* meaning, when one goes on this wicked path, We will punish him by making the evil path appear good in his heart, and will beautify it for him so that he is tempted further." (End of quote from ibn Katheer)

The Messenger of Allaah, praise and salutations be upon him and his family, made clear the importance of adhering to his guidance and that of the rightly guided predecessors in the following authentic hadeeth, on the authority of al-Irbaad ibn Saaryah who said, *"Allaah's Messenger, may Allaah's praise and good mention be upon him, gave us an admonition which caused our eyes to shed tears and the hearts to fear, so we said, "Oh Messenger of Allaah, this is as if it were a farewell sermon, so with what do you advise us?"*

So he , may Allaah's praise and His salutations be upon him, said, {I have left you upon clear guidance, its night is like its day, no one deviates from it except one who is destroyed, and whoever lives for some time from amongst you will see great differing. So stick to what you know from my Sunnah and the Sunnah of the rightly guided caliphs. Cling to that with your molar teeth, and stick to obedience even if it is to an Abyssinian slave since the believer is like the submissive camel; wherever he is led, he follows.}

(An authentic hadeeth found in "Sunan Abu Daawood" 4607, "Sunan Ibn Majah" 43,44, "Sunan at-Tirmidhi" 2676, "al-Musnad Ahmad" vol. 4/126 and other collections. The wording is that of at-Tirmidhi)

And in another authentic hadeeth:

{My Ummah will split into seventy three sects, all of them in the Fire except one and it is al-Jamaa'ah.} It was said, "Who are they, Oh Messenger of Allaah?" He, praise and salutations be upon him, replied, {That which I and my Companions are upon today.} (Authentic hadeeth reported by at-Tirmidhi (no.2643), al-Laalikaa'ee in "as-Sunnah" (no.147) and others)

Differing from the People of the Book

Indeed, we are commanded to differ from all of the disbelievers, as the Messenger of Allaah, may Allaah's praise and salutations be upon him, said,

{He who resembles a people is one of them.} (Abu Daawood, Ahmad, Sa'eed ibn Mansoor, and al-Qadaa'ee. Ibn Taymiyyah, may Allaah have mercy upon him, said, "Its chain of narration is good." in "al-Iqtidaa", page 72)

Sheikh al-Islaam, Ibn Taymiyyah, may Allaah have mercy upon him, said, "The least of the conditions of this hadeeth is that it necessitates the prohibition of resembling them, and its apparent meaning is that it demands that the one who resembles them has disbelieved, as is found in His saying, the Most High, ❲*And if any amongst you takes them as Auliyaa' (friends, protectors, helpers) then surely, he is one of them.*❳"-(Surat al-Maa'idah, From Ayat 51)

So this warning against resembling the disbelievers is a very strong one, mash'Allaah, and one that we must take seriously in every aspect of our lives. And this is strengthened in the case of the sahoor, as the Messenger of Allaah, may Allaah's praise and salutations be upon him, commanded us specifically to differ from the people of the Book in this matter. And Allaah knows best.

Sheikh Fauzaan, may Allaah preserve him, said,

"Some of the people go against the Islamic legislation concerning the sahoor and the iftaar. Some of the people- no, many of them- stay up all night and when they are tired, they eat sahoor, and it is long before Fajr. And they sleep and ignore the Salaat al-Fajr and its time, and do not pray with the congregation. And this involves a number of mistakes.

1. They fasted before it was time to fast
2. They leave off the praying of Fajr in congregation
3. They leave the Fajr prayer until past its time, and they do not pray it until they wake up- sometimes not until Dhuhr.

And some of the misguided groups, after this, leave off their iftaar until long after the setting of the sun and do not break their fast until the stars are out. ("Majaalis Shahr Ramadhaan al-Mubaarak wa Itihaaf ahl Eemaan bi Duroos Shahr Ramadhaan" Page 143)

Family Time

The Story of the Prophet Saalih

Thamud were a people who lived after the people of Aad. They lived in great cities between Tabuk and al-Madinah in what is now Saudi Arabia. They were even more skilled than Aad in building great palaces. They carved huge, beautiful palaces out of rock! They decorated them with skilled designs and carvings. Anyone who entered their city would be amazed by the tall, beautiful palaces, carved from rock and lavishly decorated, and the lush, green gardens and fields around them.

Even though Allaah had granted them all these beautiful things, they would not do anything except disbelieve in him. They worshipped idols, just like those who had been destroyed before them had done. They did not thank Allaah for what He gave them. They did not think that they would be brought to account in front of Allaah for what they had done. They seemed to think that they would never die and be taken from their great palaces and gardens.

We see here how Allaah provides for the disbelievers as well as the Muslims. He grants them wealth, power, strength, and other things, just like he does for the Muslims. However, whatever good that they get, it is in this life only- in the Hereafter they will be punished for not worshiping Allaah alone and thanking Him for the blessings He gave to them. The Muslims, on the other hand, will be rewarded in the Hereafter with things more beautiful and amazing than anything they have ever seen or anything that they can imagine- so we should thank Him and do all that we can to please Him in this life so we can get those rewards, insh'Allaah.

Allaah sent to them a prophet from amongst them named Saalih, may Allaah's salutations be upon him. He was the most noble of them, the one with the best manners and greatest intelligence. All of his people greatly respected him. They hoped that he would be a great man because of his strong intellect. When he was sent to them by Allaah, He commanded them to worship Allaah alone. This is the message that all of the prophets, all the way to our Prophet Muhammad, may Allaah's praise and salutations be upon him, brought to their people.

He reminded them of the many blessings that Allaah had granted them. First, Allaah brought them forth from the earth, because He created their father, Aadam from earth. Then He settled them in the earth, and made them prosperous on it. Saalih told them to ask forgiveness for their previous sins, and to turn to Allaah in repentance in the future. He told them that Allaah is near to them in His knowledge, for He knows everything, and that Allaah responds to those who call on Him.

The people told Saalih that, before, they used to have hope in him, but now that he was saying this, they were doubtful of him. They said, *Do you now forbid us the worship of what our fathers have worshipped? We are really in grave doubt as to that which you invite us.*-(Surat Hud, Ayat 62)

They asked him to bring them a miracle, if he was truthful. They pointed to a solid rock, called al-Kaatibah. They told him to bring a pregnant camel out of the rock. They promised him that, if he did this, they would all believe that he was a prophet and in his message. When they promised him this, Saalih started praying and invoking Allaah to bring that miracle. All of a sudden, the rock began to move, and then broke apart. A she-camel came out, with a baby camel moving in her stomach, exactly as they had asked. They were all astonished. The chief of Thamud, Jundu' Ibn Amr, immediately believed in Allaah, as did some of those who followed him. All of the noblemen of Thamud wanted to believe as well, but three evil men stopped them. They were named Dhu'aab, al-Habbaab, and Rabbaab. They managed to persuade them to remain in their disbelief.

Look again at how important it is to have good companions and friends!! Imagine seeing the camel come out of solid rock after Saalih asked Allaah for this miracle. Isn't it amazing that anyone could not then believe in Allaah?!?! But these evil men, for their own evil reasons, convinced some of the noble people of Thamud to stay disbelievers. Think how strong the ones who stood firm in belief in Allaah were. Don't you wish that you were that strong? Well, ask Allaah to make you strong and firm in your faith, and to increase you in knowledge and love of Islaam, and insh'Allaah you will be that strong. And the success is with Allaah. Look and see again, how later in this story, some evil people caused other people to do bad things. Think of this story when you want to play with children who you know will try to get you to be bad. Instead, look for friends who help you to do good, insh'Allaah.

The camel remained in the city. The camel used to drink from the well on one day and then leave it for the people on the next day. On the day that she drank, the people of Thamud would milk her and fill their containers with the milk. The camel would graze in the valleys, and all of their cattle would be frightened of her when they saw her. This was because she was a tremendous animal, with a strikingly beautiful appearance. Saalih warned them not to do anything bad to the camel. He said, *Oh my people! This she-camel of Allaah is a sign to you, so leave her to graze in*

Allaah's land, and do not touch her with evil, lest a near torment should seize you.- (Surat Hud, Ayat 64)

Allaah gave them another miracle with the coming of the camel- every other day, the people of the entire community would milk her, and fill up their containers with milk. Think of how much milk that would have to be, and it all came from this one camel, mash'Allaah.

In Thamud there were nine evil men who caused mischief in the land, and they would not reform. They were tired of the camel, and they decided to kill her so that they would get to drink from the well every day. They were chiefs of their people, so they lured all of them into agreeing that the camel should be killed.

They all went and slaughtered the camel which Allaah had sent to them as a sign. Soon, the news reached Saalih, and he went to them where they had gathered. When he saw the dead camel, he cried out, *Enjoy yourselves in your homes for three days. This is a promise that will not be belied.*-(Surat Hud, Ayat 65) He was telling them that an awful punishment was going to come to them after three days, and that this threat would surely come true.

The nine wicked people killed the camel on a Wednesday, and that night they conspired to kill Prophet Saalih as well. They swore that they would make a secret night attack on him and his family. They decided that afterwards when his relatives inquired in to the matter, they would lie and tell them that they did not see what happened, and that they were telling the truth. That night, as they gathered to carry out their evil plan, Allaah rained down stones and smashed the heads of these nine people before the rest of the tribe.

See again, how once you do one bad thing, it is easy to do another. These evil people went from killing a camel that was a miracle from Allaah, to planning on killing Allaah's prophet, Saalih! This is one reason we have to try not to do bad things, as so often one bad thing leads to another and it hard to stop and get back on the right track. But also remember Allaah's mercy- He is always willing to forgive you and help you be good if you ask Him to.

On Thursday, the first of the three days, the people awoke to find their faces were all pale yellow. On the second day, they woke up and found their faces had turned red. On the third and last day, they woke up to find their faces black. On Sunday, they awaited Allaah's Torment, and we seek Allaah's refuge from it. They did not know what would be done to them, nor from where the punishment would come. When the sun rose, a Sayhah, or loud cry, came from the sky, and a tremor came from below, and their souls were captured. No one from Thamud remained, except Prophet Saalih and those who believed in him.

A long, long, time later, the Prophet Muhammad, may Allaah's praise and salutations be upon him, passed through the ruins of the homes of Thamud. This was in the ninth year after the Hijrah, when he was on his way to Tabuk. He camped near them, and he told the people not to use the water from their wells, because they were people who were destroyed by Allaah's punishment. He told them to dump out the pots of water that they had filled, and to take the dough they had made with that water to feed their camels. He told them that they should not go through this area unless they were crying, for fear that Allaah's punishment would come to them as well. He, may Allaah's praise and salutations be upon him, said, *{Do not enter upon these who were tormented, unless you do so while crying. If you are not crying, then do not enter, so that which befell them does not befall you as well.}* The basis of this Hadeeth is mentioned in Bukhaari and Muslim. We seek refuge in Allaah from His punishment.

Points of Benefit

1. Worshipping Allaah alone, and not worshipping others along with Him, is the only way to true success, both in this world and the next

2. The Shaytaan always wants to guide people astray by making them worship others than Allaah.

3. You should never be pleased with yourself because of the good things you have, because if you are not thankful for them then they may be taken from you.

4. The disbelievers will have an awful punishment, in this world and the next.

5. Allaah always protects the Believers from evil and destruction in this world, and from His punishment in the next.

Hands on Activities

1. Make the page for prophet Saalih in your prophet book. Write the prophet's name with hollow letters and color them in as you like. Draw a little picture or write a verse from the Qur'aan from the story to remind you of who he was and what he did.

2. Show your pages to someone in your family, or to a friend, and tell them all that you can remember about the story of Saalih and the people of Thamud.

3. In Saudi Arabia today, the remains of the houses of the people of Thamud can still be seen. We know where they are because of the hadeeth of the Prophet above, alhamdulillah. They are huge stone houses, carved right from stone.

We should not look at these pictures and think how great the people were for being able to create them- we should instead remember that they were only able to create them because Allaah gave them the ability to do so- and we should remember what ultimately happened to these people, who were completely and utterly destroyed by Allaah for their arrogance and evil. So we should ask Allaah to protect us from falling into their mistakes of being proud and ungrateful and disbelieving in Allaah.

Why don't you take some cardboard boxes and use your scissors to try to make some houses similar to those that Thamud built? You can cut out windows and doors, and cut out designs and tape or glue them to the outside. Then you can decorate the houses with magic markers or paints or construction paper.

4. Allaah sent the she-camel as a miracle for the people of Thamud. Have you ever seen a camel? In many parts of the world camels still play a very important role in people's lives. They are used as riding animals, just like horses- there are even countries in which they have camel races, just like horse races! They are used to carry things from place to place. Allaah made them to be the perfect desert animals, as they do not need a lot of water and are very strong and can travel great distances. They are used to move the millstone to grind wheat into flour. They are used for meat as well as milk. Camel meat does not taste like beef or chicken. It has a strong taste all its own. The camel's urine is even used by some people mixed with milk as a medicine. That sounds strange to us, but there is an authentic hadeeth in "Saheeh al-Bukhaari" in which the some people came to the Prophet and they became sick. He sent them out to where his flocks of camels were, and told them to drink the milk and urine of the camel to get better. People still do this today in different parts of the world!

Let's think about how camels were used for transportation. They carried people and things through the hot, dry desert. Use your imagination to come up with some sort of vehicle that would serve more than one purpose, like the camel does for these people. For example, what kind of vehicle would be good for a farm? What would it have to be able to do? Or what if you wanted to be able to drive and fly with your vehicle? Draw a picture of your imaginary vehicle and color it in.

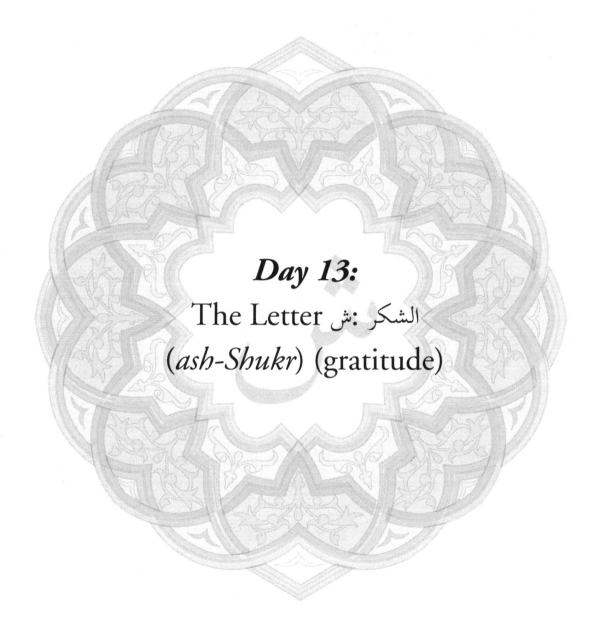

Day 13:

The Letter ش: الشكر

(*ash-Shukr*) (gratitude)

Verily from being grateful to Allaah for His Bounties is not using them to disobey Him. For example, wasting His blessings and bounty upon us.

And when we examine other people's situations we find that they prepare for Ramadhaan by purchasing great amounts of food and drink which they do not have in other than Ramadhaan; and then they fall short in being thankful for these blessings.

From the women are those whose main occupation in Ramadhaan is preparing many different varieties of food for the breaking of the fast in an amount which far exceeds the needs of their household- and then most of this may end up in the garbage can.

What is obligatory is to take a middle course in this, as Allaah, the Most High, said, *...and eat and drink but waste not by extravagance, certainly He (Allaah) likes not al-musrifoon (those who waste by extravagance).*-(Surat al-A'raaf, From Ayat 31)

Remember, oh my sister, that gratitude increases your blessings. Allaah, the Most High, says, *And (remember) when your Lord proclaimed: "If you give thanks, I will give you more (of My Blessings); but if you are thankless, then verily, My punishment is indeed severe.*-(Surat Ibraaheem, Ayat 7)

Further Points of Benefit

Ibn Qayyim, may Allaah have mercy upon him, defined shukr, saying, "It is manifesting the blessings of Allaah, Glorified and Exalted, with the tongue, thanking and acknowledging Him; and in the heart, bearing witness and having love for Allaah; and with the limbs, with submission and obedience to Him." ("al-Mudaraj" Vol. 2, Page 244)

ash-shukr is from the attributes of Allaah. He, the Most High, says,

Why should Allaah punish you if you have thanked (Him) and have believed in Him. And Allaah is Ever All-Appreciative (of good), All-Knowing.-(Surat an-Nisaa, Ayat 147)

And we understand that this shukr in regards to Allaah does not resemble or compare to that of His creation.

And also, Allaah has described the prophets and messengers and the righteous people as having ash-shukr. He, the Most High says,

Oh offspring of those whom We carried (in the ship) with Nuh! Verily, he was a grateful slave.-(Surat al-Israa, Ayat 3) And He, the Most High, says,

Thus do We explain variously the ayaat (proofs, evidences, verses, lessons, signs, revelations, etc.) for a people who give thanks.-(Surat al-A'raaf, from Ayat 58)

And Allaah, Glorified and Exalted, has commanded us to be thankful. He, the Most High, says,

❬Oh you who believe! Eat of the lawful things that We have provided you with, and be grateful to Allaah, if it is indeed He Whom you worship.❭-(Surat al-Baqarah, Ayat 172) And He, the Most High, says,

❬Therefore remember Me (by praying, glorifying). I will remember you, and be grateful to Me (for My countless favors on you) and never be ungrateful to Me.❭-(Surat al-Baqarah, Ayat 152)

And Allaah, Mighty and Majestic, joined ash-shukr and worship together, as can be seen in His, the Most High, saying,

❬So eat of the lawful and good food which Allaah has provided for you. And be grateful for the Graces of Allaah, if it is He Whom you worship.❭-(Surat an-Nahl, Ayat 114)

And Abu Hurairah, may Allaah be pleased with him, said that the Messenger of Allaah, may Allaah's praise and salutations be upon him, said, *{Verily, the one who eats and is thankful to Allaah, has the same reward as a patient fasting person. }* (Ahmad, and it is authentic)

The meaning of this hadeeth is that the one who eats and is thankful- and this a general statement, not referring specifically to Ramadhaan, but rather the entire year- has the same reward as the patient fasting person.

Abu Hurairah, may Allaah be pleased with him, also narrated that the Messenger of Allaah, may Allaah's praise and salutations be upon him, said, *{He who is not thankful to the people, is not thankful to Allaah. }* (Ahmad, and it is authentic)

We see in this the importance of showing our gratitude to the people as well as to Allaah, knowing always that whatever good has come to us has come ultimately from Allaah, the Most High. Keeping this in mind, though, we must show gratitude to the people as well, according to our capability, through such things as supplicating for them, thanking them, or giving something to them or doing good for them in return.

'Ali ibn Abi Taalib, may Allaah be pleased with him said, "Verily, blessing is connected to gratitude, and gratitude is connected to the increase of blessing. They are interrelated. And more blessings from Allaah will not be severed until the slave stops being grateful." ("'Udat as-Saabireen" Page 123)

So increase, my sister, in being grateful to Allaah for all that He has blessed you with in this life, both large and small, and the result will be that more blessings will come to you- and the success is with Allaah.

Family Time

Special Ramadhaan Meal Number Two:

Last week we cooked and ate some food from Egypt. This week we are going to another Muslim country to sample some of what they eat. Again, remember that it is the Sunnah to break your fast with dates and water, so do that first, and then eat your meal later, insh'Allaah.

This week we are going to try some food from Pakistan. Look at a map or globe and find Pakistan. Is it a large country, or a small one? What are some of the countries around it? What are some of its bigger cities? See if you can get a book, or go to a website that has photographs from Pakistan. If you like, try to decorate the room you eat in to make it look like a Pakistani home!

If you don't make all of these recipes, at least try one or two, insh'Allaah, to see how they taste, so you know how your Pakistani brothers and sisters eat. Like with the Egyptian food, we tried to choose recipes that are not too fancy, but are commonly eaten by the people. If you don't have some of the ingredients, do the best you can with what you have, insh'Allaah, it will still be good.

These recipes are from a sister who lives in Pakistan. She was born in America, but now lives in Pakistan with her husband, her son, and her husband's family. She even usually dresses like a Pakistani! She does something pretty neat. When she writes out her recipes, she uses both the English words and the Urdu words for the ingredients. Her family there speaks Urdu, so she is learning that language as well, alhamdulillah. See if you can learn some Urdu when you use her recipes.

This first recipe is for a snack food that is eaten in Pakistan. It would nice to have it right after you have broken your fast, insh'Allaah, like how we often eat samosas or falafel.

Ande ya Aloo pakoras...Egg or Potato Pakoras

You will need:

3-4 medium Aloo(potatoes)

3-4 boiled Ande (hard boiled eggs)

about a cup of besan(gram/chickpea flour)

1 Tbsp lal mirch(red chili powder)

namak(salt) to taste

One karahi(a heavy/deep skillet for frying), with 2 cups tel(oil) The tel should be on a medium/high flame, if it is too high then the pakora will burn outside and be raw inside. If the tel is not hot enough then the pakoras will absorb the oil and instead of being crispy, they will be mushy.

Step 1-Wash the aloo, peel if you want to(I don't, but a lot of people do), and then slice finely. They should be less than a quarter of an inch otherwise they won't cook properly.

Step 2-After removing the shell from the eggs, cut into slices. Unlike the aloo, the ande should be about 1/4 to 1/2 thick otherwise they fall apart.

Step 3-Place the besan, mirch and salt in a bowl and slowly add water while mixing to form a paste that is about the consistency of pancake batter.

Step 4-Carefully place the ande in the besan, and using a fork cover them with the mixture.

Step 5-Using the fork, carefully pick the egg up from underneath, and place into the tel in the karahi. Fry the ande in batches of 8-10.

Step 6-Flip the ande while frying, you should fry until they start to brown and get crispy.

Step 7-When they are finished frying remove from the tel, and place in a colander or on some paper to drain the oil. Follow the same steps for the aloo, the fork is optional because the aloo don't fall apart, but you may want to use it any way for your own safety.

Pakoras make a very tasty snack for tea time, serve with ketchup and chutney

Roti
One of the most important things of almost all Pakistani meals is the bread.

Step 1-Here are the tools that you would need to make roti-

a large bowl, a plate with extra flour for dusting, a tawa(like a cast iron skillet), a chimta(tongs), a chukla(like a raised cutting board), a bailen(rolling pin), and a rumal(bread cloth). You will also need two cups of atta(wheat flour), and 3/4 cup of water. It is better to use a gas stove if you are lucky enough to have one, but if you don't then it's not a big deal.

Step 2 is to make the dough, put the atta and the water in the bowl and use your hands to mix.

Step 3- Knead until you get a somewhat stiff dough, it shouldn't be very dry but it shouldn't stick to your hands either.

Step 4-Divide the dough into six balls, take one in one hand and using the tips of your other finger, push the edges of the ball towards the center-

Step 5-now with the same hand hold your hand in the shape of a C and move it in a circular motion. Both of these steps are important to help make a nice round shape in your bread.

Step 6-Next roll your ball in the extra flour,

Step 7-And use your hands to flatten it a bit-

Step 8-Put your dough on your chukla(board), and using your rolling pin flatten it out to about 4-5 inches across-

Step 9-If it seems like it might stick to your board you should dip it in your extra plate of flour-

Step 10-and then continue rolling until it is about 8-9 inches across.

Step 11-Pick the round up carefully and then flip it from right hand to left hand and back a few times-

This serves two purposes, one to knock off any extra flour and to widen the circle a bit.

Step 12-After that you flip the dough onto your pre-heated tawa-and if there are any wrinkles then just flatten them a bit.

Step 13-On a medium heat the bread will darken (and it won't look doughy) in about a minute, then use your chimta to flip your bread over.

Give the second side about the same cooking time as the first side then comes a bit of a tricky part.

Step 14-Move your tawa to the side of the flame and using your chimta hold the bread over the flame. Don't leave it in one place, rotate the bread so that the flame touches all parts of the bread. The bread should have turned mostly white with small charred spots, but with no dark dough spots. If you are using an electric stove you will skip this last step and instead use a small clean folded kitchen towel to press on the bread to help get it to cook evenly(gets rid of the dark spots that take a bit longer to cook)

Step 15-Now your bread is finished, put it inside your rumal(bread cloth, if you don't have one a clean dishtowel would work). Then fold the corners over your bread to keep it warm while you cook the rest.

Keema aloo- Ground Beef with Potatoes

Keema aloo is a tasty main dish.

Ingredients:

1 kilo Keema(ground beef), thoroughly washed and drained.

6 medium Aloo(potatoes), cubed

3 medium piyaz(onion), finely sliced

3-4 medium timater(tomatoes), diced

1-2 tablespoons lesan(garlic) paste

1-2 tablespoons adrak(ginger) paste

6-8 hari mirch(green chilies), cut into one inch pieces

1 2" stick dal cheeni(cinnamon)

6-8 whole kali mirch(black peppercorns)

1 bari ellichi(black cardamom)

6-8 loung(cloves)

1 tablespoon lal mirch(red chili powder)

1 tablespoon (or to taste) namak (salt)

1 teaspoon haldi(turmeric)

1 teaspoon dhania(coriander powder)

1/4 to 1/3 cup tel(cooking oil)

2-3 tablespoons ghee(clarified butter)-this is optional and sometimes I don't use it in this recipe)

Step 1-Add the tel to the pot, then the piyaz.

Step 2-When the piyaz have turned golden brown, add the adrak and lesan paste, fry for 20-30 seconds.

Step 3-Add the timater to the pot.

Step 4- Add the lal mirch, namak, haldi, and dhania, mix well.

Step 5-Fry until the tel rises to the top, if you are using ghee then add it at this point.

Step 6-Add the keema.

Step 7- Fry the keema, stirring often, for 6-8 minutes to brown it a bit.

Step 8-Add the aloo, stir well.

Step 9-Add one glass pani, stir well.

Step 10-Cover and cook on a low to medium heat until the keema is thoroughly cooked and the aloo is just about done

Step 11-Add the hari mirch, stir, cover and cook an additional 5 minutes, or more to cook off any excess pani. It should not be too soupy.

Serve with rotis.

Palli alloo- Stringbeans with Potatoes

Palli Aloo is a tasty veggie dish, that works well as a main course or as a side dish.

Ingredients-

1 kilo gawar ki palli(string beans), de-string the beans and cut into 1 inch pieces

6 medium aloo(potatoes), cut into small cubes, you can peel them if you like but I don't usually.

2-3 piyaz(onions), finely sliced

1 tbsp lesan(garlic) paste

1 tbsp adrak(ginger) paste

a 2 inch dal cheeni(cinnamon stick)

8-10 kalli mirch(black peppercorns)

1 bari ellichi(large brown cardamom)

6-8 loung(whole cloves)

1 tbsp lal mirch(red chili powder)

namak(salt) to taste, I use a bit less than a tbsp

1 tsp dhania(coriander) powder

1 tsp haldi(turmeric)

1/4 cup cooking oil

2-3 tbsp ghee(clarified butter), optional

Step 1-Add your tel and piyaz to the pot, then add the whole masalas(loung, kali mirch, dal cheeni, ellichi)to the piyaz

Step 2-When the piyaz start to turn golden, add adrak and lesan paste to piyaz, fry for about 30 seconds

Step 3-Add timater, mix well.

Step 4-Add powdered masalas, mix well.

Fry until the tel starts to separate from the sauce.

Step 5-Add 2-3 tablespoons ghee, this is totally optional and only really for flavor.

Step 6-Add the palli and aloo.

Mix well so that all sauce coats the palli and aloo.

Step 7-Add one glass pani(water), mix well.

Step 8-Cover and cook on a low flame until the palli and aloo are soft.

The Palli Aloo is finished, if you like you can garnish with fresh dhania leaves. This dish is best served with roti.

Day 14:
The Letter ص: صيام الصغير
(*Siyaam as-Sagheer*)
(the fast of the young person)

Be vigilant, oh my Muslim sister, in encouraging your children to fast from a young age so that they become acquainted with and accustomed to that, taking your example from the prayer. This is so that when they become mature and fasting is obligatory upon them, it will not be harmful for them.

You have an excellent example in the salaf, the righteous predecessors; for the Companions, may Allaah be pleased with them, would have their small children fast and they would give them toys of wool- then if they asked for food, or one of them cried from hunger, they gave him those toys to distract them until they finished their fast.

al-Haafidh ibn Haajar, may Allaah have mercy upon him, mentioned that this is a proof that training the children to fast is legislated in Islaam.

From the important questions connected to the fasting of the children is that if the child becomes mature during the day in Ramadhaan, or becomes fifteen that night, it is written down for him as a good deed (because he is fasting at that time). And the first part of such a day is not seen as that which is obligatory, while the second part of the day is obligatory.

Further Points of Benefit

Sheikh Muhammad ibn Saalih al-Utheimeen, may Allaah have mercy upon him, was asked, "Should the young people be commanded to fast if they are under the age of fifteen, such as is the case with the obligatory prayer?"

He, may Allaah have mercy upon him, replied, "Yes- command the young people who have not become mature to fast if he is able to endure it, as this is what the Companions, may Allaah be pleased with all of them, did with their children.

The people of knowledge have stated that the guardian command those children over whom he has supervision with fasting in order that they become trained and accustomed to it, and that the foundations of Islaam become a part of their own characters, so that they are instinctual for them.

However, if it is unbearable for them, or causes them harm, then do not persist in that.

Indeed, I am going to bring up here a matter which some of the fathers and mothers engage in, and it is that they forbid their children from fasting- and this is the opposite of that which the Companions, may Allaah be pleased with all of them, did. They claim that they are forbidding them out of mercy for them, and to show compassion for them. And the truth is that mercy to the children is with commanding them to follow the commands of the Islamic Legislation, and accustoming them to it, and establishing them upon it. As this, without doubt, is from the good, beneficial raising and educating of the children and from the perfection of their care and guardianship. And the saying has been confirmed from the Prophet, may Allaah's praise and salutations be upon him, {*Indeed the man is the guardian over the people of his household, and he is responsible for those under his care.}* (al-Bukhaari (853) and Muslim (1829))

And that which is incumbent upon the one who is in charge of the affairs in regards to those whom Allaah has placed under his care from family and children is that they fear Allaah, the Most High, concerning them, and command them with that which they are commanded to enjoin upon them from the Islamically legislated matters." (From "Kitaab ad-Da'wah", 1/145-146, as quoted in "Ahkaam at-Tifl", Page 71)

So we see that it is necessary for us to command our children with the fast- and this is in addition to using wisdom along with it. For example, one would not require that a baby or toddler fast. What I have found to be the most effective with the children is encouragement and setting a good example. If we want our children to fast and love the fast, then we have to fast and love the fast, and they will learn through this. Also, by making clear to them the benefits and blessedness of the fast and of the month of Ramadhaan- children want to do good, alhamdulillah, and if you explain these things in a manner which is appropriate to their age and understanding, then usually they will enthusiastically attempt the fast. Using rewards and keeping them involved and interested also helps, as the Companions would give the children toys to play with when they cried while they were fasting. In addition to this, the younger children can sometimes fast half days, or every other day, or whatever you find to be in their capability, insh'Allaah. This allows them to participate in the fast, and to begin to accustom themselves to it, without being harsh on them or harming them.

And again, if you see that they are being harmed by this, or it is too much for them, then do not force them to fast, mash'Allaah. We must choose the moderate way, following the example of the Companions, and using wisdom as well, insh'Allaah. And Allaah knows best.

Family Time

The Story of the prophet Shu'ayb

Madyan was a tribe from the Arabs like Aad and Thamud, whom Allaah had given many blessings. He gave them many children, and gave them strength. He gave them fruit trees and gardens. However, just like those who came before them, they did not thank Allaah for these blessings. They followed the whisperings of the Shaytaan. They worshipped a big tree called al-Aykah instead of Allaah. They would prostrate themselves in worship to this tree that could not hurt them or bring any good to them. They thought that this was better than worshipping Allaah.

Madyan were also a people who cheated. They would lighten the scales that they measured people's goods with, so that the people would get less than they paid for. They did not like to measure justly. In addition, they were highway robbers, causing mischief and corruption in the land. They would set up blockades on the roads, and then when any travelers came by, they would threaten to kill them if they did not give up their money. If they gave them their money they would let them go, but if they did not they would murder them.

Madyan people were not only unjust to themselves due to their disbelief, they were unjust to others by cheating them and robbing them. All they thought about was themselves, and how they could make themselves more wealthy. Have you ever cheated at anything? Don't answer that out loud, but think about it. Did you get caught cheating? When a person cheats another person and gets caught, then the other person will never trust him again. Think how sad that would be, to never be trusted. It is like lying- once a person is known to lie, people will assume that he is lying again. It is a terrible feeling to know that no one trusts you or believes you. You know that you want people to be fair to you and tell you the truth, don't you? You should remember to treat people the way you want to be treated, mash'Allaah, and they will usually treat you in a good way as well. Think back again to when you cheated. If you think you didn't get caught, then you are wrong. Allaah knows exactly what you did, because you can't hide anything from Allaah. And after all that Allaah has given to you, you should never want to displease Him- you should do all you can to please Him, and He will reward you for this. And, when we do evil or bad things, Allaah will make sure that we are punished for this as well- and we should seek Allaah's protection from that punishment, and ask His forgiveness. Remember, Allaah is always ready to forgive us if we turn to Him and ask Him for forgiveness.

Allaah sent Saalih, may Allaah's salutations be upon him, to the people of Madyan. He was the most noble of them in lineage. He told them to stop worshipping their tree, and to worship Allaah alone, with no partners. He told them that if they did not believe in him, then all of the good things that they were enjoying would be taken away, and they would be punished severely. He said to them, *Oh my people! Give full measure and weight in justice, and do not reduce the things that are due to the people, and do not commit mischief in the land, causing corruption.*-(Surat Hud, Ayat 85)

He also said that if they were just to the people, then that which they gained would be better for them than that which they took unjustly. He told them to look at the punishment that came to the disbelieving nations before them, like Nuh's people, Aad, and Thamud. Didn't they see what awful punishment had come to them because they would not believe in the messenger that Allaah sent them?

We should always remember that none of our good deeds will be unrewarded. There are angels who write down all of our deeds, and of course Allaah knows all that we do before they even write it down. And Allaah is the most Just- He will reward those who deserve to be rewarded, and He will punish those who deserve to be punished. Remember that the reward or punishment can come in this life, or in the Hereafter- but it will come, as Allaah wills it to.

Shu'ayb's people were not impressed by what he was telling them. They did not think that it was any of his business how they ran their stores. They said to him, *You are only one of those bewitched! You are only a human being like us, and verily, we think that you are of the liars!* -(Surat Ash-Shu'araa', Ayat 186) So just because he was calling them to believe in Allaah, they said that he had been affected by witchcraft, and that he was lying to them on purpose! They mocked him and laughed at him.

Yet again most of the people chose to disbelieve in Shu'ayb and his message, just like Hud and Saalih and so many of the prophets. They accused him of bad things such as witchcraft and magic, and said that he was lying to them. This is exactly what the disbelievers said about our Prophet Muhammad, may Allaah's praise and salutations be upon him, even though he was known to be from amongst the truthful people before and after he delivered his message from Allaah. The disbelievers make things up and try to hurt the prophets, mash'Allaah. In your life as a Muslim, people will probably do this to you as well, and you have to remember the prophets and messengers when this happens. You are in good company, and you have a good example in them as to how to deal with the people. They did not worry about what they said, they were patient and just continued to deliver their message for as long as Allaah wanted them to do this.

Finally, the people threatened Shu'ayb, saying, *Oh Shu'ayb! We do not understand much of what you say, and we see that you are weak among us. Were it not for your family, you would have been stoned, and you are not powerful against us.* -(Surat Hud, Ayat 91) They could not hurt him, even though they wanted to, because his family had a powerful position among them.

Shu'ayb said to them, *Oh my people! Is my family of more weight with you than Allaah?* -(Surat Hud, Ayat 92) Meaning: You would leave me alone out of respect to my people, but not out of respect for the greatness of your Lord, The Most Blessed and Exalted? Should not your awe for Allaah keep you from hurting His prophet?

Shu'ayb's people refused to believe in him and follow him. They blindly preferred the darkness of disbelief to the light of faith. They made fun of him, and challenged him to bring down a punishment from Allaah on them. They said to him, *So, cause a piece of the heaven to fall upon us, if you are of the truthful.* -(Surat Ash-Shu'araa', Ayat 187)

In the Qur'aan, Allaah compares faith and belief to light, and disbelief to darkness. Think of the difference between light and darkness. In the light we can see clearly and move around without running into things or harming ourselves or others. In the darkness, on the other hand, we bump into things, we can't see clearly and don't know where to go to stay safe and get where we want to go. We hurt ourselves and we hurt others. See how this is like faith and disbelief? With faith we know where we are going (Paradise) and how to get there (do all that Allaah and His Messenger have commanded, and leave off all of which they have forbidden). We are given the Qur'aan and Sunnah and the lives and works of the pious people who have come before us to help us, and the scholars and people of knowledge to look to for help as well. When we do not believe in Allaah and His Messenger and follow the religion of Islaam, it is like we are in the dark, not knowing where we are and how to get out, hurting ourselves in the process. May Allaah make us and keep us people who are in the light of faith, Ameen.

Shu'ayb told the people that Allaah knew best about them, and if they deserved this punishment, then he would send it upon them. Verily, Allaah does not treat anyone unjustly. And this is what happened to them. Allaah gave them a fair punishment for what they did. Allaah saved Shu'ayb and those who were with him, and punished all the others for their disbelief.

First, Allaah caused intense heat to overwhelm them for seven days. Nothing could protect them from this heat. Then, He sent a cloud to shade them, so that they all ran towards it, thinking it would protect them from the heat. When all of them had gathered under it, Allaah sent down from it fire, flames and a tremendous light. Then he caused an earthquake underneath them, shaking them, and a Sayhah, or loud cry, descended on them from the heavens, capturing their souls.

So three punishments were sent down to them: The heat, the fire, and the earthquake and sayhah. After the torment seized them, it looked as though they had never even lived there. When Prophet Shu'ayb saw them all lying there, still, as if they had never been alive, and had never lived in their city, he turned away from them, and said, ❨*Oh my people! I have indeed conveyed my Lord's message to you, and I have given you good advice.*❩-(Surat Al-A'raaf, Ayat 93) He did not feel any sorrow or pity for them, as they had only gotten what they deserved, and they had been fairly warned.

Points of Benefit

1. All of the prophets came with the same message to their people: to worship Allaah alone, with no partners.

2. You must never cheat anybody or treat them unfairly. You should always treat people with justice, just as you like to be treated.

3. You must never steal from other people, or take anything that does not belong to you.

4. All of the disbelievers will come to the same end: destruction and torment.

5. All of the believers will also come to the same end: safety in this world, and entering Jannah, or Paradise, in the next.

Hands on Learning

1. Make the page for prophet Shu'ayb in your prophet book. Write the prophet's name with hollow letters and color them in as you like. Draw a little picture or write a verse from the Qur'aan from the story to remind you of who he was and what he did.

2. Show your pages to someone in your family, or to a friend, and tell them all that you can remember about the story of Shu'ayb.

3. Remember the exercise where we pretended to be blind when we learned about Prophet Ya'qub? He could not see, but he had the light of faith in Allaah to guide him, alhamdulillah. Think about how it felt to not be able to see, and how you bumped into things and felt unsure and maybe a little afraid. Alhamdulillah, Allaah has given you the gift of Islaam, so you have guidance to follow and light to guide you.

Draw a picture of a lamp to remind you of the blessing of faith in your life. There are many different kinds of lamp- you could draw an old fashioned metal oil lantern and decorate it, or a kerosene lantern, or a lamp that stands on the floor, or sits on a table, or hangs from the ceiling. You could even draw a candle. Draw this lamp putting out beautiful, clear light. When you are unsure of something, you can think of this light, and let it remind you of the light of faith and ask Allaah to guide you to that which is best for you to do, insh'Allaah. And remember if you believe in Allaah and His Messenger and the religion of Islaam, then you have a lamp inside of you all the time, shining- the light of faith!

Day 15:
The Letter الضعف: ض
(*ad-da'f*) (weakness)

Bodily weakness- whether it is from an illness which is not chronic, pregnancy, or nursing if the mother is afraid for herself or her child- removes the obligation to fast at that time, and one can make it up later. Sheikh 'Abdul-'Aziz ibn Baaz, may Allaah have mercy upon him, said in a ruling when this question was put to him, that the ruling of the pregnant women for whom fasting is difficult, is the ruling of one who is ill. Similarly, the nursing woman, if it is hard for her to fast, then she is allowed to not fast and to make it up. As Allaah, Glorified and Exalted says, *...and whoever is ill or on a journey, the same number [of days which one did not observe saum (fasts) must be made up] from other days..."*-(Surat al-Baqarah, From Ayat 185)

And some of the Prophet's, may Allaah's praise and salutations be upon him, Companions were of the opinion that they only had to feed a poor person for each day. And the more correct opinion is the first, which is that the ruling is the same as that of the sick person because the foundational principle is that it is obligatory to make up the days. There is nothing that proves otherwise. One of the proofs of this is what Anas ibn Maalik al-Ka'bee narrated, that the Prophet, may Allaah's praise and salutations be upon him, said, *{Verily Allaah removed the obligation of fasting, and half of the prayer, for the traveler, and for the pregnant and nursing woman He removed the obligation of fasting.}* (Narrated by Ahmad and other than him, and Sheikh al-Albaani and Sheikh Muqbil declared it to be authentic)

This proves that they are like the traveler in that they don't fast, and then make up the fast later. However, in the case of being unable to fast due to old age or chronic illness, they do not fast and feed a poor person for each day. Allaah, the Most High, said, *And as for those who can fast with difficulty, (e.g. an old man), they have (a choice either to fast or) to feed a needy person (for every day)."*-(Surat al-Baqarah, From Ayat 184)

Ibn Abbaas, may Allaah be pleased with him, said, *{Allaah revealed the permission for the old man and woman who cannot fast, that for every day they feed a poor person.}* (al-Bukhaari)

Further Points of Benefit

Sheikh Muhammad ibn Saalih al-'Utheimeen, may Allaah have mercy upon him, was asked, "Is it permissible for the breastfeeding woman to break her fast? When should she make up for it? May she feed (the poor people instead of fasting)?

He, may Allaah have mercy upon him, answered, saying, "If the breastfeeding woman fears that the fasting will harm her child by reducing the milk, then she may break her fast. However, she must make up for it later, as she is in a similar situation to the person who is ill, about whom Allaah, the Most High, says,

...and whoever is ill or on a journey, the same number [of days which one did not observe saum (fasts) must be made up] from other days. Allaah intends for you ease, and He does not want to make things difficult for you.-(Surat al-Baqarah, From Ayat 185)

143

Then once the danger is past, she may make it up, either during the Winter when the days are shorter and the weather is cooler. Or, if she is unable to do this in the winter, then in the following year. As for feeding the needy people it is not permissible unless in the situation where that which prevents her from fasting, or her excuse, is continuous and is not expected to be removed. Under these circumstances, she may feed the poor people instead of fasting." ("Fataawa Arkaan al-Islaam")

And again, it is recommended that she make up the fast before the next Ramadhaan if possible, according to the hadeeth of 'Aishah mentioned previously. But as the Sheikh said, it is permissible for her to make it up whenever she is able, even if it is the next year. It is a good idea to keep track of the missed days so that you are certain of what you have to make up, or, if your circumstances permit, the number of poor people you must feed.

Also, if you are not afraid that you or your baby will suffer harm, then it is permissible for you to fast the month within its time. And Allaah is the Giver of Success.

Family Time

The Story of the Prophet Lut

When Ibraaheem, may Allaah's salutations be upon him, called his people to worship Allaah alone, one of those who believed in him was his nephew, Lut. He was the son of Ibraaheem's brother, Haraan. Allaah also made Lut a prophet, and sent him to the people to deliver the message of tawheed. He left with his uncle and first went to Sham with him. Then he went to a town called Sadum, lying to the east of the Jordan River, where he began to call the people to Allaah.

These people were the worst of people. They had evil manners and bad intentions. They did not keep away from any sin or evil that they wished to do. They would stop anyone who traveled by their town and steal all that he was carrying, leaving him with nothing to allow him to finish his journey. They were never ashamed of anything, and they would not listen to anyone who wished to advise them. They would not marry women, but only did evil deeds that no one before them had ever thought of.

The people that Lut was sent to call to worship Allaah alone were a very evil people. They only followed their desires. This is a very bad way to live your life. If you think about it, at first it seems like it might be nice to do whatever you want whenever you want without worrying about anyone else. But think about this a minute. If you are able to do this, then everyone else could do this as well! Imagine what a terrible place it would be if everyone just did whatever they wanted. For example, if your cousin wanted to beat you up and take all of your toys then he could do this- no one could stop him because the only thing that would be important is what he himself wanted. Allaah knew that this would be an evil, bad situation, so He has created laws that we must follow so that we can be good individual people who will someday be rewarded with Paradise in the Next Life. His laws were also revealed to make sure that our families and our societies are good and righteous. If everyone follows Allaah's commands, performing what He tells them to do, and staying away from what He tells them not to do, then the whole society benefits by this, not just one person. Do you see why Allaah's way is better than just following your own desires? It is really very clear when you think about it, isn't it? Alhamdulillah.

Allaah sent Prophet Lut to them, to call them to the right path, and to warn them away from all of these evil deeds. But these people were so evil that they did not want to hear anything that he was telling them. They preferred to be misguided and follow the Shaytaan. They did not respond to him at all.

Lut did not despair of getting them to believe in him. He kept calling them to worship Allaah alone, and to have faith in Him and obey Him. He told them to stop committing their evil deeds, and to turn to Allaah in repentance.

Again we see how honorable and patient Allaah's prophets are. Lut, like his uncle Ibraaheem and all of the other prophets and messengers, kept calling the people to worship Allaah alone, even though they continued to do evil deeds and did not listen to him. Allaah even tells us in the Qur'aan that all the prophets and messengers, and all that we can do, is call people to the truth and teach them about Islaam. Only Allaah can guide their hearts to the right path.

The people only answered by saying to each other, ❰*Drive out the family of Lut from your city. Verily, these are men who want to be clean and pure!*❱-(Surat An-Naml, Ayat 56)

Because they insisted on remaining on their evil ways, Allaah sent his punishment down upon them. It was brought by three angels. They are the angels that stopped to give glad tidings of a son to Ibraaheem and Saarah. When Jibreel and the other angels came to Ibraaheem, they told him that they were going to destroy the people of Lut. He said, ❰*But there is Lut in it.*❱-(Surat Al-Ankabut, Ayat 32)

They answered ❰*We know better who is there. We will, verily, save him and his family, except for his wife, she will be of those who remain behind.*❱-(Surat Al-Ankabut, Ayat 32)

The angels left and set out to destroy the people of Lut that very night. They came to Lut, and asked him to host them. He did not know who they were, as they looked like handsome young men. When Lut saw them, he felt sad, as he was afraid that the people would harm them. He said to them, ❰*By Allaah, I do not know of any people on the face of the earth more wicked and disgusting than these people (of this land- Sadum).*❱He said the same thing four times, in an effort to make them go away.

Lut, like Ibraaheem, did not know that his guests were angels- he thought they were handsome men who were in need of his hospitality. Because of this he was afraid for them. He knew how evil the men of that land were, and he was afraid that they would do evil things to these travelers. He tried to warn them away four times!

This shows also how important it is to treat guests well- he did not turn them away. Just like his uncle, Ibraaheem, he took them into his house and tried to help them. Think of this when someone needs your help, insh'Allaah, and see if there is some way you can help them out too.

When Lut's people heard that he had guests, they rushed to his house. They tried to push their way in so that they could harm his guests, saying, *Didn't we forbid you from entertaining mankind?*-(Surat Al-Hijr, Ayat 70) meaning, "Didn't we tell you not to have any guests?"

Lut tried to protect his guests, and he said to his people, *Fear Allaah, and do not disgrace me with regards to my guests. Is there not among you a single right-minded man?*-(Surat Hud, Ayat 78)

Then the angels told him who they were and reassured him, saying, *Oh Lut! Verily, we are the messengers from your Lord! They (the evil people) shall not reach you.*-(Surat Hud, Ayat 81)

The people were rushing at Lut's door, trying to break in, and he was standing at the door and trying to repel them. Then, Angel Jibreel came out and struck them with his wing. This blow blinded their eyes, so they went away, unable to see.

Mash'Allaah, how exciting that must have been! The evil people were trying to break in the door of Lut's house, while he stood there, trying to push them away. Then Jibreel, who before this had looked like a man, took another form which angels can take, and he hit the evil people with his wing, blinding them. They stumbled off, not able to see or to attack Lut's house anymore.

Then, Lut and his family left the town and traveled away from it, and none of them looked back at the town, because Allaah had commanded them not to. The only one who stayed behind was Lut's wife. She was an evil old woman, and she stayed behind with her people and shared their torment.

At sunrise, the sayhah, or loud piercing cry, came down from the heavens and overtook them. Then, Jibreel uprooted the city from the depths of the earth, lifted it up to the sky, and then threw it upside down on top of them. Allaah rained down upon them big, strong stones of hard baked clay, until the city turned into a foul-smelling lake. Not one of the people remained. All of them had been destroyed for their evil deeds.

Points of Benefit

1. Those who do evil deeds will be given destruction and torment in this world and the next.

2. Allaah saves the Believers and destroys the disbelievers

3. You must always honor your guests and never allow any harm to reach them, just like Lut did with his guests.

4. It is only good deeds that keep you from being punished, not being related to anybody. Lut's wife was from the disbelievers, so the fact the she was Lut's wife did not benefit her, and she was destroyed with all the others.

5. Angels can take more than one form. In this story we see them looking like very handsome men, and we read about Jibreel having wings, and being able to uproot the whole city from its foundations and throw it upside down on top of the evildoers. We don't know exactly how he looked when he did this, but alhamdulillah, we can see how strong and powerful he must have been. And remember, Allaah gave him this strength and power, and Allaah has more strength and power than him! He and the other angels are simply creations of Allaah, alhamdulillah.

Hands on Learning

1. Make the page for Lut in your prophet book. Write the prophet's name with hollow letters and color them in as you like. Draw a little picture or write a verse from the Qur'aan from the story to remind you of who they were and what they did.

2. Show your pages to someone in your family, or to a friend, and tell them all that you can remember about the story of Lut.

3. Allaah rained down upon the evil people of this land big, strong stones of hard baked clay, until the city turned into a foul-smelling lake. Take a minute to think about rain. Sometimes rain can be gentle and soft, sometimes it is steady and strong, and sometimes it can be very hard and driving. Some seasons there is too much rain for things to grow well, and some seasons there is not enough, mash'Allaah, for them to grow well. In the case of the people of Lut, Allaah punished them by raining down stones of clay instead of just water.

Do you know what you say when it begins to rain? The supplication for when it rains goes like this:

Allaahumma sayyiban naafi'an

Oh Allaah, provide for us a beneficial rain

And after it rains, you say,

Mutirnaa bifadli Allaahi wa rahmatihi

We are granted rain through Allaah's bounty and mercy

Both of these supplication are found in "Saheeh al-Bukhaari", alhamdulillah.

So we ask Allaah to make the rainfall beneficial for us and not harmful, and then we express our thankfulness to Him for bringing it to us, alhamdulillah.

Do you know how much it rains where you live? You can make a really easy rain gauge and put it outside to get an idea of just how much rain falls in your area. First you take a small plastic water or soda bottle- not the large 2 liter size, but the smaller .75 or one liter size. Remove the cap. Cut off the top of the bottle about ¼ of the way down, turn it over, and place it back into the bottle so that the neck of the bottle is now inside the lower piece, hanging down. That's it! You have made a rain gauge. If you have a yard, take it out and dig it into the soil a bit so it won't tip over. Don't place it under the eaves of the house, or you won't get much rain in it. You can put it out on a balcony, or hang it out a window- but try to make sure that it is fairly stable, or you'll lose the water that goes in. Check your gauge after a week and measure how much water is in it. Don't dump the water out. Check the gauge again after a month, and you'll know how much it rained in the whole month. This monthly rainfall is interesting to keep track of, and it is very helpful if you are thinking of planting things on your balcony or in your yard, mash'Allaah.

Another interesting thing to do is to think of ways to collect your rainwater. Now, the water may not be clean enough to drink if you live in a city, but if you can collect it, it can be used to water plants, for washing clothes, and many other things. Why not see if you can come up with a way to save your rainwater to use it in your house or yard, and try this out? This is an important part of being thankful to Allaah- finding ways to use His bounty in as many ways as we can, and being thankful for it all the time.

4. Why not draw a picture of the destruction of the people of Lut? Of course you can't draw the people, or the angels, but you could draw the stones pouring down from the sky, and the huge piece of land up in the sky, turned over. Use your imagination. Think of how powerful Allaah is that He was able to do this to the evil people. And remember, Allaah is very merciful and wants good for us- so we should ask Him to have mercy upon us, and guide us to the right path, and to forgive us when we do that which displeases him.

Day 16:
The Letter ط: الطهر
(*at-Tahr*) (purification)

From the matters which it is obligatory for the women to be concerned with in the month of Ramadhaan is purification from the menses or post-childbirth bleeding. And from the most important of these matters is what follows:

1. If a woman becomes purified and then sees a cloudy or yellow discharge after this, then this does not affect her prayer and worship. Purification has a clear sign which is known to the women which is when the cotton of the menstrual pad is white (قصة البيضاء) meaning, showing no traces of menstrual blood. (Translator's note: Imaam al-Bukhaari, may Allaah have mercy upon him, said in The Book of Menses, Chapter: The Beginning and the End of Menstrual Periods: Some women used to send the pads of cotton with traces of yellowish discharge to 'Aishah (to know whether they had become pure from the menses or not). And 'Aishah, may Allaah be pleased with her, would say, {Do not be hasty; wait until you see the cotton pad is white (meaning the disappearance of menstrual discharge or the presence of a white discharge).}

So if the woman sees this (the lack of menstrual discharge on the pad, or a whitish discharge) then it is a sign of the end of the period and the beginning of purity. Concerning that, Umm 'Atiyyah, may Allaah be pleased with her, said, {We did not attach any relevance to the cloudy or yellow discharge.} (al-Bukhaari, Abu Daawud, and Sheikh al-Albaani has declared it to be authentic)

2. If the woman becomes pure during the day in Ramadhaan, it is upon her to stop eating, according to the most authentic of the two opinions of the scholars. This is because of the removal of the excuse (for not fasting). And she must make up that day. (Summarized from "Majmoo' al-Fataawa" of the Esteemed Sheikh Ibn Baaz, may Allaah have mercy from him Vol. 4, No.213)

3. If the woman becomes pure before Salaat al-Fajr she must fast, as there is no barrier to stop her from putting off the ghusl from her menses until after Fajr. However, she should not put it off until after the sun rises; rather it is obligatory upon her to make ghusl and pray Fajr before the sun rises. And the case is the same for the one who has engaged in sexual intercourse. (Summarized from "Majmoo' al-Fataawa" of the Esteemed Sheikh Ibn Baaz, may Allaah have mercy from him Vol. 2, No.147)

4. It is permitted for the woman to use pills to stop the menses during the time of hajj, if she fears that she will be forced to stop the hajj (due to her menses). This should only be after consulting a doctor specializing in women's health. And also in Ramadhaan, if she wishes to fast with the people. (This is the ruling of the Standing Committee of Scholars in their book "Fataawa al-Islaamiyyah" Vol. 1, No. 241)

Further Points of Benefit

Sheikh Muhammad ibn Saalih al-'Utheimeen, may Allaah have mercy upon him, was asked, "If a menstruating woman becomes pure (her menses finishes) before Fajr, and she makes ghusl after it has come in, what is the ruling concerning her fasting?"

He, may Allaah have mercy upon him, replied, "Her fast will be valid if she is sure that she did indeed become pure before Fajr. The important thing is that she be certain that she was pure, because some women think that they have become pure and they have not. Due to this, women used to come to 'Aishah, may Allaah be pleased with her, with a piece of cotton to show her the signs of having been purified from the menses. She would say to them, *{Do not be hasty, wait until the cotton is white.}* (al-Bukhaari)

So a woman must be patient until she is sure that she has become pure, and once she has become pure, she should make the intention to fast, even if she did not perform ghusl until the advent of Fajr. She is also obligated to observe the prayer- so, she should perform ghusl in a timely fashion in order to offer the Fajr prayer in its allotted time.

We have been informed that some women become clean after the advent of Fajr, or before the advent of Fajr, yet they delay performing the ghusl until after sunrise, using the excuse that they want to make a more complete, cleaner and more pure ghusl. This is a mistake, whether during the month of Ramadhaan or in any other month. This is because it is an obligation upon her to make ghusl in a timely manner in order to offer the prayer in its allotted time. She may restrict herself to the minimum obligatory ghusl in order to perform the prayer, and then, if she wishes, she may increase on her purification and cleansing after the sun has risen. There is no sin upon her. The menstruating woman is like the one who is in a state of major ritual impurity, who did not perform ghusl until the advent of Fajr; there is no sin upon her, and her fast is valid. Likewise, if a man was in a state of ritual impurity, and he did not perform the ghusl for it until after the advent of Fajr, there would be no sin upon him for that. It has been confirmed from the Prophet, may Allaah's praise and salutations be upon him, that he would still be in a state of ritual impurity due to having had sexual intercourse with his wife, and Fajr would come in. He would fast and perform the ghusl after the advent of Fajr. (al-Bukhaari, 1930, Muslim 1109) And Allaah knows best. ("Fataawa Arkaan al-Islaam" Vol. 2)

We also see from the story of the women going to 'Aishah, may Allaah be pleased with her, how the female Companions rushed to become pure in order to resume their prayers and fasting- they would check to see if they were pure and want to make their ghusl as soon as possible afterwards. One of the mistakes of many of the women today is that they do not take such care with this matter, often delaying the making of the ghusl until long after they have become purified. May Allaah rectify the Muslims and make us steadfast and hasten to perform good deeds.

Family Time

The Story of the Prophet Moosa Part 1

One of the rulers of Egypt was a very evil man, called Fir'awn. He wanted the people under him to worship him. He was deceived by his kingdom and power into thinking that he had power over everything. He especially hated Bani Israa'eel. They were from the descendants of Prophet Ya'qub. Remember reading about the prophet Ya'qub and his sons? One of Ya'qub's other names was Israa'eel. Bani means sons, so they were the sons of Israa'eel. Fir'awn made them work as slaves for the other people, the Copts, in Egypt.

One day, Fir'awn saw in his sleep a dream that disturbed him. When he asked his interpreters what it meant, they told him that a child would be born from Bani Israa'eel who would take away Fir'awn's power and kingship. Fir'awn immediately told his soldiers to kill all of the boy babies born in Bani Israa'eel, and to leave the girls alive.

Fir'awn thought he was in charge of everything and could do as he liked. He thought that he could order whomever he wanted to be killed, just as a shepherd would do, slaughtering some of his sheep and leaving others. As soon as a baby boy was born, the soldiers took him and killed him. Thousands of babies were killed in front of their mothers and fathers.

Some of the people became afraid that if all of the boy babies were killed, then Bani Israa'eel would die out. Who would do their hard work for them if they killed all of their slaves? They would end up having to do the work themselves, and they did not like that idea! So then Fir'awn issued orders that the boys should be killed one year, and left alone the next year. Only Coptic women were allowed to be midwives. They would go around, and if they saw that any woman was pregnant then they would write down her name. When it came time for her to have her baby, they would come, and if it was a girl they would go away again. However, if it was a boy, the soldiers would come with their sharp knives, and kill him.

But Allaah was stronger than Fir'awn. Fir'awn was only a man. All of his precautions did not avail against the decree of Allaah. The baby was born that Fir'awn feared. The baby was born that would free Bani Israa'eel from the clutches of Fir'awn. Moosa Ibn Imraan was born, and lived, despite all of Fir'awn's precautions.

We see that no matter what the evil people do, Allaah will always be the only One with the power over all things, including life and death. Fir'awn made his people worship him like he was a god. He tried to act like he had power over life and death by ordering the baby boys to be killed. But look how Allaah foiled his plans, as truly Allaah sees everything, hears everything, knows everything, and He is the One with power over everything.

When Moosa's mother became pregnant with him, it was in the year when the babies would be killed. His brother, Haarun, had been born in a year when they were saved. She did not look like she was pregnant, so none of the midwives knew. But when she had a boy, she became very distressed and scared. She loved Moosa very much, and she did not want Fir'awn's soldiers to find out about him and kill him.

Allaah inspired into her heart and mind what she should do. Her house was on the banks of the Nile, and so she took a box and made it into a cradle. She would take care of Moosa and nurse him. Then, when anyone came to the house that she was afraid of, she put him into the box, and put it into the river and tied it with a rope so it would not float away.

One day, she forgot to tie it, and the water carried Moosa away, past Fir'awn's house. Some servant women saw the box and brought it to Fir'awn's wife. When she opened it, she saw a beautiful baby inside. Allaah filled her heart with love for him. When Fir'awn saw him, he wanted to kill him, because he was afraid that he might be from Bani Israa'eel. His wife, Aasiyah, came to the baby's defense, and told Fir'awn, ❴*A comfort of the eye for you and me. Kill him not, perhaps he may be of benefit to us, or we may adopt him as a son.*❵-(Surat Al-Qasas, Ayat 9) Fir'awn let her keep Moosa, not realizing that this was the child that he so dreaded.

When they brought Moosa to their house, he would not nurse from any of the women whom they brought to nurse. This is because Allaah decreed that he should not nurse from anyone except his own mother. They did not know what to do with him. Finally, they took him out to the marketplace to look for a woman to nurse him. Moosa's mother had sent his sister out to look for Moosa. When she saw them taking him to their house, she watched them from a distance. When they took him out to the market, she followed, and came to them saying, ❴*Shall I direct you to a household who will rear him for you, and look after him in a good manner?*❵-(Surat Al-Qasas, Ayat 9)

They took her to their house, and Moosa's mother was brought. They did not know that she was really the baby's own mother. As soon as she took him in her arms, he began to nurse. The people all rejoiced and sent the glad tidings to Fir'awn's wife. She called for Moosa's mother, and treated her kindly and rewarded her. She let Moosa's mother take him home with her to nurse him and take care of him. When she weaned him, he was taken back to Fir'awn's house, where he was raised like one of their children.

It would have been very hard for Moosa's mother to keep hiding him, especially as he got older and wanted to go out. So Allaah made a way for Moosa to escape being caught and killed. And by making it so Moosa would only nurse from his own mother, Allaah also showed mercy to her, as she was able to care for and nurse her own baby whom she had saved from death. Truly Allaah is the Best of Planners.

When Moosa grew older, Allaah gave him great strength, wisdom and religious knowledge. One day, Moosa came into the city in the middle of the day, when the people were all in their houses resting. He saw two men fighting. One was an Israa'eeli and one was Coptic. The man from Bani Israa'eel asked Moosa to help him so Moosa struck the Coptic man with his fist. Even though Moosa only hit him once and did not want to kill him, the man died.

Moosa turned to Allaah in repentance, and said, ❧*Oh Allaah, verily I have wronged myself, so forgive me.*❧-(Surat Al-Qasas, Ayat 16) So Allaah forgave him. Moosa became afraid of what would happen to him because of what he had done. He went about in the city, watching out for the consequences of his action to befall him. When he went out, he saw the same man from Bani Israa'eel who was fighting yesterday, fighting another Coptic man, and calling for Moosa to help him. Moosa was angry, and said to him, ❧*Verily, you are a plain misleader.*❧-(Surat Al-Qasas, Ayat 18) Then Moosa intended to grab the Coptic man, but the man from Bani Israa'eel because of his own weakness and cowardice, thought that Moosa was angry with him and wanted to hit him. He said, ❧*Oh Moosa! Is it your intention to kill me as you killed a man yesterday?*❧-(Surat Al-Qasas, Ayat 19)

Here is another example of how other people can draw you into their badness- look how this man got Moosa into trouble! First he called on him to help fight the other man, then after Moosa accidentally killed the other man he called him again to fight somebody else. Then he became afraid and made it known what Moosa had done. So see how you have to be careful when other people try to get you involved in something that is not good. It is best just to have friends and companions who will help you be good, as you help them to be good.

Before this no one had known about it except him and Moosa, but when the other Coptic man heard it he went to the gates of Fir'awn with this news, and told Fir'awn about it. When Fir'awn heard, he became very angry, and decided to kill Moosa. He sent people after him to bring him in. One courageous man who wanted to help Moosa found out about it, and took a shorter path than the one Fir'awn's people were taking. He ran to Moosa and told him, ❧*Oh Moosa! Verily, the chiefs are taking counsel together about you, to kill you, so escape. Truly, I am one of the good advisors to you.*❧-(Surat Al-Qasas, Ayat 20)

Again, see the value of good people? This person risked his own safety to help Moosa, alhamdulillah!

When Moosa heard that they were plotting against him, he left Egypt all by himself. He was not used to being alone, because before that he had lived a life of luxury and ease, having been in a position of leadership. He looked around him in fear, and he called on Allaah, saying, ❧*My Lord! Save me from the people who are wrongdoers!*❧-(Surat Al-Qasas, Ayat 21)

When Moosa left Egypt, he traveled toward Madyan. When he reached there, he went to drink from its well. He found a group of men watering their flocks of sheep, and he saw two women, waiting and keeping their sheep back. When Moosa saw the two women, he felt sorry for them, and asked them why they did not water their flocks with the others. They answered, ❧*We cannot water our flocks until the shepherds take their flocks, and our father is a very old man.*❧-(Surat Al-Qasas, Ayat 23) They did not have anyone to help them, as their father was too old. Moosa watered their flocks for them, and then he returned to the shade, and said,❧*My Lord!*

155

Truly I am in need of whatever good you bestow upon me.❯-(Surat Al-Qasas, Ayat 24)

Their father was surprised when the two women came back so quickly. They told him about Moosa helping them, and so he sent one of them to ask Moosa to come and meet him. One of the women came to Moosa, walking shyly, putting her garment over her face. She said to him, ❮*Verily, my father calls you so that he may reward you for having watered our flocks for us.*"-(Surat Al-Qasas, Ayat 25) When Moosa came to him and told him his story, he said, "*Fear you not. You have escaped from the people who are wrongdoers.*"-(Surat Al-Qasas, Ayat 25)

Then, one of the man's daughters, the one that had walked behind Moosa, said, ❮*Oh my father! Hire him! Verily, the best of men for you to hire is the strong, the trustworthy.*❯-(Surat Al-Qasas, Ayat 26) The old man told him that he would marry one of his daughters to him if he would take care of his flocks for eight years. He told him that if he wanted to give him two extra years to make ten, he could, but if not, then eight was enough. Moosa accepted, married his daughter, and served him for ten years.

The women were shy to be taking their animals for water because it meant that they had to mix in with the men. They must have been good women, because they hung back, away from the crowd, and Moosa noticed this. He came to their aid, and watered their flocks for them. Then he supplicated to Allaah, asking for good. He did not help the women in order to get anything from them, alhamdulillah- he just did it because it was the right thing to do. And look how Allaah rewarded him. He found a home, a job, and a wife, just through this one act of kindness, mash'Allaah.

Hands on Learning

1. Think about Moosa's mother and how she saved him by putting him in the basket out in the river Nile. Did you look up Egypt when you made the Egyptian food last week? If not, look it up now. See how long the Nile River is? Alhamdulillah that Allaah inspired Moosa's mother to save him in this way. It is a strong, big river- and Allaah protected him when the basket was not tied and broke free. He only went a little ways and then was found. Do you think you could make a basket? What are some ways that you could do this? You could weave one out of construction paper, or maybe make one out of a box. There are many ways you could make a basket. Try to make one. It doesn't have to be big enough to fit a baby in, but it will be fun to make anyway. If you don't think you can make one, why not draw a picture of the basket in the water, or use construction paper and glue to make the picture? Use your imagination and have fun, insh'Allaah.

2. Look at how Moosa was rewarded for his kindness to the two women. How
    often do you do things for other people, not because you want a reward,
    or because you are afraid of getting into trouble, but just because it is a
    good thing to do? Why not try to be kind and do good things for people
    as often as you are able? See how many times today you can do something
    for someone else, without asking for any reward. You will be rewarded by
    Allaah every time you do something, as long as you are doing it to please
    Allaah alone. And it is very likely that even though you don't ask anyone for
    any sort of reward, some of them will reward you anyway- maybe by doing
    something nice for you!

Day 17:
The Letter ظ: الظمأ الحقيقي
(*adh-Dhama' al-Haqeeqee*)
(the true thirst on the Day of Judgment)

Ponder, oh my sister, the hadeeth of the Prophet, may Allaah's praise and salutations be upon him, *{How many of the fasting people do not receive anything from their fast except for thirst? And how many of the people who stand up to pray at night do not receive anything from their standing except for weariness?}* (ad-Daarimee, and Sheikh al-Albaani has said that it has a good chain of narration)

And to understand the loss of he whose limbs do not fast due to evil deeds or sins, remember that if you feel thirst when you are fasting, you must remember that the true thirst is on the Day of Judgment- the Day of Sorrow and Regret. Remember that deliverance on that Day is for the one who held tight to the Sunnah of the Prophet, may Allaah's praise and salutations be upon him, as he, may Allaah's praise and salutations be upon him, said, *{I will go before you to the pool of al-Kauthar. Whoever comes (after me) will drink. And whoever drinks will never feel thirst afterwards. Some people will be turned away from me- people whom I know, and they know me. And we will be separated. I will say, "They are from me." And it will be said, "You do not know what they innovated in the religion after you." I will say, "Away with those who change the religion after me!"}* (Agreed upon)

And it has been related in a narration that Ibn Mubaarak, may Allaah have mercy upon him, came to the well of Zamzam and got a drink and said, "Oh Allaah, verily ibn al-Mawaal narrated to us from Muhammad ibn al-Munkadir on the authority of Jaabir that the Prophet, may Allaah's praise and salutations be upon him, said, *{The water of Zamzam is for that which it is drunk for.}* and I am drinking this to keep me away from the thirst on the Day of Judgment." And then he drank it. " ("Siyaar 'Alaam an-Nubala", 8/393)

Further Points of Benefit

Another thing to remember, my sister, when you are feeling the thirst from the fast, is that the reward for your fast is very great, and insh'Allaah you will someday be in Paradise, where you will feel no thirst at all, and be given the best of beverages to drink.

Sheikh Saalih Fauzaan, when describing the drinks that will be found in Paradise, said,

"Allaah, the Most High, mentions some of the beverages of the people of Paradise in the verse,

{The description of Paradise which the muttaqoon (the pious) have been promised (is that) in it are rivers of water the taste and smell of which never change, rivers of milk of which the taste never changes, rivers of wine delicious to those who drink, and rivers of purified honey (clear and pure); therein for them is every kind of fruit, and forgiveness from their Lord."} (Surah Muhammad, From Ayat 15)

These beverages are, in name, similar to the drinks of the people of this world. And although their meaning is the same, and their name is the same, their description and their reality is different. As the beverages which are in this world are finite; but the drinks of the people of Paradise are infinite and never-ending. In addition, the drinks of this world are in small amounts compared to the drinks which are in Paradise, in flowing rivers. And the drinks which are in Paradise never change or spoil.

For example, the water in this world, if it stagnates it becomes corrupt, and emits a foul odor. As for the water in Paradise, it will never change and will never become corrupt of spoiled- whether it is running or standing still.

In addition, the milk which is in this world- if it is left it spoils and becomes sour and curdles- or perhaps it will even ferment. But the milk of Paradise never changes taste no matter how long it stands without being used- as it is always good and does not change.

The wine which is in this world is harmful and smells strongly, and it intoxicates and destroys one's intellect. It causes affliction to the one who drinks it and is the mother of all evil things. Allaah, the Most High, and His Messenger, may Allaah's praise and salutations be upon him, have forbidden it, as have all the previous revealed religions. Also, it causes illness in the body and destroys it. As for the wine in Paradise, then it does not cause any harm or distress, and it does not intoxicate... it is delicious, in contrast to the wine of this world...

Also from the drinks of Paradise is honey. In this world it is the most beneficial and delicious of beverages, and it heals, as Allaah, the Most High says in His Book. In addition to this it is delicious and good. However, the honey of Paradise is far better than the honey of this world, and the honey of this world only resembles it in name. Due to this Allaah says in the above verse, "...purified honey..." because the honey of this world is cloudy and must be purified, and poured into containers after it is collected. This is in contrast to the honey of Paradise, which is originally pure and does not need to be poured into containers to remain good. Also, the honey of this world is found in small amounts, and is expensive. As for the honey of Paradise, then it is in running streams...

Likewise, all of that which is in Paradise, from fruit and produce and other than these, is greatly different from that which is in this world to an extent only known to Allaah, Glorified and Exalted, and it is explained to the people in this world through comparing it to what they are familiar with in this world, as none can describe what is in Paradise except Allaah, Glorified and Exalted." (From "Majaalis Shahr Ramadhaan al-Mubaarak wa Itihaaf ahl Eemaan bi Duroos Shahr Ramadhaan" Pages 34-38)

Family Time

The Story of Prophet Moosa Part 2

After Moosa had served his father-in-law for the agreed time, he missed his family and his relatives, so he decided to go and visit them secretly. He took his family and his flocks, and started out on a cold, rainy night. They lost their way, and stopped to camp, but he could not start a fire. Then he saw a fire from the direction of the Mount Tur. He said to his family, *Wait, I have seen a fire, perhaps I may bring you some information, or a burning firebrand to warm yourselves.*-(Surat Al-Qasas, Ayat 29)

When Moosa headed for the fire, he found it burning in a green bush on the side of the mountain adjoining the valley. He stood, amazed at what he was seeing, as green wood does not burn. Then his Lord called him from the right side of the valley, in the blessed place, from the tree. He called, *Oh Moosa ! Verily I am Allaah, the Lord of all that exists. And throw your stick!*-(Surat Al-Qasas, Ayat 30-31) Allaah told Moosa to throw down his stick that he leaned on, and that he used to beat down the branches for his sheep.

When Moosa did as he was commanded, the stick turned into a snake! The snake moved very fast, even though it was so big. Its mouth was huge, and jaws snapping, as it swallowed every rock it passed. When Moosa saw that, he turned and began to run away, as it is human nature to run from such a thing. Allaah said to him, *Oh Moosa! Draw near, and fear not. Verily, you are of those who are secure.*-(Surat Al-Qasas, Ayat 31)

Then Allaah said, *Put your hand into the opening of your garment, it will come forth white without a disease.*-(Surat Al-Qasas, Ayat 32) Moosa put his hand into his garment, and when he pulled it out, it was shining like a piece of the moon. It was still just as healthy as it had been before, with no trace of a disease. Allaah told Moosa, *Draw your hand close to your side to be free from fear.*-(Surat Al-Qasas, Ayat 32) So after that, whenever Moosa felt afraid of anything, he put his hand on his side, and he was not afraid anymore. Perhaps, if a person does this following the example of Moosa, and puts his hand over his heart, his fear will disappear or be lessened, if Allaah wills, and in Allaah we place our trust.

Then Allaah told him to go to Fir'awn with these two proofs of his prophethood, and call them to the worship of Allaah alone. Moosa said, *My Lord! I have killed a man among them, and I fear that they will kill me. And my brother Harun-he is more eloquent in speech than me, so send him with me as a helper to confirm me. Verily, I fear that they will deny me*-(Surat Al-Qasas, Ayat 33-34) Moosa wanted his brother Haarun to keep him company in this immense task. He wanted him to help him explain his message to Fir'awn and his people, as Haarun spoke more clearly than Moosa did. This was because when Moosa was a baby, he had mistakenly picked up a burning coal, and put it in his mouth. Then Allaah took this defect away from him, and made it so he could speak clearly. He also made Haarun a prophet and messenger to Fir'awn and his people.

Moosa and Harun came before Fir'awn and his chiefs, and showed them the miracles and proofs that Allaah had given them to show that they were telling the truth. They told them that Allaah was One, and that they must worship Him alone and obey His orders. Even though Fir'awn and his chiefs knew that Moosa and Haarun were really prophets sent by Allaah, they refused to believe in them. They were too proud and arrogant to admit that what they had been brought was the truth. They tried to use false arguments against them. They said that they had never seen any of their forefathers before them worshipping Allaah alone. They also said that the miracles that Moosa brought them were only magic.

Fir'awn said, *Oh chiefs! I know not that you have a god other than me.*-(Surat Al-Qasas, Ayat 38) Fir'awn tried to fool his people into believing that he was their god, and worshipping him. They listened to him because their minds were weak and foolish.

Fir'awn and his chiefs decided to try to defeat Moosa and Haarun with sorcery and magic. They gathered all the sorcerers from every city and every region of the kingdom. They fixed a day for the contest between Moosa and the sorcerers. A huge pavilion was erected for Fir'awn, and everyone had gathered to watch. Fir'awn promised the sorcerers that he would give them a great reward and make them from the people who sat with him in his court if they won against Moosa.

The sorcerers said, *Oh Moosa! Either you throw first, or we will be the first to throw.*-(Surat Taahaa, Ayat 65) Moosa told them to throw first. They threw down their sticks and ropes, and they looked like they were crawling, moving fast. This was an illusion, fooling the people's eyes. Then Moosa threw down his stick, and it truly turned into a huge, frightening snake. It had a gigantic mouth, and it caught up all of the sorcerers' ropes and sticks, and swallowed them up. It did not miss even one.

When the sorcerers saw this, they were amazed. They realized that this was from the heavens, and was no magic, so they fell prostrate to Allaah, and said, *We believe in the Lord of all that exists. The Lord of Moosa and Harun.*-(Surat Ash-Shu'araa', Ayat 47-48) Fir'awn was very angry when he saw that the magicians believed before he had given them permission to do so! He said that they had plotted with Moosa and agreed to let him win, even though he knew that this was a lie.

He began to threaten them, trying to get them to turn away from Allaah. He said that he would cut off their hands and feet and then crucify them. But they were not afraid. They knew that Allaah would give them a wonderful reward in the hereafter if they believed in Him, no matter what Fir'awn did to them in this world. Fir'awn tormented them and killed them, but they did not turn away from their belief in Allaah. How amazing their story is! They started the day as disbelieving sorcerers, and ended it as honorable martyrs!

When Fir'awn and his people persisted in their disbelief, Allaah sent many punishments upon them. He sent on them floods that stayed for a long time, locusts to eat all of their crops, and weevils that ate all of their grain. He tormented them with frogs, so that a person would be sitting in a crowd of frogs up to his chin, and he could not open his mouth without a frog jumping in. He filled their rivers and wells and drinking containers with blood, so they had nothing to drink. Every time a punishment afflicted them, they would go to Moosa and tell him that they would believe in him if he invoked Allaah to take it away from them. Then, when it was gone, they would stay in their disbelief, so Allaah would send another torment down upon them.

Then Allaah commanded Moosa to take Bani Israa'eel, and leave Egypt in the night. The next morning, when Fir'awn found out that they had all left, he was filled with anger. He called all of his troops together, and started chasing Bani Israa'eel with a huge army. Fir'awn's army caught up with Bani Israa'eel near the shores of the Red Sea. Bani Israa'eel stood there afraid, not knowing what to do. They thought that they were sure to be caught, because Fir'awn was behind them and the sea in front of them. There was nowhere to go. Moosa told them not to be afraid, as this was where his Lord had told him to bring them.

Finally, when Fir'awn's army came very near to them, Allaah commanded Prophet Moosa to strike the sea with his staff. By the will of Allaah, the water rose up like solid walls on either side, and they could walk across on the dry sea bed. Moosa's people all went into the sea bed and walked safely to the other side. Then Fir'awn's people tried to go across as well, to catch Moosa. As soon as all of the people in Fir'awn's army had entered the sea, Allaah sent the waves crashing down on them and they were all drowned. Not one of them remained alive; Allaah destroyed every single one of them.

This is only the beginning of the story of Moosa. There are still many more stories about Moosa and his people: When Moosa goes up to Mount Tur, when his people worship the calf, Moosa and al-Khidr, and many more stories. You should try to read them all, and learn more about this prophet and messenger of Allaah, insh'Allaah.

Points of Benefit

1. Allaah brings whatever He wills to pass, no matter what people do to try and prevent it.

2. The Muslims will be saved if they believe in Allaah and follow His messenger.

3. Arrogance and pride lead to humiliation.

4. Every oppressor will be put down eventually, even if it takes a long time.

5. Belief in Allaah is much better than the whole world and all that it contains.

6. You must be patient if you are harmed in the way of Allaah.

7. You must never be fooled into thinking that people are powerful. You must remember the immense power of Allaah.

8. You must be ready to sacrifice everything, even your life, for Allaah, just as the sorcerers did.

9. Gentleness and good manners are very important when you are calling to Allaah.

Hands on Learning

1. Make the page for Moosa in your prophet book. Write the prophet's name with hollow letters and color them in as you like. Draw a little picture or write a verse from the Qur'aan from the story to remind you of who they were and what they did.

2. Show your pages to someone in your family, or to a friend, and tell them all that you can remember about the story of Moosa.

3. Allaah parted the waters of the Red Sea, and it was easy for Him to do this. Look on a map or globe and find the Red Sea. What countries are near it? Think about Moosa and his people, running from Fir'awn, and coming to that large body of water- they must have been scared, but alhamdulillah, Moosa had faith in Allaah and trusted Him to get them to safety. Again he was commanded by Allaah to use his staff, or stick, and the water parted for them!! This is an amazing thing, it is a miracle that Allaah performed for Moosa and his people.

4. Take a cake pan and fill it over halfway with water. See if there is any way that you can part that water, like Allaah parted the mighty Red Sea. You can use whatever you can think of to try to do it. Write down what happened in your journal. And remember that Allaah parted a great Sea, and that it was easy for Him to do this. Isn't Allaah truly the Mighty and Majestic, with power over all things? Alhamdulillah that He made you a Muslim, and you worship Him alone- no one or nothing else can do the things that Allaah can do, and all that He does is easy for Him. So when you need help, call on Allaah.

5. Draw a picture of the Red Sea parting. You know it is not permissible to draw animals or people, but you can draw the mighty walls of water drawing back to allow Moosa and his people to enter. If you like you can draw the Sea after it came back down and swallowed up Fir'awn's people. There would probably be carts and wheels and swords and all sorts of things in the water afterwards, as Fir'awn and all of his people drowned as punishment for what they had done, mash'Allaah.

Day 18:
The Letter ع : العمرة
(*al-'Umrah*)
(the lesser pilgrimage)

Ibn 'Abbaas, may Allaah be pleased with him, narrated that the Prophet, may Allaah's praise and salutations be upon him, said to a woman of the Ansaar who was called Umm Sinaan, *{What has prevented you that you from performing Hajj with us?}* *She answered, "The father of so and so (meaning her husband) had only two camels. One of them had been taken away by him and his son for Hajj, and the other one is used by our boy to carry water." Upon this he (the Prophet), may Allaah's praise and salutations be upon him, said, {'Umrah during the month of Ramadhaan would be equal in reward to Hajj or Hajj along with me.}* (Muslim)

Imaam an-Nawawi, may Allaah have mercy upon him, mentioned that the meaning of {...is equal in reward...} is simply that the reward is the same, as it does not count as the obligatory Hajj.

And Sheikh al-Islaam ibn Taymiyyah, may Allaah have mercy upon him, mentioned that it was disliked to repeat the 'Umrah often due to the consensus of the Pious Predecessors. Also, the 'Umrah in Ramadhaan is not specific to the beginning, middle or end of the month.

From the common mistakes mentioned by Sheikh ibn 'Utheimeen, may Allaah have mercy upon him, is that many of the people come to perform 'Umrah in the beginning of the month (of Ramadhaan) and when it reaches the middle of the month they go out to at-Tan'eem and make another 'Umrah, and in the end of the month they go out yet again to at-Tan'eem and come with another 'Umrah- and this deed has no basis in the Islamic Legislation.

Further Points of Benefit

Sheikh Muhammad ibn Saalih al-'Utheimeen, may Allaah have mercy upon him, was asked, "What is the ruling on repeating 'Umrah during Ramadhaan? Is there any particular amount of time that must elapse between the performance of one 'Umrah and the next?"

The Sheikh, may Allaah have mercy upon him, replied, "Repeating the 'Umrah during the month of Ramadhaan is an innovation, because performing 'Umrah more than once in the same month is in opposition to the practice of the Pious Predecessors.

Indeed, Sheikh al-Islaam, ibn Taymiyyah, may Allaah have mercy upon him, said, as quoted in "al-Fataawa," that it is disliked to perform 'Umrah repeatedly, according to the consensus of the Pious Predecessors, especially if one repeats it during the month of Ramadhaan. If this was something that was considered desirable, then the Pious Predecessors would have been more conscientious about performing it than we are, and they would have repeatedly performed the 'Umrah.

The Prophet, may Allaah's praise and salutations be upon him, was the person who had the most taqwa (who was the most aware of Allaah, and feared Him the most), and he loved performing good deeds more than anyone, and he remained in Makkah for nineteen days in the year of its conquest, shortening his prayers- and yet he did not perform 'Umrah. When 'Aishah, may Allaah be pleased with her, asked the Prophet, may Allaah's praise and salutations be upon him, to permit her to perform 'Umrah, he ordered her brother, 'AbdurRahman ibn Abi Bakr, may Allaah be pleased with both of them, to accompany her from the sacred precincts to the place of commencement, so that she could perform 'Umrah. He, may Allaah's praise and salutations be upon him, did not advise 'AbdurRahman, may Allaah be pleased with him, to perform the 'Umrah as well. If it were legislated, then he would have advised him to perform it. If it were known among the Companions, may Allah be pleased with all of them, that it was legislated, 'AbdurRahman ibn Abi Bakr, may Allaah be pleased with both of them, would have performed it, as he had gone out to the starting place.

In regards to the specific amount of time that would lapse between the performance of one 'Umrah and another, according to Imaam Ahmad, may Allaah have mercy upon him, one should wait until his head becomes like charred wood, meaning, until his head has become black (from the hair growing back from the last one)." ("Fataawa Arkaan al-Islaam", Vol. 2)

We see in this the danger that can come from trying to surpass that which the Prophet, may Allaah's praise and salutations be upon him, and his Companions did. As the Messenger of Allaah was the most pious and best of men, and set the example for his Companions, who were the best of people after him. Thus we should follow their example in all that we do, insh'Allaah, as this is the balanced and most correct path. And Allaah knows best.

Family Time

The Story of the Prophet Daawud

After Musa, May Allaah's praise and salutations be upon him, died, Bani Israa'eel remained on the right path for a period of time. Then, they began to innovate, or change things, in the religion and some even worshipped idols. Allaah sent many prophets to them, calling them to the right path. Some of Bani Israa'eel believed in the prophets, but others remained on the path of ignorance. When Bani Israa'eel committed these evil things, and turned away from the message that Allaah had sent them, Allaah let their enemies defeat them and rule them. Their enemies captured a lot of them, and took away their land.

One of the prophets that Allaah sent to Bani Israa'eel was Shamweel. He called them to Allaah, and told them to worship Him alone. They asked him to appoint a king for them, so that they could fight their enemies under his command. Allaah chose Taalut as a king over them. He was a knowledgeable, honorable, strong, handsome, and patient man. He had great skill in combat and warfare. But Bani Israa'eel did not want him to be their king. They thought that he was too poor, and he was not the son of any previous king. They had always had kings from one family among them, and he did not belong to that family.

Their prophet answered them saying, ❴*Verily Allaah has chosen him above you, and has increased him abundantly in knowledge and stature. And Allaah grants His kingdom to whom He wills.*❵-(Surat Al-Baqarah, Ayat 247) Taalut also brought them a wooden box as a sign from Allaah. It contained Musa's stick, and the remnants of the Tablets that Musa brought to them. When he was given this sign, they followed him and obeyed him.

Taalut marched forth with his soldiers to fight a huge enemy army that was under the command of a man called Jaalut. Allaah tested the strength of the soldiers with a river. They were very thirsty from marching, when they came to a river. Taalut told his men that whoever drank freely from the river could not come with him to fight, and had to stay behind. Only those who took a little water in their hands to drink could come with him. Almost all of the soldiers were too weak to restrain themselves from drinking. They gulped down the water, and were left behind.

When Taalut crossed the river, he had only about three hundred and ten soldiers with him. All the rest stayed behind. Some of the soldiers thought that they were too few to fight such a big army as Jaalut's. But those who had knowledge among them reminded them that triumph comes from Allaah alone. If Allaah decreed that they would win and Jaalut would be defeated, then it did not matter if they were only a few.

When the little army of believers came face to face with Jaalut's huge army, they invoked Allaah, saying, ❴*Our Lord! Pour forth on us patience, and set firm our feet, and make us victorious over the disbelieving people.*❵-(Surat Al-Baqarah, Ayat 250)

When the battle began, Jaalut came forward and called for someone to duel with him. He was a huge strong man, and all of the believing soldiers felt afraid to go and fight him. Taalut promised that whoever killed Jaalut would marry his daughter and inherit the kingship after him. Still, no one stepped forward to fight. Finally, a shepherd boy named Daawud came forward and said that he would fight Jaalut. Even though Daawud was so young and small, he was very brave and he had strong faith in Allaah, so he placed all of his trust in Him.

Allaah strengthened Daawud, and gave him the power to kill the tall, powerful disbelieving commander. Jaalut's army could not believe their eyes when they saw that the little shepherd boy had killed their great commander. The Muslims easily defeated them and overwhelmed them.

This shows you how being big or strong or having a lot of people on your side will not help you win- Allaah is the One who grants success. So you have to be strong in your faith and love and certainty in Allaah, and insh'Allaah you will always be a winner in the long run. There are many instances in Muslim history where a much smaller group of Muslims defeated a large group of disbelievers, and this is because they believed in Allaah and He made them win. They had to be brave enough and trust Allaah enough to be strong and go in and fight even though there were more of the enemy than of them.

This is the case with any sort of struggle that we have in this life. Belief in Allaah will always make it easier, and we have to remember that only Allaah can assist us and make us overcome whatever obstacles we face.

Daawud not only married Taalut's daughter and inherited the kingship; Allaah also granted him prophethood, and gave him great wisdom. Daawud had a very beautiful voice. When he recited the book he had been given, az-Zabur, the birds would all come, attracted by his beautiful voice. They would stop and hover in the air over him and repeat after him, and the mountains would respond and echo his words. Allaah says, *And We subjected the mountains and birds to glorify Our praises along with Daawud.*-(Surat Al-Anbiyaa', Ayat 79) Allaah also taught him how to make chain-mail armor. He was the first person to make this, and they used it to protect themselves while fighting.

Allaah also blessed him with a son named Sulaymaan. Sulaymaan was also given the prophethood. Allaah granted Sulaymaan wisdom and knowledge like He had granted to Daawud, and He gave him a wonderful kingdom as well. Later, Inshaa' Allaah, you will learn about the story of Sulaymaan as well.

One day, two women came to Prophet Daawud asking him to judge between them. There was an older one and a younger one, and they had each had a baby. One day, a wolf came and ate one of the babies. That baby's mother went and took the other woman's baby, and said it was her own. They came to Daawud, each saying that the baby was hers. Daawud did his best to find out what the truth was, and then he ruled that the older woman could have the baby.

However, Allaah made his son, Sulaymaan, understand the case better, and he called the two women back to him. Sulaymaan said to the women, "Give me a sword and I will divide him up between you." When the older woman heard that he was going to cut the baby in half, she did not say anything. But the younger woman, who was really the baby's mother, could not bear to have her little baby sliced in two. She would do anything to save him, even give him up to the other woman. She immediately said to Sulaymaan, "May Allaah have mercy on you! He is her child, do not cut him up!" Sulaymaan knew that no mother would watch her baby be cut into two pieces and not say anything to save him. He knew that the younger woman must really be the baby's mother, so he gave the baby to her. Daawud was very happy when he saw the wisdom Allaah had granted his son.

Daawud ruled the kingdom fairly and justly until his death. When he died, his son Sulaymaan inherited it after him. He ruled justly as well, following the example of his father, may Allaah's salutations be upon them both.

Points of Benefit

1. You should always be willing to do whatever Allaah has commanded you to do. You must never turn away and disobey Him because the command is not what you want to do.

2. Allaah chooses whichever of His servants He wishes, and grants them all the blessings that He wishes.

3. Whoever has faith and certainty in Allaah, he will be the winner. Physical strength and power have nothing to do with it.

4. You should always remember to praise and glorify Allaah, wherever you are and whatever you are doing.

5. You should never be afraid to ask the advice of someone younger than you, as Daawud did with his son.

6. Just because someone is older than another person, does not always mean that they are right.

Hands on Learning

1. Make the page for Daawud in your prophet book. Write the prophet's name with hollow letters and color them in as you like. Draw a little picture or write a verse from the Qur'aan from the story to remind you of who they were and what they did.

2. Show your pages to someone in your family, or to a friend, and tell them all that you can remember about the story of Daawud.

3. In this story you read that Daawud was a shepherd boy before he became a prophet. The people of knowledge say that all of the prophets and messengers were shepherds at some point in their lives. Sheikh Suhaymee, may Allaah preserve him, says in his class on "Akhlaq an-Nabi" that being a shepherd and taking care of flocks of animals helps prepare them to teach and guide people when they are prophets and messengers. There are many animals that need to be watched by shepherds. There are sheep, camels, goats, and cows, to name a few.

4. Look up sheep in a reference book or on the internet. Think what it would take to take care of a large flock of sheep. They graze on grass, but sometimes you also have to feed them and give them water- and you have to take them to the fields to eat and find them water to drink no matter what. You would have to protect them from wolves and other animals that would want to kill them and eat them. You would have to protect them from people who wanted to steal them. You would have to wash them and make sure that they did not have worms or fleas or other things that could harm them. You would have to be patient in working with them because they are animals and can't

understand you. There are a lot more things you would have to do to take care of those sheep as well. Take a piece of paper and draw a line all the way down it from top to bottom. Put "Shepherd" on one side, and "Prophet" on the other. Write down the things that shepherds do, and what characteristics you think a shepherd would need to be a good one, under "Shepherd." Do the same for what a prophet must do and what characteristics they would have to have, on the side under "Prophet." Look how alike they are, and also see any differences. Do you think it would be easy to be a shepherd? How about a prophet? Allaah had to choose strong, wise, intelligent, patient men to be prophets, alhamdulillah, and we should strive to be like them in any way that we are able, insh'Allaah.

5. If you can get a group of friends together, take turns being the shepherd and being the sheep. See how difficult it is to get everyone to do what you want them to do!!

Day 19:
The Letter غ : الغفلة
(al-Ghaflah)
(heedlessness)

From that which is to be regretted is that many of the Muslim men and women in our present time have fallen into a high degree of heedlessness concerning remembrance of Allaah. Also, they have screened themselves from taking advantage of the seasons of good such as the month of Ramadhaan, which is the month of forgiveness and of release from the Fire.

From that which demonstrates this heedlessness which will lead to the hardening of the hearts:

1. Staying up late at night and sleeping during the day, which causes them to miss the legislated time of many of the daily prayers so they pray them after their set times.

2. Wasting time uselessly by watching television programs and daily serials night and day and abandoning provisioning themselves with good deeds for the Hereafter.

3. Often visiting on the nights of Ramadhaan and gathering for idle speech, vain amusement, and evil deeds.

Sheikh 'Abdul 'Aziz ibn Baaz, may Allaah have mercy upon him, said that what is obligatory upon the Muslims is to fear Allaah, Glorified is He, concerning what he comes to, as well as what he leaves, at all times. Also, to stay away from that which Allaah has prohibited from watching films devoid of benefit in which are shown many forbidden things such as pictures of things with souls, singing with musical instruments, and misguiding calls, due to what this contains of watching evil deeds and performing an evil deed, and also the hardening of the hearts and causing them (the hearts) to become diseased, and causing the people to make light of the Legislation of Allaah and to become reluctant to perform that which Allaah has made obligatory.

Further Points of Benefit

And this has become common amongst the Muslim Ummah today, mash'Allaah. Ramadhaan is seen as a month of increased visiting, talking, shopping, eating, and indulging in desires. The people stay up late engaging in idle pursuits, then sleep away half of the day- and when they awaken they do not read Qur'aan or do something of benefit; rather, they call up friends, or watch television, or go shopping, or spend hours making expensive, luxurious dishes for the breaking of the fast. We are accountable for how we spend our time every day of our lives- should we not take care that we spend it in ways and manners which are pleasing to Allaah? And to waste the blessings and virtues which are offered to us in this blessed month of Ramadhaan is even worse, mash'Allaah. This is not to say that we should not spend time with family and friends, or make a special treat now and then- but we should always be aware of what we are doing, and why, and make the conscious effort to make sure that it is pleasing to Allaah, the Most High, Who granted us this beautiful month and the blessings within it.

Sheikh Saalih ibn Fauzaan ibn 'Abdullah ibn Fauzaan, may Allaah preserve him, said,

"Indeed, the virtues and merits of Ramadhaan are many and varied. And the people are benefitted by these virtues as much as Allaah grants them success to benefit from them. For some of them get the complete benefit; and this is the state of the Pious Predecessors. They would be gladdened despite the fact that during the course of the whole year they exerted themselves by praying during the night and fasting during the day and also making jihaad in the way of Allaah, and seeking knowledge and striving to perform good deeds; despite this, they would be happy about the coming of this month (Ramadhaan) due to that which it contains of extra good and benefit. And they loved good and all that led to good. The Pious Predecessors would rejoice at the coming of this month and single out this month for greater exertion in the performance of good deeds. They would stop other work in order to perform them. They would ask Allaah to bring it (this month) to them, and then ask Him to accept their good works from them.

As for those who benefit to a lesser degree than them, then they are benefitted by this month to the extent that Allaah allows this, if they do not ruin their fast through performing evil deeds and being heedless. As the month of Ramadhaan has many virtues- for Allaah singled it out for obligatory fasting which is a pillar from the pillars of Islaam. And this pillar must be performed in this month- and without any other virtues, this alone would be enough to distinguish this month.

From its virtues is that Allaah revealed the Qur'aan in it. As Allaah, the Most High, says,

❴*The month of Ramadan in which was revealed the Qur'aan...*❵-(Surat al-Baqarah, From Ayat 185) And this is a great virtue, because this time was designated by Allaah for the revelation of a Book of Allaah from the Books of Allaah- and this is the noble and great Qur'aan. And it can be taken from this that reciting the Qur'aan in this month is better than reciting it in other months; and the Muslim should recite the Qur'aan often in all the months and in all the days. However, the fact that the Qur'aan was revealed in this month gives its recitation extra merit. And also, it is the month in which Jibreel would study the Qur'aan with the Prophet, may Allaah's praise and salutations be upon him. This does not mean that one should single out this month only for reciting the Qur'aan, as he should recite the Qur'aan year round, for every letter counts as a good deed, and the good deed is multiplied ten times, and it is multiplied more in the month of Ramadhaan.

The fasting person who allows his eyes to gaze upon that which is forbidden and does not look away from that which is prohibited, or goes out to the markets and the meeting places of the women and other places of fitnah (trial) and allows his sight to look at that which is forbidden by looking at women or other things which are unlawful to look at, or sits in his house and turns on the television or a video coming from Europe or America and from every trash bin in the world- what is found there is fornication, lewdness, shamelessness, nudity, and evil deeds- and he sits there staring at the screen and he is fasting!!- this person has no fasting left worth mentioning. All he has left is hunger and thirst, and this will not benefit him with Allaah, Glorified and Exalted.

Likewise, the fasting person does not keep his hearing away from listening to that which Allaah has prohibited. So he listens to music and musical instruments, and evil speech such as name calling, cursing, slander and backbiting. This one is not fasting a fast which will benefit him with Allaah. His fast has no benefit. However, he is not commanded to make it up because he is outwardly fasting- but he has no reward with Allaah, Mighty and Majestic. So this fasting is like a torn and broken shield that will not protect a weak spot, or even look good…

…and the one who is fasting must remember that the Prophet, may Allaah's praise and salutations be upon him, advised him to keep his tongue from that which is forbidden, even if one speaks to him and calls him names and abuses him- he should not respond to him…even if generally, answering back would be allowed because it is similar to the case of qisaas (the principle that one can return a harm done to him back upon the one who harmed him). So if this is the case in that which is allowed, then what about the case of one who starts it, and attacks someone with name calling, abuse, slander and backbiting?! (From "Majaalis Shahr Ramadhaan al-Mubaarak wa Itihaaf ahl Eemaan bi Duroos Shahr Ramadhaan" Pages 8-9 and 17-18)

Family Time

The Story of the Prophet Sulaymaan

Daawud had a great many sons, as he had one hundred wives. Out of all of Daawud's sons, Allaah chose Sulaymaan to inherit the kingship and the prophethood. Allaah gave Sulaymaan complete authority and power over mankind, the jinn, and the birds. Even the strong winds obeyed him. He had a huge mat made of wood, and all of his horses, camels, tents, and soldiers would get onto it. Then he would command the wind to carry it wherever he wanted it to go. It went so fast that it traveled a whole month's journey in one morning, and another month's journey in the afternoon.

All of the shayaateen and jinn had to obey him too. Do you remember what jinn are? Remember Iblees in the story of Aadam? Iblees was of the jinn. Jinn are beings which Allaah created from fire, just as He created men from clay and angels from light. Some of them are good, believing jinn, and some of them are evil, disbelieving jinn. Some of them dove into the water and got out pearls and jewels for Sulaymaan. Others built beautiful palaces with high rooms and huge fountains. Any jinn who refused to work was tied up in chains as punishment. Sulaymaan could understand the language of the birds and animals, which was something that was not given to any other human being, as far as we know from the Qur'aan and Sunnah.

These amazing things which Sulaymaan could do were all gifts from Allaah to him. They are not made up stories, or things that someone imagined- they are true! This is one reason that we have to be careful about reading about pretend people who can do wonderful things. First of all, they are not true, so you are reading about lies. Secondly, the reality of what Allaah can do is more wonderful and amazing than anything that anyone could make up for someone to be able to do. Allaah can do anything He wishes, and He gives special blessings and abilities to certain righteous people when He wants to.

One day, all of Sulaymaan's troops of jinn, men and birds were gathered together. Sulaymaan marched in the front, then came the men, followed by the jinn. The birds flew overhead and sheltered Sulaymaan from the heat with their wings. They were all in battle formation, and no one was allowed to step out of place. As they marched, they came to a valley where some ants lived. Sulaymaan heard one of the ants shouting, *Oh ants! Enter your dwellings, lest Sulaymaan and his armies should crush you, while they do not notice!*-(Surat An-Naml, Ayat 18) Sulaymaan understood what she was saying, and smiled, amused at what she had said. Then he gave thanks to Allaah for all of the favors that he had bestowed upon him and his parents, so that he could even understand the speech of an ant.

Remember this story from the life of the prophet Sulaymaan the next time you step on an ant or a bug. Insects and animals are not like humans, but they are creations of Allaah, and they deserve to be treated in a good way, unless they may hurt you or are causing harm in some way. Think how surprised you would be if one of them spoke and you understood it! And yet this was one of the gifts Allaah gave to His prophet, Sulaymaan.

One afternoon, some beautiful, well-trained horses were brought to Sulaymaan for him to look at. He was so busy looking at them and admiring them that he missed the time of 'Asr prayer. He was so upset with himself when he realized that he had missed the prayer that he ordered that the horses be slaughtered, even though he liked them so much. This was so that he would never again be so absorbed in them that he would forget to worship his Lord at the correct time. Because he did this for the sake of Allaah, Allaah gave him something even better and swifter than them. He made the wind obey him and take him wherever he wanted to go.

We must always try to remember that we have obligations to Allaah. That is, there are things that we must do because Allaah commanded us to do them. One of these is the prayer. Can you think of another of these obligations? How about the fast of Ramadhaan? Look at how upset Sulaymaan was when he realized that the time for the prayer had passed by. Also, look at how Allaah rewarded him for repenting and turning to Him. We must remember that whenever we do a good deed for the sake of Allaah, we will be rewarded by Allaah for it.

Among the birds, the hoopoe was an expert at finding water. Whenever Sulaymaan wanted water, and there was none to be found, he would send for the hoopoe. When the hoopoe showed him where the water was, Sulaymaan would tell the jinn to dig there until they found it. One day Sulaymaan checked on the birds and he did not see the hoopoe. He said, *What is the matter that I do not see the hoopoe? Or is he one of those who are absent? I will surely punish him with a severe punishment, or slaughter him, unless he brings me a clear reason (for his absence).*- (Surat An-Naml, Ayat 20-21)

The hoopoe was only gone for a short time. When he came back, the other birds asked him, "What kept you? Sulaymaan has vowed to shed your blood." The hoopoe said, "Did he say 'unless'? They said, "Yes, he said, "Unless he brings me a clear reason."" The hoopoe said, "Then I am saved." He told Sulaymaan that he had come to know something that Sulaymaan and his troops did not know, and that he had come from the land of Saba' with true news. Saba' was a dynasty of rulers in Yemen. He told Sulaymaan, *I found a woman ruling over them, and she has been given all things, and she has a tremendous throne. I found her and her people worshipping the sun instead of Allaah, and Shaytaan has made their deeds seem fair to them, and has prevented them from the (right) way, so they have no guidance. They do not prostrate themselves before Allaah, who brings light to what is hidden in the heavens and the earth, and knows what you conceal and what you reveal. Allaah, La Ilaaha Ila Huwa, The Lord of the supreme throne!*-(Surat An-Naml, Ayat 23-26)

Even the hoopoe called to what is good, and for people to prostrate to Allaah alone. The scholars have said that this is why it is forbidden to kill a hoopoe. The Prophet Muhammad, may Allaah's praise and salutations be upon him, forbade us to kill four kinds of animals: ants, bees, hoopoes, and sparrow hawks.

Sulaymaan said to him, *We shall see whether you speak the truth or whether you are of the liars.*-(Surat An-Naml, Ayat 27) Sulaymaan wrote a letter to the queen, Bilqees, and her people, and gave it to the hoopoe to deliver. The hoopoe took the letter on his wings and went to their land. When he found Bilqees' palace, he went to her private chambers and threw the letter in a small window. Then he stepped to one side out of good manners, and waited.

The queen was amazed when she saw a bird delivering a letter to her like that. She picked it up and read it. She gathered her chiefs and commanders together and said to them, *Oh chiefs! Verily, here is delivered to me a noble letter. It is from Sulaymaan and it reads, 'In the Name of Allaah, the Most Gracious, the Most Merciful. Do not be exalted against me, but come to me submitting as Muslims.'*-(Surat An-Naml, Ayat 29-31)She asked her people's advice, and they told her that they had power and strength to fight, if she saw fit. But she preferred to resort to peaceful means, and said, *I am going to send him a present, and see with what the messengers return.*-(Surat An-Naml, Ayat 35) She hoped that he would accept the gift and leave them alone, or make them pay a tax, and not fight against them. She sent him a huge gift of gold, jewels, pearls, and other things.

When the messengers came to Sulaymaan bringing the gift, he did not even look at it. He turned his back to them, and said, *Will you help me in wealth, when what Allaah has given us is better than that which he has given you? Nay, you rejoice in your gift. Go back to them. We will verily come to them with armies that they cannot resist,*

179

and we shall drive them out from there in disgrace, and they will be abased.-(Surat An-Naml, Ayat 36-37) He told them that he would not accept anything except Islaam or the sword. If they would not become Muslim, then he would fight them.

When the queen's messengers came back to her, she and her troops came to Sulaymaan, intending to honor him and follow him in Islaam. Before she set out, she ordered that her throne be locked up. It was made of gold, and inlaid with rubies, pearls, and other precious gems. It was placed in the innermost of seven rooms, one within the other, and all of the doors were securely locked. Then she set off to Sulaymaan with her army.

When she had almost gotten there, Sulaymaan gathered together the jinn and humans under his command and said, *Oh chiefs! Which of you can bring me her throne before they come to me surrendering in obedience?*-(Surat An-Naml, Ayat 38) A giant Ifreet from the jinn said, "I will bring it to you before you rise from your place. And verily, I am indeed strong and trustworthy for such work."-(Surat An-Naml, Ayat 39)

Then, a believer from the humans stood up. His name was 'Aassif. He was Sulaymaan's scribe, and had knowledge of the Scripture. He said, *I will bring it to you within the twinkling of an eye!*-(Surat An-Naml, Ayat 40) Then he stood up, made wudhu, and prayed to Allaah. When Sulaymaan saw it before him, he said, *This is by the grace of my Lord, to test me, whether I am grateful or ungrateful.*-(Surat An-Naml, Ayat 41)

Sulaymaan told them to disguise the throne, to see whether she would recognize it. When she came, they asked her, *Is your throne like this?" She said, "It is as though it were the very same.*-(Surat An-Naml, Ayat 42) So she replied with wisdom. She did not say quickly that it was hers, as hers was so far away. And she did not quickly deny that it was hers either.

Then they told her to enter the palace. The palace was built of glass, and water was flowing under it. The floor looked like it was water, and so she tucked up her skirts, so they would not get wet. Sulaymaan said, *Verily, it is a palace sturdily constructed of glass.*-(Surat An-Naml, Ayat 44) When the queen saw for herself what Allaah had given Sulaymaan and how majestic his position was, she submitted to the command of Allaah and acknowledged that he was a noble prophet. She said, *My Lord! Verily, I have wronged myself, and I submit, together with Sulaymaan, to the Lord of all that exists.*-(Surat An-Naml, Ayat 44) When she became a Muslim, all of her people followed her, and also submitted to Allaah.

When Allaah decreed death for Sulaymaan, he was sitting in his chair, leaning on his stick. He did not look like he was dead, and so the jinn who used to work for him thought that he was still alive. He stayed like that for nearly a year, until a tiny worm ate through his stick, and he fell. Then it became clear to the jinn that if they had really known the unseen, as they liked to claim, they would have known that he was dead. They had remained there working for him, as though he were alive, when in reality he was dead, and they could have left long ago.

May Allaah's praise and salutations be upon Prophet Sulaymaan, and upon every one of the prophets and messengers.

Points of Benefit

1. Allaah chooses whomever he wishes and honors him with the prophethood and the Message.

2. When Allaah grants a favor to his servant, it is to test him as to whether he will he be grateful or ungrateful.

3. Even the weakest of Allaah's creation might have knowledge that the strongest one does not have, like the hoopoe and Sulaymaan.

4. All of the animals have their own languages, and they speak between each other. However, no one can understand them except Allaah, and whoever He chooses to gift with this ability, like Sulaymaan.

5. You must always call to Allaah, and search for people of wrongdoing, in order to call them to the right path.

6. No one except Allaah alone knows the unseen.

7. Allaah is the only one who can cause harm to anyone or benefit them.

8. If you supplicate to Allaah, and turn to Him alone, then He will help you.

Hands on Learning

1. Make the page for Sulaymaan in your prophet book. Write the prophet's name with hollow letters and color them in as you like. Draw a little picture or write a verse from the Qur'aan from the story to remind you of who they were and what they did.

2. Show your pages to someone in your family, or to a friend, and tell them all that you can remember about the story of Sulaymaan.

3. Think about the story of Sulaymaan and the ants. What do you know about ants? Did you know that there is a whole surah in the Qur'aan named "The Ants"? Why not look ants up in a book, or on the internet, and learn more about these amazing insects. Then, take some time to really watch the ants around your house. You will see that they amazing little creatures. They can carry things much larger than themselves. They work together to get things done. They are very interesting and amazing, and Allaah created them in this way. Write down some of the interesting things that you have seen or read about in your journal.

4. Try to imagine the throne of Bilqees. A throne is a very fancy chair that kings and queens sit in. Her throne sounds like it was very fancy, doesn't it? Why not try to either build a model of what you imagine her throne could have looked like, using lots of different materials. Or, draw or paint a picture of it, or use construction paper to make a picture of it. Use your imagination. We don't know what her throne really looked like, but you can have fun thinking about it!

Day 20:
The Letter ف: الفطر
(*al-Fitr*) (the breaking of the fast)

When you hear the adhaan of Maghrib, remember, oh my sister, that from the Sunnahs of breaking the fast are:

1. Breaking one's fast early in order to differ from the Jews and the Christians, as the Prophet, may Allaah's praise and salutations be upon him, said, *{The religion will remain manifest as long as the people break their fast early, because the Jews and the Christians break their fast late.}* (Abu Daawud and Sheikh al-Albaani has declared it to be authentic)

2. Breaking the fast with fresh or dried dates, as in the hadeeth of Jaabir, may Allaah be pleased with him, in which he said that if the Prophet, may Allaah's praise and salutations be upon him, had fresh dates he did not break his fast except with those fresh dates. If he did not have fresh dates, he would not break his fast except with dried dates.

3. Making the supplication for the breaking of the fast with the supplication which is in the narration transmitted in the hadeeth of Ibn 'Umar that the Prophet, may Allaah's praise and salutations be upon him, when he broke his fast, said, *{The thirst has gone, the veins are moistened, and the reward is certain, if Allaah so wills.}* (Abu Daawud, and Sheikh al-Albaani has declared it to be hasan)

4. Supplicating for the one who fed you that which you broke your fast with. 'Abdullah ibn az-Zubair, may Allaah have mercy upon him, narrated that the Prophet, may Allaah's praise and salutations be upon him, when he broke his fast with the people, he said, *{The fasting people have broken their fast with you, and the angels have sent you their salutations.}* (at-Tabaraani, and Sheikh al-Albaani has declared it to be authentic)

Further Points of Benefit

Alhamdulillah, the time when we break our fast should be one of joy and thanksgiving, hoping for the reward of Allaah and enjoying the relief and pleasure of drinking and eating again. We should hasten to break the fast when Maghrib arrives, as this sets us apart from the people of the Book as well as being a mercy from Allaah, the Most High, to this Ummah.

Often people break their fast immediately with a large meal- if we look at the manner in which the Prophet, may Allaah's praise and salutations be upon him, broke his fast, we will see how this differs with his actions. He would break his fast with dates and water, mash'Allaah. Alhamdulillah, this is a very healthy way to break our fast, as well as being in conformance with the Sunnah, as the dates provide us with some instant nutrition and energy, and the water begins the process of rehydration. Ibn Qayyim, may Allaah have mercy upon him, says that this is also beneficial because the dates are hot and sweet.

Sheikh Saalih Fauzaan, may Allaah preserve him, said,

"…and from the etiquette of fasting is breaking the fast as soon as the sun has properly set, as the Prophet, may Allaah's praise and salutations be upon him, said, *{ The people will remain in a good state as long as they hasten to break their fast. }* (Agreed Upon)

Meaning, that this Ummah will be manifest and in a good state as long as they adhere to this Sunnah.

Also from the etiquettes of fasting is to break the fast on fresh dates, and if these are not found, then on dry dates, because the Prophet, may Allaah's praise and salutations be upon him, used to break his fast upon fresh dates before he would pray. If there were no fresh dates available, he would break it with dry dates. If there were no dry dates then he would have a few swallows of water. (Abu Daawud (2356) at-Tirmidhi (543) Ahmad (164) al-Haakim (342) and al-Haakim said it is authentic on the conditions of Muslim)

And one should not be excessive in what they have to break their fast from different types of foods and drinks, as this is against the Sunnah and keeps one away from the congregational prayer." ("Majaalis Shahr Ramadhaan al-Mubaarak wa Itihaaf ahl Eemaan bi Duroos Shahr Ramadhaan" Page 160)

There is also a great reward for the one who provides the food for others to break their fast with, alhamdulillah, so this is another matter in which we can strive, especially in this blessed month of Ramadhaan. This does not mean that we have to be very extravagant or lavish in feeding the people- rather it is best to take the middle road in this, insh'Allaah.

Family Time

Special Ramadhaan Meal Number Three

Last week we cooked and ate some food from Pakistan. This week we are going to another Muslim country to sample some of what they eat. Again, remember that it is the Sunnah to break your fast with dates and water, so do that first, and then eat your meal later, insh'Allaah.

Have you ever heard of a country called Yemen? I am pretty sure that you have, insh'Allaah. Look for Yemen on a map or globe. What countries are near it? What seas are around it? There are many scholars and people of knowledge in Yemen. Sheikh Muqbil ibn Haadee al-Waadi'ee was from Yemen, may Allaah have mercy upon him. Many of his students teach there now, like Sheikh Muhammad al-Imaam, and Sheikh Muhammad ibn 'Abdul Wahaab al-Wasaabee, among others, alhamdulillah. There are centers of learning in Damaaj, Ma'bar, Ibb, and other villages and cities in Yemen. Look in a book or on the internet to find some photographs of Yemen.

Samboosah (Meat Filled Pastries)

This is common snack food in Yemen, especially in the month of Ramadhaan. It is often served at the iftaar, when people are breaking their fasts. It can be dipped in hot sauces or ketchup, if you like. We like to make them with potatoes, or sometimes tuna, instead of the meat.

Ingredients:

For the dough:

4 cups flour

1/3 cup oil

¼ tsp salt

Water

Mix the salt with the flour, and then stir in the oil. Add enough water to make a soft dough. Knead it until smooth, cover it, and set it aside to rest. While it is resting, make the filling.

For the filling:

Ingredients:

½ kilo ground beef

2 onions, diced

½ cup parsley, chopped (optional)

1 hot pepper, seeds removed, diced (optional)

Salt and pepper to taste

Brown the ground beef and the onions in a little bit of oil. Add the remaining ingredients and a small amount of water. Cover and cook until done.

Make the dough into walnut- sized balls. Roll out into a circle. Put a spoon of meat on the circle, fold it over, and press the edges shut with a fork dipped in water.

Fry in hot oil until golden brown on all sides. Set on a paper towel to drain.

Zibaadi bi al-Khiyaar (Yogurt and Cucumber Salad)

Ingredients:

2 cucumbers

2 cloves of garlic

1 container of plain yogurt

Salt and dried mint

Chop the cucumbers finely. Crush the garlic with a little salt and a little cumin if desired. Mix these with the yogurt, and sprinkle with the dried mint.

Al-'Aqada (Chicken Stew)

Ingredients:

1 diced onion

3 cloves of garlic, crushed

3 diced tomatoes

1 hot pepper, seeds removed, diced (optional)

1 potato, cut as for French fries

2 spoons of tomato paste

Salt and pepper to taste

1 chicken, boiled and cut up

Diced parsley (optional)

1 tsp cumin

1 tsp curry powder

½ tsp ground coriander

Sauté the onion in a small amount of oil. Add the garlic and stir. Add the spices (not the parsley) and the potato and sauté for another five minutes. Add the tomatoes and tomato paste. Add the chicken pieces. Add water to about halfway up the chicken. Cover and simmer for ½ hour, until the potatoes are tender and the flavors melded. Add the parsley and serve. This is usually eaten with bread, but you can eat it with rice, if you like.

Biskweet (Cookies)

These are a very common cookie in Yemen, they are often served with coffee or tea for a snack.

Ingredients:

1 ½ cups of butter

½ cup oil

3 eggs

1 cup powdered sugar

½ cup unsweetened coconut

3 tablespoons of powdered milk

1 tablespoon baking powder

4 cups flour

Cream the butter, oil, and sugar together. Beat in the eggs, one at a time. Add the remaining ingredients and stir until well mixed. If it is sticky, add some more flour to make it easier to shape. Cover with plastic and refrigerate the dough for two hours. Roll out the dough on a floured board. Use cookie cutters to cut out pretty shapes. Here they use a cookie press- so if you have one, you can use the cookie press and skip the rolling and cutting. Bake 350 degrees for about 10-12 minutes- keep an eye on them so that they do not get too browned. Remove and let them cool (if you can. You might have to eat one right away!!)

Day 21:

The Letter ق: قراءة القرآن

(*Qura'at al-Qur'aan*)

(reading and reciting the Qur'aan)

Reciting the Qur'aan in the month of Ramadhaan is from the most obvious signs of exerting oneself in worship, which it is proper to increase and do much of in the depths of the night as well as in the beginning and end of the day.

However, one should pay close attention and take care not to fall into the following mistakes.

1. Hastily reciting the Qur'aan as some people do, and this is similar to reciting poetry- as they do not take care in its recitation or ponder its meanings or rulings. Their purpose in this is reaching the end as quickly as possible, which is in opposition with the saying of Allaah, the Most High, *And recite the Qur'aan (aloud) in a slow (pleasant tone and) style.*-(Surat al-Muzzammil, From Ayat 4) And His, the Most High, saying, *Do they not then think deeply in the Qur'aan, or are their hearts locked up (from understanding it)?*-(Surat Muhammad, Ayat 24)

    What is obligatory is that one combine the two goods of reading much Qur'aan and reciting it slowly and well while pondering its meanings and implementing its rulings in this noble month (as well as outside of it).

2. Many people pay attention to reading the Qur'aan during the day in Ramadhaan and forget all about it during the night. There is no proof that reciting the Qur'aan during the day is any better than reciting it at night.

3. Many people turn away from reading the Qur'aan after the end of Ramadhaan; and there are some people who act as if they do not even know of the Qur'aan except during Ramadhaan.

Further Points of Benefit

Sheikh Saalih Fauzaan, may Allaah preserve him, says concerning this,

"Oh servants of Allaah, fear Allaah, the Most High, and thank Him for the faith which He has blessed you with, and for the revelation of the Qur'aan. As the Qur'aan is the great Qur'aan and the wise remembrance and the straight path.

It is the only speech which is not resembled by any other speech, and evil cannot come to it from in front of it or from behind it. It is revealed by the All Wise, Who is Worthy of All Praise. Allaah commanded us to memorize it so it would not decrease or increase, and it is also written in the Lawh al-Mahfoodh and in the musaahif, and memorized in the hearts and recited by the tongues and made easy to learn and contemplate. *And We have indeed made the Qur'aan easy to understand and remember; then is there anyone who will remember (or receive admonition)?*-(Surat al-Qamr, Ayat 17)

It is easy to memorize for anyone, even a foreigner who does not know its language, or a small child. Also, it is difficult to become tired of reciting it, or have enough of listening to its sweetness and enjoyable sound. And the scholars do not tire of contemplating it and understanding its meanings.

Mankind and the jinn have still been unable to create that which is similar to even the smallest surah, because it is an eternal miracle (sent down to the Prophet), and the proof which will always remain. Allaah commanded us to recite it and contemplate it, and made it a blessing, as He said, *◆A Book (the Qur'aan) which We have sent down to you, full of blessings, that they may contemplate its Verses, and that men of understanding may remember.◆*-(Surat Saad, Ayat 29)

And the Prophet, may Allaah's praise and salutations be upon him, said, *{ Whoever recites a single letter from the Book of Allaah, then it is written down for him as a good deed, and a good deed is multiplied by ten times. And I do not mean that alif laam meem is a letter; rather, that alif is a letter, and laam is a letter, and meem is a letter. }* (at-Tirmidhi, and he said that this hadeeth is hasan Saheeh)

And Allaah has distinguished and given extra virtue to those who have memorized the Qur'aan and who act upon it. The Prophet, may Allaah's praise and salutations be upon him, said, *{ The best of you is he who learns the Qur'aan and teaches it. }* (al-Bukhaari (5027)) And he also said, *{ The example of the believer who recites the Qur'aan is like the citron- it smells and tastes pleasant. And the believer who does not recite the Qur'aan is similar to a date- it has no smell, but its taste is good. And the hypocrite who recites the Qur'aan is like basil- it smells good, and tastes bitter. And the hypocrite who does not recite the Qur'aan is like the colocynth it has no smell and a bitter taste. }* (al-Bukhaari (5427) Muslim (797))

…and he (the Prophet) has divided the people in regards to the Qur'aan into different categories. The best of them is he who recites it properly and takes care to learn it and implement it. And those are the true people of the Qur'aan. And there are those who turn away from it and do not learn it or implement it. And those have had a stern warning. Allaah, the Most High, says,

◆And whosoever turns away blindly from the remembrance of the Most Gracious (Allaah) (i.e. this Qur'aan and worship of Allaah), We appoint for him Shaytaan to be a companion to him.◆-(Surat az-Zukhraf, Ayat 36) And He also said,

◆But whosoever turns away from My Reminder (i.e. neither believes in this Qur'aan nor acts on its teachings), verily, for him is a life of hardship, and We shall raise him up blind on the Day of Resurrection." He will say: "Oh my Lord! Why have you raised me up blind, while I had sight (before)." (Allaah) will say "Like this Our ayaat (proofs, evidences, verses, lessons, signs, revelations, etc.) came to you, but you disregarded them (i.e. you left them, did not think deeply in them, and you turned away from them), and so this Day, you will be neglected (in the Hell-fire, away from Allaah's Mercy)."-(Surat Taa Haa, Ayat 124-126)

And from the people are those who memorize the Qur'aan but neglect it- and this is distancing oneself from the Qur'aan and depriving one's soul from the great reward, and will be a cause for it to be forgotten. And it is worried that he may enter into the above verse." (From "Majaalis Shahr Ramadhaan al-Mubaarak wa Itihaaf ahl Eemaan bi Duroos Shahr Ramadhaan" Pages 186-188)

Family Time

The Story of the Prophets Zakariyyah and Yahya

There was once a righteous woman, who was the wife of Imraan. Imraan was the Imaam of his people. When his wife was going to have a baby, she vowed to make her child serve Bayt Al-Maqdis (The masjid in Jerusalem), and concentrate on worshipping Allaah. But when she had her baby, she saw that it was a baby girl. She knew that a boy is not the same as a girl, because a boy is stronger, and more able to serve the masjid in Jerusalem. However, Allaah wanted a bright future and great distinction for this baby girl. He accepted her because of her mother's vow, and He gave her good manners, and made her righteous.

Her mother named her Maryam, and then carried her to the people who were in charge of taking care of the masjid. They all fought over who had the most right to take care of the baby. They all wanted her, as she was the daughter of their Imaam. Zakariyyah was married to her aunt, her mother's sister, so he thought that he had the most right to her. They would not agree to this, and proposed to cast lots. They went to the Jordan River, and decided that they would all throw their pens into the water. The owner of the pen that remained floating and idle would get to take Maryam and take care of her. When they threw their pens into the river, the water took all of the pens under except that of Zakariyyah.

Remember how we talked about casting lots in a previous story? Here it is again, mash'Allaah. In this way the people do not make a decision themselves; rather, they leave the decision totally up to Allaah, and cast lots, as Zakariyyah and the others did here.

Zakariyyah was the scholar, Imaam, chief, and prophet of his people. He was a carpenter, and ate from the money he had earned with his own hands. He took Maryam and raised her and taught her. One day, he noticed that whenever he entered the place where she used to worship to visit her, she would have food with her. He had not brought it to her so where had it come from? In the winter, she would have fruits that were only available in the summer, and in the summer, fruits that were only available in the winter. He asked her about it, saying, ❲*Oh Maryam! From where have you gotten this?" She replied, "This is from Allaah.*❳-(Surat Aal-Imraan, Ayat 37)

All of the prophets and messengers were men- but this does not mean that women cannot be good, righteous people who are blessed by Allaah. Look at Maryam, who Allaah provided food for. And not just any food. He would provide her with summer fruits in the winter, and winter fruits in the summer. Remember that back then you could not go to a big grocery store and buy whatever you wanted. People had to eat what grew in each season, in that season. So it is even more of a miracle- Allaah blessed her with fruit that would not have been available in the markets.

Also, see how Maryam knew exactly Who to thank for providing for her in this wonderful way. When Zakariyyah asked her, she simply said, "This is from Allaah."

When Zakariyyah saw how Allaah provided food for Maryam, it made him want to have a righteous child of his own. He was afraid that the people after him would be a wicked generation, so he wanted a son who would be a prophet after him, and guide them. He called out to his Lord in secret, *My Lord! Indeed, my bones have grown feeble, and gray hair has flamed up on my head, and I have never been unblessed in my invocation to You, Oh my Lord! And verily, I fear those who will succeed me, and my wife is barren. So give me from Yourself an heir. Who shall inherit me and inherit the posterity of Ya'qub. And make him, my Lord, one whom with you are well pleased.*- (Surat Maryam, Ayat 4-6)

He called on Allaah in secret. We can always call on Allaah, of course. But sometimes it is good to call on Him when you are alone, and you can be sure that you are only doing it for Allaah, and not to be seen by people, insh'Allaah.

Allaah answered his supplication, and gave him glad tidings of a noble son named Yahya. No one had ever been given this name before him. The scholars have said that he was called Yahya, which means he lives, because Allaah had filled his life with faith.

Zakariyyah was amazed and overjoyed when his supplication was answered. It was particularly amazing, because Zakariyyah was an old, old man, and his wife was an old woman who had never had any children in her whole life. He asked the angel who brought him the glad tiding how this was going to happen. The angel replied, *Thus says your Lord, 'It is easy for Me. Certainly, I created you before when you had been nothing!'*-(Surat Maryam, Ayat 9)

We see again how Allaah uses angels to deliver His message to His chosen prophets and messengers. Remember Jibreel? Remember the angels that visited Ibraaheem, and Lut? Here again, an angel came to tell Zakariyyah that he was going to have a son.

Zakariyyah asked Allaah to give him a sign. As a sign, Allaah prevented his tongue from speaking for three days and nights, even though he had no illness. He could recite, and glorify Allaah, but he could not speak to the people except in gestures.

Soon, the boy was born, and he was named Yahya. When he was still a child, he was given the knowledge of the book of Allaah known as the Tawraah. He was distinguished from all of the other children by his wisdom at such a young age. Allaah gave him compassion, purity, and piety. Yahya treated his parents well, and did not disobey them. He was not arrogant or disobedient. Allaah gifted him with all of these beautiful characteristics.

Allaah also gave him peace, safety, and security in the three loneliest times of a person's life. First, when he was born, and he sees himself coming out from the safety that he was in. Second, on the day he dies, when he sees people for the last time, and knows he will not see them again in this life. Third, on the day when he is resurrected, and sees himself among the great gathering of people. Allaah honored Yahya Ibn Zakariyyah by giving him peace in all of these situations.

When Yahya grew up, he was sent as a messenger to Bani Israa'eel. He called them to repent from their sins, and turn to Allaah. He was always aware of Allaah, and did not care for what he ate or drank. He would take whatever he could find, and not concern himself about it. Allaah told him to call the people to five things. Worshipping Allaah alone, without partners, the Salaat, fasting, charity, and remembering Allaah much.

We can take another lesson from Yahya here. He did not worry about what he would eat or drink- he was not picky, and he was thankful for whatever Allaah gave him, alhamdulillah. Think about Yahya the next time you don't like what your mother has made for you, and thank Allaah for it, then thank your mother for it, and then eat it, insh'Allaah.

Yahya called the people to Allaah, and was not afraid of anything. He never hid the truth, no matter what the consequences. There was an evil ruler, who wanted to marry his own niece. Yahya told him that that was forbidden, and that he could not do it. When his niece heard this, she was mad at Yahya. When her family heard that Yahya had told the ruler that he could not marry his niece, her mother told her to ask the ruler to kill Yahya. So that day, when she went to the ruler, he asked her what she wanted. She answered, "I want you to kill Yahya Ibn Zakariyya." He was afraid to kill him, so he said, "Ask for something else." She said, "I do not want anything but this." The ruler called for Yahya and a basin was brought, and the ruler ordered Yahya to be slaughtered over it.

Aren't you thankful for the blessing Allaah gave Yahya, to not be afraid when he died? Look at what this evil king did, just because an evil woman told him to do it. We should never listen to people who try to get us to do evil deeds. Instead, we should call on Allaah, like Yusuf did before, and ask Him to strengthen us and keep us from falling into wrongdoing.

Allaah's anger came down on these people who killed their own prophet. He allowed an evil king, name Bukhtanassar, to defeat them. The king oppressed them and slaughtered many of them. That is a fair recompense for the people who slew the prophet that Allaah had sent to guide them.

So we see again, how even though evil people sometimes have some success, in the end Allaah will always punish them for their evil- just as He will reward the righteous, good people, for their goodness. May Allaah make us amongst those who please Him and who will get His rewards in this life and the next.

Points of Benefit

1. Allaah gives provision to whomever He wishes.

2. Calling on Allaah alone with sincerity can cause your supplication to be answered.

3. Allaah can do anything that He wishes.

4. If you are thankful to Allaah, then that is a cause for the favors He granted you to remain.

5. Sins are a cause for hardship, and repentance causes the hardship to be lifted.

6. Allaah will seek revenge for His prophets from whoever harms them.

Hands on Learning

1. Make a page each for Zakariyyah and Yahya in your prophet book. Write their names with hollow letters and color them in as you like. Draw a little picture or write a verse from the Qur'aan from the story to remind you of who they were and what they did.

2. Show your pages to someone in your family, or to a friend, and tell them all that you can remember about the story of Zakariyyah and Yahya.

3. When Zakariyyah asked Allaah to give him a sign, Allaah made it so he could not speak for three days except to recite and praise Allaah. This was a sign from Allaah. How long do you think you could do what Zakariyyah did? Why not see how long you can go without saying anything, except for reciting Qur'aan and remembering Allaah?

4. Think of Maryam in her room, with all of her food provided for her! Draw a picture of a mat or table spread with some of your favorite kinds of food.

5. Make a list of all of the good characteristics of the prophet Yahya. Each day, try to be like him in one way. This is a good thing to do with all of the prophets, especially Prophet Muhammad, may Allaah's praise and salutations be upon him.

Day 22:
The Letter ك: كظم الغيظ
(*Kadhm al-Ghaydh*)
(controlling the anger)

As Islaam has commanded us to control our anger and forgive the one who has wronged us in every time and place. Allaah, the Most High has said, ❲*Those who spend (in Allaah's Cause) in prosperity and in adversity, who repress anger, and who pardon men; verily, Allaah loves al-muhsinoon (those who do good).*❳-(Surat aal-'Imraan, Ayat 134)

So in this month of Ramadhaan one should go to greater efforts to control his anger. The Prophet, may Allaah's praise and salutations be upon him, said in that which he narrated from his Lord, {Allaah the Most High said, *"Every good deed that the son of Aadam performs is for him except for the fast, which is for Me, and I will reward him for it. And fasting is a shield; so on the day one of you is fasting, he should not yell or use bad language. And if someone insults him or tries to fight him, he should say, 'I am fasting, I am fasting.'"*} (al-Bukhaari)

One of the mistakes that many people make during Ramadhaan is that they lose their temper and become furious over small things, and they use improper speech.

This is despite the fact that one of the reasons for the legislation of fasting is purification of the soul and the guidance of them to the best of characters. The reason for fasting is not only leaving off food and drink; rather in addition to that it is staying away from evil character, as the Prophet, may Allaah's praise and salutations be upon him, said, {*Fasting is not only from food and drink- it is also fasting from bad language and evil speech. So if someone insults you or acts ignorantly towards you, say, "I am fasting, I am fasting."*} (al-Haakim, and al-Albaani has declared it to be authentic)

Further Points of Benefit

Sheikh Saalih Fauzaan, may Allaah preserve him, said,

"And know that fasting has etiquettes which must be given attention to and implemented for the fast to be in accordance with the Islamic Legislation, and so that the one who is fasting can benefit from it. As the Prophet, may Allaah's praise and salutations be upon him, said, { *Perhaps a fasting person will not benefit from his fast except for hunger.* } (Ibn Majah (1690) an-Nasaa'i (3249) al-Haakim (431) and other than them. And al-Haakim said that it is authentic on the conditions of al-Bukhaari though he did not narrate it. And adh-Dhahabi agree with this)

…And the Prophet, may Allaah's praise and salutations be upon him, said, { *Whoever does not leave off speaking evil and acting upon it, Allaah has no need of him leaving off his food and drink.* } (al-Bukhaari (1903)) (From "Majaalis Shahr Ramadhaan al-Mubaarak wa Itihaaf ahl Eemaan bi Duroos Shahr Ramadhaan" Pages 161-163)

And remember, my sisters, that Shaytaan and his minions among the jinn and the men wish to lead us astray, and to cause us to do that which is displeasing to Allaah. They want for us to become angry and fall into all of the traps which they set for us.

Sheikh Fauzaan says, concerning this,

"Any of those of correct and sound mind will see the wisdom in Allaah's commands and prohibitions, in that they will bring them benefit. And if they act upon them, they will be benefitted quickly and eternally. And if they ignore them, then they are harmed, quickly and eternally- and they are only destroying themselves and losing their own way; for they have turned away from the obedience of Allaah, Mighty and Majestic, and they can only benefit themselves by obeying Allaah. So the evil that they do will return to them, and the good that they do will return to them. So where are their minds, and where are their intellects (meaning, those who follow the Shaytaan)?? It is as if their minds have been stricken, so they do not benefit their owners. As Allaah, the Most High, says,

And surely, We have created many of the jinn and mankind for Hell. They have hearts wherewith they understand not, and they have eyes wherewith they see not, and they have ears wherewith they hear not (the truth). They are like cattle, nay even more astray; those! They are the heedless ones.-(Surat al-A'raaf, Ayat 179)

Meaning that they do not understand in a manner which will benefit them, and do not hear that which will benefit them; rather, they only see and hear like animals which see, but do not comprehend. As an animal may do something which will destroy it, but it does not know. And likewise a person whose intellect, hearing and sight do not benefit him. So he is far more misguided than the animals, because animals are not held accountable for what they do. And the person is held accountable, and will have to account for his actions. And he will be punished or rewarded. "They are like cattle, nay even more astray" And Allaah is calling to people to Paradise, and Shaytaan and his supporters call them to the Hellfire. Allaah, Glorified and Exalted, says,

Surely, Shaytaan is an enemy to you, so take him as an enemy. He only invites his followers that they may become the dwellers of the blazing Fire.-(Surat Faatir, Ayat 6)

So how great is the difference between the call of Allaah and the call of Shaytaan and his helpers?!?!" (From "Majaalis Shahr Ramadhaan al-Mubaarak wa Itihaaf ahl Eemaan bi Duroos Shahr Ramadhaan" Pages 43-44)

Family Time

The Story of the Prophet 'Isa

Do you remember the story we read yesterday, of how Zakariyyah took care of Maryam? Now you are going to hear more about Maryam. Maryam was one of the righteous female worshippers, known for her devotion and worship. One day, when she was alone, Allaah sent Angel Jibreel to her. He came to her in the form of a man. When she saw him suddenly come in to where she was praying alone, she was afraid. She said, *Verily, I seek refuge with the Most Gracious from you, if you fear Allaah.*-(Surat Maryam Ayat 18) Jibreel said to her to remove her fear, *I am only a messenger from your Lord, to announce to you the gift of a righteous son.*-(Surat Maryam Ayat 19)

When Maryam heard this, she was amazed. How could she have a son when she was not married? The angel said, ❮*Thus says your Lord: "That is easy for Me"*❯-(Surat Maryam Ayat 21)It was easy for Allaah to make a baby without a father. He created Aadam without a father or a mother, and he created Hawwa from AAadam, without a mother. Angel Jibreel told Maryam that her son would be named al-Maseeh, 'Isa Ibn Maryam. He was going to be a mercy to his people, and a righteous prophet. When Maryam heard this, she submitted to the decree of Allaah. Jibreel blew into the sleeve of her garment, and she became pregnant with 'Isa.

Allaah can do anything He wants to- He is the only One who can create something out of nothing. He is the One Who gives things life, and He is the One who causes them to die. Remember how He made the camel come out of the rock? Remember how He created Aadam and Hawwa- Aadam from clay, with no parents, and Hawwa from Aadam? Remember how He gifted Ibraaheem and Saarah, and then Zakariyyah and his wife, with a child even though the women were too old to have babies? Always remember that Allaah can do anything and everything He wants to do, and thank Him for all that He does for you, and worship only Him.

When Maryam felt that the baby was going to be born, she went away from her people. She knew that she was going to be tested with the birth, that nobody would help her, and that when they saw the baby they would not believe her story of how he was born. She went under the trunk of a date palm for shelter, and said, "Would that that I had died before this, and had been forgotten and out of sight."-(Surat Maryam Ayat 23)

Then, Jibreel called out to her from the bottom of the valley, ❮*Do not grieve, your Lord has provided a stream under you. And shake the trunk of the date palm towards you, it will let fall fresh ripe dates upon you. So eat and drink and rejoice. And if you see any human being, say, 'Verily, I have vowed a fast for the Most Gracious, so I shall not speak to any human being today.'*❯-(Surah Maryam Ayat 24-26) So she ate the dates and drank the water.

After she had her son, she took him and carried him back to her people. When they saw her with a baby, they made a big deal about it and protested, because she was not married. They said, ❮*Oh Maryam! Indeed you have brought us a mighty thing!*❯-(Surat Maryam Ayat 27) They reminded her that she was from a good, pure family, well-known for their righteousness and worship. They slandered her and falsely accused her. She did not answer them at all, but only pointed to baby 'Isa. They said, ❮*How can we speak to one who is a child in the cradle?*❯-(Surat Maryam Ayat 29)

Then the baby began to talk. He said, ❮*Verily, I am a servant of Allaah, He has given me the scripture and made me a prophet. And He has made me blessed wherever I am, and has enjoined on me Salaat and Zakaat, as long as I live. And to be dutiful to my mother, and made me not arrogant, unblessed. And Salaam (peace) be upon me the day I was born, and the day I die, and the day I shall be raised alive.*❯-(Surat Maryam Ayat 30-33)

Look at how Allaah blessed Maryam, alhamdulillah! Remember how He used to provide her with food and drink when she was under the care of Zakariyyah? Then He gave her the gift of a baby, even though she was not married. Next, He provided food and drink for her again, when she was going to have her baby. And He told her not to speak to the people at all- so when they accused her of committing wrongdoing, she did not answer them. Instead, 'Isa, who was just a tiny baby, spoke to them!! How amazing that must have been, alhamdulillah! Allaah defended Maryam by giving 'Isa this miracle of speech when he was a baby, and it was a sign to the people that he was a prophet of Allaah. Allaah also honored Maryam by making her the mother of a prophet and messenger, and 'Isa said that he would always be dutiful to her.

'Isa said that he was the servant of Allaah, and not his son, as some people say. Even in his cradle he called the people to worship Allaah alone, He said, *And verily, Allaah is my Lord and your Lord, so worship Him. That is the straight path.* -(Surat Maryam Ayat 36) Even after this was explained to them, the people differed regarding him. Some of them said that he was the son of Allaah and deserved to be worshipped. Some said the truth, that he was a prophet and servant of Allaah.

When 'Isa grew up, Allaah sent him as a prophet to his people. Many of Bani Israa'eel had gone astray, and 'Isa was sent as a mercy to them. Allaah gave him a book called the Injeel. 'Isa called to the right path, and ordered them to do good and forbade them to do evil, no matter where he was. They did not want to hear this from him. They would rather keep on doing all the evil that they wanted to. They disbelieved in his message and asked him to prove to them that he was a prophet.

Allaah gave 'Isa amazing miracles to prove his prophethood to them. By Allaah's leave, he could make a bird out of clay, and blow into it, and it would turn into a real bird. He could heal those who were born blind, and lepers. Allaah even gave him the miracle of bringing the dead back to life. He could tell those around him what they had just eaten, and what food they were saving in their houses for the next day. All of these things were proof that 'Isa was a prophet sent by Allaah.

However, Bani Israa'eel were adamant in their disbelief. When 'Isa saw this, he said, *Who will be my helpers in Allaah's cause?* -(Surat Aal-Imraan, Ayat 52) Some of Bani Israa'eel helped him, and believed in him, and gave him their support. They were called the Hawariyyun.

One day, the Hawaryiyyun asked 'Isa to supplicate to Allaah to send down for them a table of food, that they could eat from. Then they would be stronger and more able to perform acts of worship. 'Isa was afraid that it would be a trial for them, so he said, *Have Taqwa of Allaah, if you are indeed believers.* -(Surat An-Nisaa', Ayat 112) They said, *We wish to eat thereof, and be stronger in faith, and to know that you have indeed told us the truth, and that we ourselves be its witnesses.* -(Surat An-Nisaa', Ayat 113) They wanted it to strengthen their faith when they saw the table come down to them, as a proof that 'Isa had indeed told them the truth.

So 'Isa supplicated Allaah for a table to be sent down from the heaven, and Allaah answered him. He sent a table down to them, as a sign from Him. They ate from it as much as they wanted, and the food never ran out. Then, some of them stole from it, saying that they were afraid that the food would be gone tomorrow. When they did this, Allaah made the table go back up into the sky, as a punishment.

The evil people in Bani Israa'eel tried to kill 'Isa by conspiring to defame him and crucify him. He could not stay in one place for very long, because they wanted to kill him. He moved around to many different cities with his mother, Maryam. But they would not be satisfied with anything but 'Isa's death. They complained about him to the disbelieving king. They told him that 'Isa misguided the people, told them not to obey the king, and caused division between them. They told the king many evil lies about 'Isa, that will be part of their burdens on the Day of Judgment. The king was furious, and he sent his soldiers to torture and crucify 'Isa.

They came in the night and surrounded Prophet 'Isa's house. When 'Isa felt sure that the people would soon get into the house, he said to his companions, "Who will volunteer to be made to look like me, and then he will be my companion in Paradise?" A very young man, the youngest among them, volunteered. 'Isa thought that he was too young, and asked him to sit down. He asked the question a second and a third time, but each time no one answered but the same young man. Finally, 'Isa said, "Well then, you will be that man." Allaah made the young man look exactly like 'Isa. A hole opened up in the roof of the house, and 'Isa was made to sleep. Then Allaah raised him up from the house to heaven. When the evil people saw the young man who looked like 'Isa, they thought that he was 'Isa. They captured him, humiliated him and crucified him. They placed a crown of thorns on his head. For the amazing sacrifice that this man showed, he will be the companion of 'Isa in paradise. The evil people did not realize that they had been deceived. 'Isa was not dead at all; rather, he was with his Lord in the heavens. Allaah saved his Prophet, raised him up to Him, and left them in disarray, thinking that they had achieved their goal. Allaah made their hearts hard, and made them defiant. He disgraced them so completely that they will remain disgraced until the Day of Resurrection.

The Christians believe that 'Isa was killed on that day. They also believe that he was the son of Allaah, or even that he was Allaah himself. Do you see how silly that is? How could Allaah die? We know that Allaah cannot die, just as He was never born. The true story is what you have read here. 'Isa was raised into Heaven without them killing him. Think about that young man who put himself in 'Isa's place- even though he was very young, he was very brave, and he truly believed in Allaah and the message which 'Isa brought from Allaah to the people. So remember this man when you have to be brave- it didn't matter that he was young, he was a noble, good servant of Allaah.

At the end of time, Prophet 'Isa will come down to the earth. He will come down close to the white minaret, to the east of Damascus, wearing two garments lightly colored with saffron. He will rule justly according to the Qur'aan and the

Sunnah of Prophet Muhammad, may Allaah's praise and salutations be upon them both. He will break the crosses, and kill all of the pigs. He will make it so that all of the disbelievers have to accept Islaam or be killed. No money will be accepted from them. 'Isa will save the people from the Dajjaal and kill him. He will supplicate to Allaah to save the people from Ya'juj and Ma'juj, and they will be saved from them. Then the world will be filled with peace and prosperity, until Allaah sends a wind that will take the souls of every Believer and Muslim, leaving none but the evildoers. On these evil people, the Hour will begin, and the Trumpet will be blown.

Points of Benefit

1. If you have faith in Allaah and trust in Him, then He will provide for you, as when Maryam was given food.

2. 'Isa and his mother are free from all the lies that the Jews and Christians forge about them.

3. All of the prophets call to the same message: To worship Allaah alone, with no partner.

4. No matter how young you are, you should always be brave, and ready to defend the Believers. The man who was made to look like 'Isa was the youngest among them, and he was the bravest.

5. 'Isa, may Allaah's salutations be upon him, is not dead, he is in the heavens, and he will come down at the end of time, when Allaah wills.

6. From the characteristics of the Jews is that they betray and kill their prophets, and disbelieve in the signs of Allaah.

7. Allaah saves His believing servants from all evil.

Hands on Learning

1. Make a page for 'Isa in your prophet book. Write his name with hollow letters and color them in as you like. Draw a little picture or write a verse from the Qur'aan from the story to remind you of who he was and what he did.

2. Show your pages to someone in your family, or to a friend, and tell them all that you can remember about the story of 'Isa.

3. Draw a picture of where Maryam waited to have her baby, with a beautiful date tree full of dates and a stream nearby. Think again of how Allaah provided for her, both when she was with Zakariyyah, and now when she was going to have 'Isa.

4. Write a newspaper report about Prophet 'Isa's amazing life. Remember that when we talk about the prophets we should only say what has been authentically said about them- we can't add things to their stories, or make them say or think things that Allaah did not let us know that they said or did.

5. Draw a picture of the table spread with food sent down by Allaah as a miracle from 'Isa. Think of how the people could eat and eat and there was always more food, mash'Allaah.

Day 23:

The Letter ليلة القدر : ل

(*Laylat al-Qadr*)

(the Night of Decree)

Laylat al-Qadr has been distinguished with great excellence over the other nights of Ramadhaan. Allaah, the Most High, says, *The Night of Decree is better than a thousand months (i.e. worshipping Allaah in that night is better than worshipping Him a thousand months.*-(Surat al-Qadr, Ayat 3)

The Prophet, may Allaah's praise and salutations be upon him, said, *{Indeed this month has come upon you, and in it is a night which is better than a thousand months; the one who is forbidden from its good is forbidden from all good, and no one is forbidden from its good except that he is one to whom all good is forbidden.}* (Ibn Maajah, and Sheikh al-Albaani has declared it to be hasan)

Regarding the reward of standing up to pray during Laylat al-Qadr, the Prophet, may Allaah's praise and salutations be upon him, said, *{The one who has stood up to pray during Laylat al-Qadr with faith and seeking the reward of Allaah- all of his previous sins will be forgiven.}* (Agreed upon)

And from the wisdom of Allaah, the Most High, is that He did not make the exact date of Laylat al-Qadr known to the people so that they would strive more diligently in performing good deeds during all of the last ten nights.

The Prophet, may Allaah's praise and salutations be upon him, said, *{ Seek Laylat al-Qadr in the odd nights of the last ten days of Ramadhaan. }* (al-Bukhaari)

However Allaah, Mighty and Majestic, has given it distinguishing characteristics. The Prophet, may Allaah's praise and salutations be upon him, said, *{ Laylat al-Qadr is gentle and calm, neither hot nor cold. The sun rises the following morning weak and red. } (al-Baihaaqi, and Sheikh al-Albaani has declared it to be authentic) (Translator's note: A corresponding authentic hadeeth is found in Ahmad, which states, {Verily Laylat al-Qadr, its sign is that it is glowing and pure as if there were a bright, tranquil, calm moon during this night. It is neither cold nor is it hot, and no shooting star is permitted until morning. Its sign is also that the sun appears on the following morning smooth, without rays, similar to a full moon at night. Shaytaan is not allowed to come out with it upon this day.}*

And in another of hadeeth *{And from its signs is that on its day the sun rises without rays. }* (at-Tabarani, and Sheikh al-Albaani has declared it to be hasan)

Do not forget to make du'a often during these last ten nights. 'Aishah, may Allaah be pleased with her, narrated that she said, "Oh Messenger of Allaah, if I realized which night is Laylat al-Qadr, what should I say (how should I supplicate) during it?" He said, *{Say: Oh Allaah, verily you are forgiving and love forgiveness, so forgive me. }* (Ahmad, and Sheikh al-Albaani has declared it to be authentic)

Further Points of Benefit

Sheikh Saalih Fauzaan, may Allaah preserve him, says, concerning Laylat al-Qadr,

"For Laylat al-Qadr is a great night. Allaah has made it of tremendous importance, and mentioned it in His book, and described it with magnificent description…

…in any case, it is a tremendous night, and Allaah has described it as being better than one thousand months; meaning, that worship in it is better than the same worship being performed for one thousand months which did not include Laylat al-Qadr. So what do you think must be done in a night which is equal to a thousand months?

One must spend it in obedience to Allaah, Glorified and Exalted, and that is because, if Allaah gave this Muslim success in finding Laylat al-Qadr and being diligent in performing prayer and other acts of worship within it, then Allaah will write for him the reward similar to the reward of the one who prayed for one thousand months or more.

And this night is in Ramadhaan, without any doubt. As Allaah, Glorified and Exalted, has informed us that the Qur'aan was revealed in it, and the Qur'aan was revealed in the month of Ramadhaan. As Allaah, the Most High, says, "The month of Ramadhaan in which was revealed the Qur'aan" meaning that the Qur'aan began to be revealed during it, and that after that it was revealed to the Prophet, may Allaah's praise and salutations be upon him, at different times, until the Messenger of Allaah, may Allaah's praise and salutations be upon him, died, after Allaah completed the religion through him, and completed the revelation of the Noble Qur'aan. So the Qur'aan began to be revealed to the Prophet on this noble night, and because of the greatness of the Qur'aan and its high standing, Allaah made this night, the night in which it began to be revealed to His Messenger, great also.

From the virtues of this night are that in it the angels descend to the Earth- angels, the number is not known except to Allaah- to assist the Muslims in their worship; for it is known that the angels descend to the Muslims to assist in their worship as they descend to help them during the times of jihaad in the name of Allaah, Mighty and Majestic. And they descend for this purpose during this night. And regarding the "ruh": it is said that it is Jibreel, aleihi salaam, as Allaah, the Most High, says,

❧ *Which the trustworthy Ruh [Jibreel] has brought down upon your heart (Oh Muhammad) that you may be (one) of the warners,* ❧ (ash-Shu'araa, Ayats 193-194) And it is also said that the ruh is a type of angel unknown except to Allaah…

…and He described it (Laylat al-Qadr) as being peaceful until Fajr. And it is tranquil and protected from evil and it is free from blight and disease- so it is a night of peace as people are saved from evil, diseases, and pests until Fajr. Meaning, until the advent of Fajr.

There are two things which should be performed during this night.

1. The taraaweeh prayer, the tahajjud (night) prayer, and other voluntary prayers- as the door is open for whoever wants to pray more by himself or in congregation. And if he prays all night, this would not be excessive...

2. Supplication- for the Muslim should supplicate much during this night, whether in or out of the prayer. His supplicating in the prayer is better, especially the supplication which is performed during the prostration. Included in this is asking Allaah for your needs and asking for forgiveness, and repenting to Him- because the door of Allaah is always open, day and night, and especially during the last third of the night. And He says that in every night when two-thirds of the night has passed, *{Is there any one supplicating so that I can give him that which he supplicates for? Is there anyone asking for forgiveness so I can forgive him? Is there anyone repenting, so I can accept his repentance?* }...and the supplication is all good and worship for Allaah, Mighty and Majestic, and it is for all times- but even more so in the specific times when it is mentioned that it is answered, such as this night and the other nights of this blessed month." (From "Majaalis Shahr Ramadhaan al-Mubaarak wa Itihaaf ahl Eemaan bi Duroos Shahr Ramadhaan" Pages 108-121)

Family Time

The Story of the Prophet Muhammad, Part 1

Insh'Allaah we are going to end this blessed month of Ramadhaan, and our series of stories about the prophets, with the seal of the prophets- the last prophet and messenger, Muhammad, may Allaah's praise and salutations be upon him. Since Allaah has preserved the noble religion of Islaam, we know a lot about the Messenger of Allaah, alhamdulillah. So insh'Allaah we are going to take four days to talk about him- and still we cannot touch on everything about him and his noble life, mash'Allaah.

Prophet Muhammad is the best of Allaah's creation, and the most noble. He is from the descendants of Prophet Ismaa'eel ibn Ibraahim, may Allaah's praise and salutations be upon them. Remember reading about Ibraahim and Ismaa'eel? What was Ismaa'eel's mother's name? What building did he and his father build?

Our Prophet's name is Muhammad ibn 'Abdullaah ibn 'Abdul-Muttalib ibn Haashim ibn 'Abd-Manaaf. He was born in Makkah, in the year known as the Year of the Elephant, when Abraha tried to demolish the Ka'abah, and was destroyed. His mother was named Aaminah Bint Wahb.

His father, 'Abdullaah, died before he was born. When Prophet Muhammad was born, his grandfather 'Abdul-Muttalib, was very happy, and named him Muhammad. He was given to a woman named Halimah as-Sa'diyyah to nurse. She took him with her to the desert and took care of him, so that he would not become sick in the city air of Makkah. He stayed with her until he was two years old, when she weaned him and took him back to Makkah. She had come to love him so much, and he had brought so much prosperity and blessing to the family, that she could not bear to part with him. She asked his mother, Aaminah, to let him stay with her for a little while longer, so that he would get stronger. His mother agreed, and she took him back with her.

One day he went out to play with the other boys. Suddenly, two men dressed in white came to him. They were angels sent by Allaah. They split open his chest, and took out his heart. They opened his heart and took out a drop of black. That black drop was the evil that is in every person's heart. The angels took all the evil out of Prophet Muhammad's heart, and then they washed his heart with ice, and put it back in. Then he stood up, not hurt at all. When Halima heard what had happened, she was afraid, and took him back to Makkah, and gave him to his mother.

When Muhammad was six years old, his mother decided to take him to Madinah to visit his uncles who lived there. They stayed with his uncles for a month, and then started back to Makkah. But on the way home, Muhammad's mother got very sick and died at a place called Abwaa, between Makkah and Madinah.

Then his grandfather 'Abdul-Muttalib took care of Muhammad, may Allaah's praise and salutations be upon him, until he died when the Prophet was eight years old. Before his death, 'Abdul Muttalib entrusted his grandon to Muhammad's uncle, Abu Taalib. Abu Taalib raised Muhammad along with his own children. He loved his nephew very much, and always kept him at his side.

When the Messenger of Allaah, may Allaah's praise and salutations be upon him, was twenty-five years old, he went to Shaam selling merchandise for a woman from the Quraysh named Khadijah. She was a merchant from a noble family, and she asked Prophet Muhammad to take her things and sell them for her, so he would get some of the profit. He took her servant boy, Maysarah, with him to Shaam. Maysarah was extremely impressed by Muhammad's generosity, truthfulness, trustworthiness, and good manners. When he returned to Makkah, Maysarah told Khadijah about Muhammad. She was so impressed by what she heard that she sent one of her friends, Nafeesah bint Munya, to suggest to Muhammad that he marry her. He accepted, and Muhammad and Khadijah were married. Prophet Muhammad, may Allaah's praise and salutations be upon him, did not marry any other women until she died, and she was the mother of all of his children except Ibraahim. She had al-Qaasim, from whom the Prophet took his kunya, 'Abdullaah; Zaynab, Ruqayyah, Umm Kalthum, and Fatimah. All of his sons died when they were children, but his daughters grew up, accepted Islaam, and made hijrah to Madinah.

The Messenger of Allaah, may Allaah's praise and salutations be upon him, hated the idols, and knew that they were false gods. He was the most manly and well-mannered of his people, and the most kind, truthful, and trustworthy among them. His people called him al-Ameen, or the trustworthy, because of the good qualities that Allaah had given him.

The first sign of prophethood that Allaah gave him was true dreams. He would not see any dream except that it would come true. The Messenger of Allaah, may Allaah's praise and salutations be upon him, used to like to be alone to worship his Lord. He would go up to Cave Hiraa' for days at a time, all alone, to worship Allaah. One day, when he was in Cave Hiraa', the revelation suddenly came to him. Angel Jibreel came and said to him, "Read!" The Messenger of Allaah, may Allaah's praise and salutations be upon him, said, "I am not one who reads." This was because Prophet Muhammad did not know how to read. The angel seized him and pressed him so hard that he thought that he could not bear it any more. Then he let go of him and said again, "Read!" Again, our Prophet, may Allaah's praise and salutations be upon him, replied, "I am not one who reads." He did this three times, and then the angel said, *Read in the name of your Lord who has created. He has created man from a clot. Read! And your Lord is the most Generous. Who has taught by the pen. He has taught man that which he did not know.*-(Surat al-Alaq, Ayat 1-5)

Muhammad went home to Khadijah with his heart trembling. He said to her, "Wrap me up, wrap me up." So they wrapped him up in covers until his fear went away. Then he told Khadijah what had happened to him. She took him to her cousin Waraqah's house. He had become a Christian, and used to copy out the Scriptures. He was a very old man who had gone blind. When he heard what had happened, he told the Prophet that this was Angel Jibreel, whom Allaah sent to Moosa. He said, "I wish that I was young, and could live until the time when your people drive you out." Allaah's Messenger, may Allaah's praise and salutations be upon him, said, "Will they drive me out?" Waraqah told him that they would, and said that if he lived until that time then he would support the Prophet and help him. However, Waraqah died soon after this meeting.

First, Allaah ordered the Messenger of Allaah to read the revelation himself, and He did not tell him to spread it to the people. Then, Allaah ordered him to warn his close relatives and companions, then his people, then the Arabs who lived around them, then all of the Arabs, and then all of the 'aalameen, the jinn and the men. The first man to believe was Abu Bakr, the first woman was Khadijah, the first freed slave was Zayd Ibn Haarithah and the first child was his cousin, Ali Ibn Abi Taalib.

When the powerful tribe of Quraysh heard about the religion that Prophet Muhammad, may Allaah's praise and salutations be upon him, was calling the people to, they tried everything they could think of to stop the people from believing in it. They made fun of it, they made up false claims about it, they tried to stop the people from hearing the Qur'aan, they tried to pollute the purity of Islaam by trying to add the worship of other than Allaah into it, and they punished and tortured those who believed.

When they saw that the faith was still spreading, they went to Abu Taalib and tried to get him to stop Muhammad from calling to Islaam, but he refused to do this and protected Muhammad from them. They were too proud and arrogant to be patient for very long, so soon they began to harm the Messenger of Allaah, may

Allaah's praise and salutations be upon him.

An evil man named Abu Lahab, and his wife, Umm Jameel, were especially cruel to him. Even though he was the Prophet's uncle, he hated him and scorned him and his religion. When the Messenger of Allaah would go out to the people and call them to Islaam during the time of the pilgrimage, Abu Lahab would follow and shout, "Verily, he is an apostate and a liar!" His wife would place thorns in the path of the Prophet, may Allaah's praise and salutations be upon him, to harm his feet when he walked. Another man who would cause harm to him was 'Uqbah ibn Abi Mu'eet. One day, the Prophet, may Allaah's praise and salutations be upon him, was praying at the Ka'abah, when Abu Jahl and some of his companions saw him. A camel had just been slaughtered the day before, and its entrails were laying nearby. Abu Jahl said, "Who will take the entrails of the camel, and place it on Muhammad's back when he prostrates?" The worst among them, 'Uqbah Ibn Abi Mu'eet stood up and took it. When the Messenger of Allaah prostrated, 'Uqbah put it between his two shoulders.

When the punishment that the disbelievers were inflicting on the Muslims became too hard to bear, the Messenger of Allaah ordered them to make hijrah, or emigrate, to Abyssinia, where there was a just and fair king. On the first trip, twelve men and four women left for Abyssinia. On the second trip, thirty-eight men left and nineteen women.

The Quraysh tried to get the Prophet's tribe, Banu Haashim, to hand him over to them to kill, but they refused. The Quraysh wrote a pact against Banu Haashim. The Quraysh made all of Banu Haashim go into a valley, and they would not let any food get to them. They stayed in the valley for three years, until one could hear the women and children crying from hunger in the valley. Then Allaah sent worms to the pact that they had written, and they ate every word on it except the name of Allaah. When the Quraysh saw this, they had to let Banu Haashim out of the valley, to mix with the people of Makkah once again.

Six months later, Abu Taalib died, and then a few days after him, Khadijah, may Allaah be pleased with her, passed away as well. Abu Taalib had been the one who was protecting the Prophet Muhammad, may Allaah's praise and salutations be upon him, so after his death the disbelievers began to torment him more than ever.

He went to the people of the city of Taa'if to call them to Islaam, but they proved to be even worse than his own people. They lined up along the roads, and they would not let him set down his foot except that they would stone it, until he left with his feet bleeding. Allaah sent to him an angel who offered to crush the people between the two mountains, but the Messenger of Allaah refused, because he hoped that, even if they did not believe, their children might believe in Allaah after them.

Then the Messenger of Allaah, may Allaah's praise and salutations be upon him, was taken up to the heavens on the night journey called al-Israa' wal-Mi'raaj. He was taken to Jerusalem, were he led all of the previous Prophets in prayer. He was taken up to the heavens, were he saw many amazing things. On this journey, Allaah made the five daily prayers obligatory on his Ummah. He returned to Makkah on that same night, and when he told the people they called him a liar. He described Jerusalem to them, and those who had seen it had to admit that it was exactly as he said. He told them about their caravan which he had passed on the way, and told them when it would arrive, and which animal was leading it. When it arrived it was as he had said, but the people were still stubborn in their disbelief.

Hands on Learning

1. In this part of the story of Muhammad, may Allaah's praise and salutations be upon him, you read about the first time the angel Jibreel came to the Prophet with revelation from Allaah. Look at see what Surah of the Qur'aan this is from. Do you have this surah memorized? Sit down with your parents and read through the whole surah, insh'Allaah. Think about how the Prophet, may Allaah's praise and salutations be upon him, must have felt when this first revelation came to him. Mash'Allaah, we should always try to be as strong and brave as he was when we are faced with something new or strange to us. Draw a picture of the Cave of Hira. You or your parents can probably even find a picture of it in a book or on the internet- it is still there, outside of Makkah, even today, alhamdulillah.

2. You also read about Abu Lahab and his wife- they were very evil people who were great enemies to the Messenger of Allaah, even though they were his relatives, mash'Allaah. Read Surat al-Masad in the Qur'aan, and it will tell you the story of what they did to the Prophet, may Allaah's praise and salutations be upon him, and what Allaah says about this. This is a short Surah. If you have not already memorized it, insh'Allaah memorize it now.

3. Do you know what poetry is? It is when you try to write about thoughts, feelings, or events using a few well-chosen, descriptive words. It is like painting with words. Poetry was known before the time of the Prophet, may Allaah's praise and salutations be upon him, and it was known during his time, and it is known now, alhamdulillah. Why not choose one event out of this story and write a poem about it? If you can't write it down yourself, ask your parents or big brothers and sisters to help you with it.

4. Look through this story and write down some of the miracles that Allaah gave to the Prophet Muhammad during this period of his life. You should also make a list of all of the Messenger of Allaah's children and his family members, as well as his lineage, and then write down the first four people to embrace Islam after him, may Allaah's praise and salutations be upon him.

Think of what it must have been like to be one of the Prophet's, may Allaah's praise and salutations be upon him, companions at this time. Their faith was tested all the time, as the Quraysh persecuted them terribly, mash'Allaah. May Allaah be pleased with all of them.

Day 24:
The Letter م :المفطرات
(*al-Maftooraat*)
(that which breaks the fast)

The principle concerning those things which break the fast is that they do not break the fast except if they were done purposefully and were consciously chosen.

Considering that, some examples of things which do NOT break the fast are as follows: vomiting by accident, the pulling of a tooth, blood tests, nosebleed, medicinal injections (which are not nourishing or serving the purpose of food), enemas, eye or ear drops, use of asthma inhalers, swallowing one's saliva, water or other liquid reaching the throat by accident, tasting food for necessity without swallowing it, using the miswak, bathing, toothpaste- while being careful not to swallow any of it, perfume- and bakhoor is the exception (Translator's note: it is considered by many of the scholars including Sheikh 'Utheimeen, to break the fast, as one inhales the smoke of it- they compare it to cigarette smoke, and Allaah knows best), kohl (for the eyes), henna, lotion, makeup, kissing your spouse, and wet dreams.

As for that which breaks the fast, then they make it obligatory to make up the fast. They are of two categories.

1. Those things which break the fast, but all that is obligatory is making it up. These include vomiting purposefully, nose drops, I.V.'s and glucose injections, kidney dialysis, and eating and drinking when one is unsure of the sun's having set- because the general principle is that the day remains until the sun is known to have set.

2. Things which break the fast, which make it obligatory to both make the fast up and to pay expiation. These include: sexual intercourse- and the expiation is freeing a slave; and if this is not possible, then fasting two consecutive months; and if this is not possible then feeding sixty poor people- half of a saa' (a saa' is four double handfuls of an average sized man) of the food of the people of that land to each person. (These are summarized from Sheikh Bin Baaz, from the books "Fataawa Manaar al-Islaam" and "Fataawa Islaamiyyah" in the Book of Fasting)

Further Points of Benefit

Sheikh Muhammad ibn Saalih al-'Utheimeen, may Allaah have mercy upon him, was asked concerning those things which break the fast. After listing them and giving their proofs, he went on to say,

"These things which break the fast are invalidators of the fast. However, they do not invalidate it unless three conditions are met. They are:

1. Knowledge

2. Remembering

3. Intention

So a person's fast is not invalidated by these things which could invalidate it, unless these three conditions are present.

1. That he knows the ruling according to the Islamic legislation, and he knows the situation, or the time. If he is ignorant of the ruling or the time, then his fast is valid, according to the words of Allaah, the Most High,

❴*Our Lord! Punish us not if we forget or fall into error*❵-(Surat al-Baqarah, From Ayat 286) Allaah, the Most High, also says,

"I have done so."

And Allaah, the Most High, says, ❴*And there is no sin upon you concerning that in which you made a mistake, except in regards to what your hearts deliberately intend.*❵-(Surat al-Ahzaab, From Ayat 5)

These two evidences are general in their scope.

According to specific proofs concerning fasting confirmed in the Sunnah (the fast of the one who is ignorant is valid). In Saheeh al-Bukhaari it is narrated in the hadeeth of 'Adi ibn Haatim, may Allaah be pleased with him, that he fasted and placed two 'iqal under his pillow- and an 'iqal is the rope which is used to tether the leg of a camel- one of them was black and the other was white. He would eat and drink until the white one was distinct from the black one, after which he fasted. Then in the morning, he went to the Prophet, may Allaah's praise and salutations be upon him, and the Prophet, may Allaah's praise and salutations be upon him, explained to him that the meaning of the white and black threads in the verse are not the well-known threads. Actually, what is meant by the white thread is the whiteness of the daylight and the black thread is the blackness of the night. However, the Prophet, may Allaah's praise and salutations be upon him, did not command him to make up for the fast because he was ignorant of this ruling, believing that this was the meaning of the Noble Verse. (al-Bukhaari (1916) and Muslim (1090)

Concerning ignorance of the time, then it is narrated in Saheeh al-Bukhaari on the authority of Asmaa' Bint Abi Bakr, may Allaah be pleased with them both, that she said, {*We broke our fast during the time of the Prophet, may Allaah's praise and salutations be upon him, on a cloudy day, and then the sun came out.*} (al-Bukhaari (1959))

The Prophet, may Allaah's praise and salutations be upon him, did not command them to make up the fast- and if making it up had been obligatory then he would have commanded them to do so; and if he had commanded them to do so, then it would have been transmitted to the people…

2. This is that the person remembers, and the opposite of remembering is forgetting. So, if a person were to eat and drink forgetfully, then his fast is valid and he does not have to make it up, according to the words of Allaah, the Most High,

❴*Our Lord! Punish us not if we forget or fall into error*❵-(Surat al-Baqarah, From Ayat 286)

Allaah, the Most High, says, "I have done so."

According to the hadeeth of Abu Hurairah, may Allaah be pleased with him, the Messenger of Allaah, may Allaah's praise and salutations be upon him, said, *{ Whoever forgot while he was fasting and ate or drank, then he should complete his fast, as it was only Allaah Who fed him and gave him drink. }* (al-Bukhaari (1933) and Muslim (1155))

3.   The intention, which is that a fasting person chooses to perform this action which invalidates the fast. If he does not choose to do it, then his fast is valid, whether he was compelled to do it or not. This is based upon the words of Allaah, the Most High, regarding the one who is forced to do something,

Whoever disbelieved in Allaah after his belief, except for the one who is forced to do this and whose heart is at rest with his faith; but such as open their chests to disbelief, on them is the wrath from Allaah, and theirs will be a great torment.-(Surat an-Nahl, Ayat 106)

If the ruling of disbelief is removed due to coercion, then anything less than this has more right to be pardoned. Also, there is the hadeeth in which the Prophet, may Allaah's praise and salutations be upon him, said,

{ Allaah has pardoned my people for their mistakes, their forgetfulness, and the things which they are forced to do. }

Based upon this, if dust were to fly into the nose of a fasting person and he tasted it in his throat, and it went down into his stomach, it would not cause his fast to be broken because he did not intend for this to happen. Likewise, if he was forced to break his fast and he did so do to this compulsion, then his fast is valid, because he did not choose to do this. Also, if he had a nocturnal emission while he was sleeping (during the time of the fast) his fast is valid, because the one who is sleeping does not have intention. Similarly, if a man forced his wife to have intercourse while she was fasting, then her fast would still be valid because she did not choose to do this..." (From "Fataawa Arkaan al-Islaam", Vol. 2)

Family Time

The Story of Prophet Muhammad, Part 2

The Messenger of Allaah, may Allaah's praise and salutations be upon him, used to go to the pilgrims who came every year for Hajj, and call them to believe in him and his message, and protect him, but no one accepted his call. Then the Ansaar of Madinah heard about him. They had already heard from the Jews of Madinah that a prophet was expected to come to them in this time. The Jews told the Ansaar that when the expected prophet came, the Jews would follow him, and fight the Ansaar and win against them. But that is not what Allaah had decreed. The Ansaar believed in Prophet Muhammad, may Allaah's praise and salutations be upon him, and the Jews disbelieved, and they were defeated.

We should never be arrogant and sure of ourselves like these Jews of Madinah were. They knew that a prophet was coming, and were looking for him, and then when the Messenger of Allaah, may Allaah's praise and salutations be upon him, came, they disbelieved in him. Allaah puts His blessings where He will, and Allaah chose the Ansaar of Madinah to be the ones to receive the message and the Messenger of Allaah, alhamdulillah.

First the Messenger of Allaah met with a group of six of the Ansaar. He called them to Islaam, and they all accepted it from him. These six went back to Madinah and called their people to accept Islaam, until there was not a single house that did not have a Muslim in it. The next year, twelve of the Ansaar came on Hajj and met the Prophet, may Allaah's praise and salutations be upon him. When they returned he sent one of his companions, Mus'ab Ibn Umayr, back with them to teach them the Qur'aan and the religion. The third year they again came to Madinah, and they gave their pledge to the Messenger of Allaah, may Allaah's praise and salutations be upon him, that if he came to them they would protect him as they protected their own women and children.

See how this is like when the Prophet, may Allaah's praise and salutations be upon him, first began calling to Allaah and a few people accepted? Here we see how he called six people, and within one short year, every single house in Madinah had a Muslim in it, alhamdulillah!

Then the Messenger of Allaah gave the Muslims permission to emigrate, or make hijrah, to Madinah. The believers left, one by one, until no one that was able to leave was left except the Messenger of Allaah, Abu Bakr, and Ali. The Messenger of Allaah got ready to leave along with Abu Bakr, and waited for the command to come from Allaah, ordering him to go to Madinah.

The disbelievers in Makkah became afraid of what would happen if the Messenger of Allaah went to Madinah. They were afraid that he would gather strength and fight them, so they decided to murder him. Every tribe from the Quraysh chose a strong young man from their midst, and told them to all strike the Prophet, may Allaah's praise and salutations be upon him, at once as he came out of his house. This was so that no one person would hold the blame for killing him. Jibreel came to the Messenger of Allaah and told him what the Quraysh were plotting to do. The Prophet, may Allaah's praise and salutations be upon him, went to Abu Bakr and told him to get ready to accompany him that night. In the night, the disbelievers all surrounded his house, and waited for him to come out so they could kill him. The Messenger of Allaah got up, and left Ali sleeping on his bed in his place. This was so that they would not notice that he was gone. Then he walked right out in front of the disbelievers, reciting Qur'aan, and he threw a handful of clay on their heads. Allaah protected him from them, so that they did not even see him or know that he had left. Then he left with Abu Bakr for Madinah. The Quraysh chased after him, but they could not find him.

When the Messenger of Allaah, may Allaah's praise and salutations be upon him, entered Madinah, the people were filled with joy. It was the happiest and most beautiful day they had ever seen. He stayed with Abu Ayyub al-Ansaari until his masjid and house was complete. He, may Allaah's praise and salutations be upon him, helped build the masjid with his own hands, working alongside his companions. Then he built two houses next to the masjid, one for his wife Sawdah and one for his wife A'ishah.

When he was settled in Madinah, he divided the ninety men from the Muhaajreen (those who made hijrah from Makkah to live in Madinah) and the Ansaar into pairs. He gave each man from the Muhaajreen a brother from the Ansaar. Some of the poor Muslims lived in the masjid, they were called ahlus-Saffah. The Prophet, may Allaah's praise and salutations be upon him, would distribute these poor ones out among his companions, and they would take them home to eat with them.

Before he came to Madinah, the Muslims all faced Bayt al-Maqdis in Jerusalem when they prayed. They remained facing Jerusalem until the second year after the hijrah, when Allaah ordered them to face the Ka'bah.

Then Allaah ordered his Messenger to fight the disbelievers. This was in the second year after hijrah. The Prophet, may Allaah's praise and salutations be upon him, sent several expeditions out to fight against the disbelievers. Then, in Ramadhaan, he went out with three hundred and a few dozen men, to stop a caravan belonging to the Quraysh. They only had two horses in the whole army, and seventy camels. When the Quraysh heard that they had come out to stop their caravan, they were furious. All of the noblemen in Makkah formed a huge army. They also called on the tribes around Makkah to come and help them defeat Muhammad. They thought that it would be easy to crush him because he had so few men and horses, while they were many and powerful.

Meanwhile, the caravan changed its route and escaped from the Muslims. The caravan sent a messenger to the Quraysh, telling them not to go out and fight the Muslims, as they were no longer in danger. However the Quraysh decided to go ahead and fight the Muslims anyway, thinking that it would be easy to defeat them and be rid of them.

The two armies met at Badr. The Messenger of Allaah called on Allaah to grant them victory. He pleaded with his Lord, raising his hands until his cloak slipped off. During the battle, Abu Bakr, Sa'd Ibn Mu'aadh, and a group of the Ansaar fought near the Prophet, defending him from the disbelievers. The Muslims stayed firm and fought, until Allaah granted them victory. They killed seventy of the disbelievers, and took seventy of them captive.

Among them was the enemy of Allaah, Abu Jahl. Two boys from the Ansaar, named Mu'aadh Ibn Amr and Mu'aadh Ibn 'Afraa', killed him. After the fight, Abdullaah Ibn Mas'ud found him almost dead. He cut off his head, and brought it to the Messenger of Allaah. He, may Allaah's praise and salutations be upon him, praised Allaah and glorified him when he saw what an example had been made of one of the greatest enemies of Islaam.

Fourteen of the Believers were martyred. When the Messenger of Allaah, may Allaah's praise and salutations be upon him, returned to Madinah, he ransomed the prisoners to the people of Makkah. When the people of Makkah heard what had happened to their army, they were shocked. How could the little Muslim army have won against their huge army? They were humiliated, and all of Makkah mourned for their fallen leaders.

Again, Allaah will give victory and help to the Believers, alhamdulillah. Even though they were few, and did not have a lot of horses or camels, He granted the Muslims victory over the Quraysh. And look how two boys from amongst the Muslims were able to kill Abu Jahl, who had been one of the greatest enemies of the Muslims. You do not have to be big to win or to do great things, alhamdulillah, if you have faith in Allaah and ask Him for help.

In the third year after the hijrah, the Quraysh prepared a huge army to get revenge from the Muslims. It was made up of three thousand soldiers with three thousand riding animals and two hundred horses under the command of Abu Sufyaan Ibn Harb. They marched towards Madinah until they reached Mount Uhud, where they camped.

When the Messenger of Allaah heard that they were coming, he asked his companions for advice. He thought that they should stay in Madinah, and fight in the city. The head of the hypocrites at that time was 'Abdullaah Ibn Ubayy. A hypocrite, basically, is a person who acts like a Muslim on the outside but who is not really one on the inside. They are known to be liars, and to break their promises, and to be generally not trustworthy- yet on the outside they could seem to be the most religious of people. 'Abdullaah ibn Ubayy agreed with the Prophet because he thought that he could easily hide in his house and avoid fighting. He was a cowardly man who was afraid of death, However, many of the Prophet's companions advised him to go out to fight the Quraysh, and they pressed him to do this until he agreed. The Messenger of Allaah, may Allaah's praise and salutations be upon him, went into his house and put on his armor before coming back out. When his companions saw this they were afraid that they had forced him into agreeing to go out so they said, "If you think we should stay in Madinah then we will do so." He, may Allaah's praise and salutations be upon him, replied, "If a Prophet puts on his armor it is not proper for him to remove it until Allaah judges between him and his enemies." So he left al-Madinah along with one thousand of his companions.

Between Makkah and Uhud, 'Abdullaah Ibn Ubayy ran away from the Prophet's army, taking all of the hypocrites- a third of the army- with him. He pretended that he was mad because the Prophet, may Allaah's praise and salutations be upon him, had not listened to his advice. When they arrived at the battlefield, the Messenger of Allaah organized his army. He put the archers under 'Abdullaah Ibn Jubayr, and told them not to move from their stations no matter what happened. He gave the standard, or flag, to Mus'ab Ibn Umayr. He sent back some of the boys whom he thought were too young to fight, like 'Abdullaah Ibn Umar, Usaamah Ibn Zayd, and Zayd Ibn Arqam.

In the beginning, the Muslims were winning, and their enemies began to retreat. When the archers saw the enemy retreating many of them began to leave their stations to get to the booty. Their commander, 'Abdullaah Ibn Jubayr, cried out to them, reminding them that they had promised the Messenger of Allaah that they would not move, but they did not listen to him. Then the disbelievers easily began to overcome the Muslims, because the archers had left their places. They even reached the Messenger of Allaah, and wounded his face, breaking his tooth. Ten of the companions were killed defending the Messenger of Allaah. Talha Ibn 'Ubaydullaah was wounded many times and his hand was paralyzed in the defense of the Prophet, may Allaah's praise and salutations be upon him. Abu Dujanah shielded the Prophet with his back. Arrows and blows from swords would land on him and he would not move at all.

The Messenger of Allaah's uncle, Hamza, was martyred. Mus'ab Ibn Umayr was carrying the flag when the disbelievers cut off his right hand. He then took the flag in his left hand, until it too was cut off. Then he held the flag up with his shoulders and neck until he was martyred. When the battle began to quiet down, the Quraysh went away after promising to come back for another battle the next year. The Muslims went down to the battleground and found their dead and wounded. Seventy of the Muslims had been killed. The dead were buried in their clothes, without being washed or prayed over. They were buried two or three to a grave, and scented grass was placed between them to separate them. This is the way that martyrs are buried because of their high distinction.

In the following years, the Messenger of Allaah fought several more battles against the disbelievers, and sent out expeditions against them. He chased the Jews out of Madinah after they broke the agreement he made with them and betrayed him.

Hands on Learning

1. The masjid at the time of the Messenger of Allaah, may Allaah's praise and salutations be upon him, was a very simple building made of mud and clay and palm trees, mash'Allaah. The masjid you see nowadays is not the exact one built by him, mash'Allaah. Think about what his masjid might have looked like when it was built. We can't know for sure, of course, but we can imagine. You can look in books to see what buildings made out of mud and clay look like, to give you an idea. Then draw another picture of the masjid as it is today, insh'Allaah. Remember that a masjid does not have to be fancy. Masjids are houses of Allaah, and they should be built in a good way, but they do not have to be fancy or decorated in any way. They are meant as places of worship, to worship Allaah alone, and we should always treat them

with respect and help to keep them clean and nice.

2. Look on a map to see where Makkah and Madinah are located. What country are they in? What are some of the other cities you see in that country? If you have a world map or a globe, find where you are. Look to see what way you have to face in order to be facing Makkah. Trace or draw a map of Saudi Arabia, and mark clearly where Makkah and Madinah are.

3. Makkah and Madinah are in a land that has a desert climate. There are places with water and where things can grow, but much of it is very dry and hot. Find out some interesting facts about the climate and environment in Saudi Arabia, and write a report about it. Write about what you think it would be like to live there, and how living there now would be different than when the Messenger of Allaah, may Allaah's praise and salutations be upon him, lived there. You can draw some pictures to illustrate your report- or, if you are too little to do a report, just draw the pictures, using photographs and/ or your imagination.

Day 25:
The Letter ن :النسيان
(*al-Nisyaan*) (forgetfulness)

Whoever drinks or eats forgetfully when he is fasting- then his fasting is still valid. If the food or drink is still in his mouth when he remembers, he must spit it out. The proof that his fasting is accepted is the saying of the Prophet, may Allaah's praise and salutations be upon him, in the hadeeth of Abu Hurairah, {*Whoever forgot when he was fasting and ate and drank, should finish his fast; for Allaah only has fed him and given him drink.*} (Agreed upon)

And because the person is not taken account of for that which he forgets. Allaah, the Most High, says, ❧*...Our Lord! Punish us not if we forget or fall into error, our Lord...*❧-(Surat al-Baqara, from Ayat 286)

Whoever sees someone who has forgotten, then it is obligatory upon him to remind him, because this is from changing the wrongdoing, as the Prophet, may Allaah's praise and salutation be upon him, said, {*Whoever among you sees a wrongdoing should change it with his hand; and if this is not possible, then with his tongue; and if this is not possible then with his heart.*} (Muslim)

There is no doubt that the eating or drinking of the fasting person when he is fasting is wrongdoing, but it is forgiven in the case of his forgetfulness because the one who forgets is not taken account of for that which he forgot. As for the one who sees this, then he has no excuse for not correcting him (if he is able). (Sheikh 'Utheimeen, "Fataawa al-Islaamiyyah")

Further Points of Benefit

The complete ruling is as follows:

Sheikh Muhammad ibn Saalih al-'Utheimeen, may Allaah have mercy upon him, was asked, "What is the ruling concerning a fasting person who eats due to forgetfulness? And what is the obligation upon the one who saw him do this?"

He, may Allaah have mercy upon him, replied, "Whoever ate or drank forgetfully while he was fasting, his fast is still valid. However, if he remembers, he must stop, even if the morsel of food or drink is still in his mouth- he must spit it out.

The evidence that his fasting is complete is the statement of the Prophet, may Allaah's praise and salutations be upon him,

{ *Whoever forgot when he was fasting and ate and drank, should finish his fast; for Allaah only has fed him and given him drink.* }

Also, a person is not held accountable if he does something prohibited due to forgetfulness, according to the words of Allaah, the Most High,

❧*Our Lord! Punish us not if we forget or fall into error.*❧-(Surat al-Baqarah, From Ayat 286)

And Allaah, the Most High, says, "I have done so"

227

As for the one who observes him doing this, then it is necessary that he remind him, because this is part of changing what is evil, and the Prophet, may Allaah's praise and salutations be upon him, said,

{ If one of you sees an evil, he should change it by his hand. If he is unable to do that, then with his tongue. If he is unable to do that, then (he should hate it) in his heart. } (Muslim 49)

There is no doubt that eating and drinking by a fasting person during the time when he is supposed to be fasting is something wrong, but he is forgiven for it when it is due to forgetfulness, and he is not punished for it. But as for the one who observes him, then there is no excuse for him not to reproach him for it (if he is able)." ("Fataawa Arkaan al-Islaam", Vol.2)

There is one opinion that the one who forgets and eats should vomit the food back out, but the stronger opinion is that this is not necessary, as the intentional vomiting breaks the fast, while the eating out of forgetfulness does not. However, if the food or drink is still present in the mouth, then one should spit it out.

And we see the strength of the admonition to us to command the good and forbid the evil, if we see someone eating or drinking who we know is fasting, we should remind them, having the good suspicion that he has forgotten, rather than assuming right away that he is purposefully committing a wrongdoing. We should approach him in a gentle, helpful way, rather than being harsh or cruel. And if there is a chance that we may be attacked or harmed somehow, then we must at least hate this action that he has performed in our hearts, if we can't directly change it with our hands or tongues.

This allowance for forgetfulness should also remind us of the mercy of Allaah towards His creation, alhamdulillah, as we are not held responsible for that which we have no control over.

Family Time

The Story of Muhammad Part 3

One day, the Messenger of Allaah, may Allaah's praise and salutations be upon him, and his companions left for Makkah because they wanted to make 'Umrah, the lesser pilgrimage. When the Quraysh heard of this, they decided to fight them and keep them away, even though they only wanted to make 'Umrah. The Prophet, may Allaah's praise and salutations be upon him, explained to the Quraysh, telling them that his intention was not to fight them. He only wanted to visit the Ka'abah, as it was the right of all the people to do. He sent 'Uthmaan Ibn 'Affaan to meet with the chiefs. The Quraysh did not want to let the Muslims enter Makkah.

Finally, the Quraysh and the Muslims worked out a peaceful treaty, called the treaty of Hudaybiyyah. The treaty said that the Muslims could not enter Makkah for 'Umrah that year, but the Quraysh would have to allow them to the following year.

Some of the Companions felt upset over the conditions of the treaty, but they knew that the Messenger of Allaah knew better than them, and that he, may Allaah's praise and salutations be upon him, would not disobey his Lord. In the end, the treaty added greatly to the Muslims' strength.

The next year, the Muslims returned to Makkah to make 'Umrah. The Quraysh all left and went to the hills around the town. From there they watched the Muslims performing 'Umrah at the Ka'abah. When they saw the strength and power of the Muslims, they were filled with fear. The Muslims stayed for three days before returning to Madinah.

The Messenger of Allaah sent letters to many leaders and kings inviting them to accept Islaam. He sent them to the Roman emperor, the Caesar, the Egyptian king, the ruler of Bahrain, and many others. He also sent a letter with Shuja' ibn Wahb to Haarith al-Ghassani, who was the Roman ruler of Busra. When Shuja' reached a place called Mu'ta, the leader killed him. This meant that they wanted to fight with the Muslims, and so the Prophet, may Allaah's praise and salutations be upon him, sent an army of three thousand led by Zayd ibn Haarithah. He told them that if Zayd was killed, then Ja'far ibn Abi Taalib would lead, and if he was killed then 'Abdullaah Ibn Rawaahah. The Roman emperor came to fight them with an army of two hundred thousand. The Muslim army was not afraid of them, even though there were so many of them. 'Abdullaah Ibn Rawaahah told them, "March forward and you will get one of two good things: you will either be martyred or you will win and defeat them." All three of the commanders were martyred. Ja'far was found with over ninety wounds on his body, and his arms were cut off while he was trying to hold up the standard. Allaah rewarded him with wings to fly about in Paradise as he wished. Then, Khaalid ibn al-Waleed led them, and they drove fear into the hearts of the disbelievers, and defeated them totally.

In the eighth year after the Hijrah to Madinah, the Quraysh broke their treaty with the Prophet by secretly helping fight against some of his allies. After they broke the treaty, they began to feel sorry and scared of what would happen. They sent Abu Sufyaan to Madinah to try to work out another treaty with the Muslims. However, the Messenger of Allaah did not accept their offer. He set out for Makkah with all of the Muhaajireen and the Ansaar, as well as many of the tribes around Madinah. The army was made up of ten thousand men. On the way to Makkah, they met some of the chieftains coming out to embrace Islaam. They defeated the disbelieving army which was led by Ikrimah, Suhayl, and Safwan. No one fought them except that they defeated them. The Muslims entered Makkah on the tenth of Ramadhaan. The Messenger of Allaah announced that if the people did not resist then they would be safe from harm.

The people all assembled near the Ka'abah, and the Prophet asked the Quraysh, "What do you expect from me?" They knew how kind and generous he was, so they did not think he would kill them. They said, "Good. You are a generous brother, the son of a generous brother." He said, "There is no blame on you today. May Allaah forgive you." Even though the Quraysh had caused so much harm to the Prophet and his people, he forgave them freely and generously.

All of the idols in the Ka'abah were destroyed. There were three hundred and sixty five of them, and the Prophet, may Allaah's praise and salutations be upon him, helped the Companions break them. He also sent some of the Companions to break the idols in other places. The walls of the Ka'abah were rubbed with saffron, and all of the pictures were taken off them. Then the Messenger of Allaah made prayed inside the Ka'abah, and then went around it and touched the Black Stone. He ordered Bilaal to call the adhaan from the roof of the Ka'abah. All of the Muslims were filled with happiness to see and hear the adhaan being called openly in Makkah, after they had been exiled from the city for so long.

Several battles were fought after Makkah was opened. In the Battle of Hunayn, the tribes of Qays and Aylaan were defeated, and the Muslims gained a lot of booty from them. The Muslims also marched to meet the Roman Army at Tabuk, but the Romans got so filled with fear that they retreated and fled, and did not fight.

All of the Arabs began to enter into Islaam in great waves, until the Islamic state reached from the sea all the way into the plains of Yemen and Oman. All of the tribes came to the Prophet and pledged that they would obey him. He sent teachers and callers to all corners of the country, teaching the people about Islaam. After nearly a quarter of a century of struggling against the disbelievers, and bearing many hardships, the Messenger of Allaah had been granted a total victory by his Lord.

The Messenger of Allaah made the Farewell Hajj in the tenth year after the Hijrah. He left Madinah on the fifteenth of Dhul-Qa'dah. He delivered the famous Farewell Khutbah in the middle days of Dhul-Hijjah. When he returned, he prepared an army to fight the Romans in Palestine and Balqa'. He chose Usaamah Ibn Zayd to be the commander-in-chief. Some of the people did not want him to be the commander because he was only eighteen years old. The Prophet said, "By Allaah, he is well qualified to be the leader, and he is the most beloved of people to me after his father." His father was Zayd Ibn Haarithah, who was martyred in the battle against the Romans at Mu'tah. While the army was being prepared, the Messenger of Allaah, may Allaah's praise and salutations be upon him, fell ill, so he did not set off with them.

One night at midnight, the Prophet went with his freed slave to the graveyard, and supplicated for the dead there. Then he told his freed slave that he had been given the choice between all the treasures of this world, and living in it forever until entering into Paradise, or dying now and meeting his Lord and entering into Paradise. His freed slave wanted him to choose the treasures of the world and then Paradise, but the Messenger of Allaah replied, "No, By Allaah, I have chosen to meet with my Lord and Paradise."

His pain continued to get worse until he asked his wives to let him stay in 'Aishah's house until he got better. But he got worse, and he could not lead the people in prayers. He told them to ask Abu Bakr to lead. One time, the Prophet felt a little better and went out to the masjid. When Abu Bakr saw him he tried to move back so that he could lead, but the Messenger of Allaah sat down by his side. Abu Bakr followed the Prophet and the people followed Abu Bakr.

One day before his death he freed all of his slaves and gave away the few dinars that he possessed. When he died he did not leave any worldly possessions except a mule, some weapons, and a plot of land that he said was to be given away in the way of Allaah.

On the day he died, he moved the curtain of the door of 'Aishah's house. The Muslims were praying the Fajr Prayer behind Abu Bakr. He looked out and smiled at them. The people almost made a commotion; they were so filled with joy at the sight of the Prophet. He signaled to them to continue praying, and dropped the curtain again.

His daughter Faatimah came to see him, and when she saw how much he suffered she cried out, "Oh my father's pain." He answered her gently, trying to make her sorrow less, *{Your father will not suffer any more pain after today.}* He kept a pitcher of water by him, and he would wipe his face with it and say, *{Laa Ilaaha Ila Allaah. Surely, death has its pains.}* As the suffering got worse, he had to stop speaking.

While he was laying down, 'Aishah's brother 'Abdur-Rahmaan, came in with a miswaak (a tooth stick) in his hands. From the way the Prophet looked at it, 'Aishah knew that he wanted it, so she took it from her brother, softened it, and handed it to the Messenger of Allaah. He brushed his teeth with it. Then he looked upwards, and pointed his finger up. He was saying, *{Among those you have blessed: the Prophets, the foremost believers, martyrs, and the righteous. Oh Allaah, forgive me, show me mercy, and join me with the Rafeeq al-A'laa (The highest and best of companions).}* Then he said *{Oh Allaah, to the Rafeeq al-A'laa,}* three times. Those were the last words he spoke, and death came to him shortly after, may Allaah's praise and salutations be upon him. That was before noon on Monday, the twelfth of Rabi' al-Awwal, in the eleventh year after the Hijrah.

When Faatimah saw that he had died, she said, "My father! He has responded to the call of his Lord. His end will be in the Firdaws (the highest level) in Paradise. Oh my father! To Jibreel we leave the announcement of your death."

Sorrow and grief descended on all of the Muslims. It was the saddest, darkest day the Ummah will ever witness. Nothing has ever affected the Muslim Ummah, before or after, that is as bad as the death of our Prophet.

'Umar was so shocked that he could not believe that the Prophet, may Allaah's praise and salutations be upon him, had died. He argued hotly with anyone who said so. Then Abu Bakr came. He uncovered the Prophet's face and kissed him and cried. Then he went out to the people and said to them, "Whoever worshipped Muhammad, then Muhammad is dead. And whoever worshipped Allaah, then Allaah is Alive. He does not die." Then he recited Allaah's words, *{Muhammad is no* *more than a Messenger among you. Other Messengers have come before him. If he dies, or is killed, will you turn back on your heels? And Whoever turns back on his heels will do no harm to Allaah. And surely, Allaah will reward the grateful.* -(Surat Aal-Imraan, Ayat 144)

When the truth dawned upon 'Umar, he was so overcome with grief that he could not hold his weight, but fell to the ground.

The next day they bathed the bod yof the Messenger of Allaah while he was wearing his clothes. They shrouded him with three pieces of white cotton cloth. People prayed on him in groups without anyone leading the prayers. He was laid to rest in the spot where he died, in 'Aishah's house, on Wednesday.

May Allaah's praise and salutations be upon the chosen one, the best of Allaah's creation, our prophet Muhammad, and on his family and companions and whoever follows them in good until the Day of Resurrection. We all belong to Allaah, and to Him we return.

Hands on Learning

1. In the last lesson, as in this one, you read about the Muslim army carrying a "standard". This is the flag that armies would carry to identify them. It was held up above the people who were fighting, and the people would know that their people were by that flag. The Muslims had three standards. The main standard was white, and the Ansaar and Muhajireen each had a black one.

   Draw the Muslim's standards- or, if you like, design one for yourself. Remember not to use pictures of people or animals on them, insh'Allaah.

2. Think how amazing it must have been for the Muslims to hear the adhaan being called openly in Makkah for the very first time. Do you know the words to the adhaan? Only men can call the adhaan, but women should know it as well, because the Messenger of Allaah, may Allaah's praise and salutations be upon him, told us to repeat after the one who is calling the prayer. Also, one of the best times to supplicate to Allaah is in between the adhaan and the iqaama. Learn the call to prayer and what you should say after each thing the caller says, insh'Allaah. And remember to supplicate after you hear the adhaan for whatever it is you want or need from Allaah.

Allaahu Akbar (Allaah is Most Great)

Allaahu Akbar (Allaah is Most Great)

Allaahu Akbar (Allaah is Most Great)

Allaahu Akbar (Allaah is Most Great)

Ashshadu an la ilaaha ila Allaah (I testify that there is no god worthy of worship but Allaah)

Ashshadu an la ilaaha ila Allaah (I testify that there is no god worthy of worship but Allaah)

Ashshadu ana Muhammadan RasoolAllaah (I testify that Muhammad is the Messenger of Allaah)

Ashshadu ana Muhammadan RasoolAllaah (I testify that Muhammad is the Messenger of Allaah)

Hiyya ila as-Salaat (Come to the prayer)

Hiyya ila as-Salaat (Come to the prayer)

Hiyya ila al-Falaah (Come to Success)

Hiyya ila al-Falaah (Come to Success)

Allaahu Akbar (Allaah is Most Great)

Allaahu Akbar (Allaah is Most Great)

La Ilaaha ila Allaah (There is no god worthy of worship except Allaah)

It is related in al-Bukhaari and Muslim that one should repeat what the caller of the adhaan says, except when he says, Hiyyal as-Salaat and Hiyyal al-Falaah. At that time, one should say,

"la hawla wa la quwatta ila billah"

There is no power Nor might except with Allaah

3. Allaah offered the Messenger of Allaah, may Allaah's praise and salutations be upon him, the choice between all the treasures in this world, and living in it forever until he went to Paradise, or dying at that time and meeting his Lord and entering Paradise. He chose to not take the treasures of this world- he wanted to meet his Lord and enter Paradise.

Think of all the treasures of this world. What do you think of first? Do you think of things like gold and jewels and money and cars? Also, often the true things of value are not things we can hold onto even in this world. Think about your family. Think about your best friends. Think about your favorite place to sit and look at the trees. All of these things are treasures as well.

These are all passing things- while we do enjoy them in this life, and they are permissible for us, they are not important before Allaah. Allaah looks into our hearts and sees what is in them of faith and goodness, and this is how we are judged, alhamdulillah.

Make a list of all of the treasures of this life that you can think of. Then think about what Allaah will look at on the Day of Judgment. Think of how you want to go to Paradise someday. Make a list of as many things as you can think of that you can do to please Allaah and earn Jennah. When you are finished, look at the two lists, and remember that the things that please Allaah are worth much much more than the worldly things that you could want. Ask Allaah to help you to do those things which please Him.

Day 26:
The Letter ه: الهمة العالية
(*al-Hamat al-'Aaliyah*)
(the high aspirations)

The Prophet, may Allaah's praise and salutations be upon him, has set the highest example for having high aspirations in the month of Ramadhaan and especially in the last ten days.

'Aishah, may Allaah be pleased with her, narrated, *{When the last ten days of Ramadhaan came the Prophet, may Allaah's praise and salutations be upon him, would gird up his loins and stay awake at night (to pray) and wake up his family (to pray with him).}* (al-Bukhaari)

One of the best examples of the high aspirations of the Messenger, may Allaah's praise and salutations be upon him, and his noble Companions, may Allaah be pleased with all of them, is their leaving for jihaad in the way of Allaah for the first time in Islaam for the Greater Battle of Badr during the day in Ramadhaan. So where are we compared to them, when all manners of comfort are made easy for us- which they could not even have imagined?! Despite this, we slack off in regards to performing many good deeds and we lean towards laziness and apathy.

We are those who become weary of our normal work and angry about studying during Ramadhaan despite the fact that comfort is made easy for us in the places of work and school, and even in regards to transportation.

And to Allaah we must complain about our state.

Further Points of Benefit

Mash'Allaah, this is something to contemplate when we complain of the heat, as we sit in air conditioning- or complain of the food, as several dishes are arrayed before us- or complain of the difficulty of making 'Umrah, as we sit in a comfortable plane or hotel room. This is the case with so many of our acts of worship nowadays. We can perform them in relative comfort and still we sometimes feel overburdened or oppressed by them. Think of the Prophet, may Allaah's praise and salutations be upon him, and his Companions, fasting in the heat of a Saudi Arabian summer. They would pour water over their heads to find some relief. Most of us, if we do not have air conditioners, at least have fans, mash'Allaah, and we can break our fast with cold water and cool down quickly. Think about Hajj and 'Umrah at the time of the Prophet and afterwards, until only recently, mash'Allaah. People would leave their homes for Hajj, knowing that they would be gone weeks, months, even years- and knowing that their return home was uncertain at best, mash'Allaah.

Mash'Allaah, how can we complain when we can perform our acts of worship in relative comfort and ease?

Sheikh Saalih Fauzaan, may Allaah preserve him, says, concerning the levels of the people,

"Allaah, the Most High, says,

Then We gave the Book (the Qur'aan) as inheritance to such of Our slaves whom We chose (the followers of Muhammad). Then of them are some who wrong their own selves, and of them are some who follow a middle course, and of them are some who are, by Allaah's Leave, foremost in good deeds. That (inheritance of the Qur'aan) – that is indeed the great Grace. 'Adn (Eden) Paradise (everlasting Gardens) will they enter, therein will they be adorned with bracelets of gold and pearls, and their garments therein will be of silk.-(Surat al-Faatir, Ayat 32-33)

Allaah, the Most High, made clear in these verses that He gave this Great Qur'aan to those whom He chose- and they are this 'Ummah. And this 'Ummah is the best of all the nations, as Allaah, Glorified and Exalted, says,

You (true believers) are the best of peoples ever raised up for mankind...-(Surat aal-'Imraan, From Ayat 110)

And He, the Most High, also says,

Thus We have made you [true believers], a just (and the best) nation...-(Surat al-Baqarah, From Ayat 143) Meaning, the most just and the best. *"that you will be witnesses over mankind and the Messenger (Muhammad) will be a witness over you."*-(Surat al-Baqarah, From Ayat 143)

This verse is a proof of the virtue of the Ummah of Muhammad, and that Allaah has chosen those of us who have the characteristics of those who follow the Sunnah from this Ummah of believing in Allaah and His Messenger and performing good deeds and leaving off prohibited deeds. As for he who only attributes himself to them (i.e. calls himself Muslim but does not necessarily fulfill the conditions of Islaam), and then acts contrarily to Islaam and ignores the proofs of the Book and the Sunnah, then his attribution of himself to them will not benefit him. Only the one who has the characteristics of this Ummah and is upright upon its belief system, worship, and the correct methodology- then he is truly from this Ummah.

And the Ummah is divided into three types of people:

1. The one who wrongs himself; and he is the one who does evil deeds without them reaching the level of associating others with Allaah.

2. Some of them are muqtasid- and he is the one who performs that which is obligatory and leaves off that which is prohibited, but he may do some of that which is disliked by Allaah and leave off some of that which is recommended.

3. And from them is the one who hastens to perform righteous actions, and this is the highest of the three levels. Allaah, the Most High, says,

And the foremost ones [(in Islaam and in performing righteous deeds)] will be foremost (in Paradise). These will be the nearest (to Allaah). In the Gardens of Delight (Paradise).-(Surat al-Waa'qiah, Ayats 10-12)

And Allaah has informed us that the people from all three of these categories are all in Paradise. And the one who hastens to good deeds is he who performs all that is obligatory and recommended, and abandons all that is forbidden of disliked, and also some of what is allowed (but is he has doubt about it) out of fear that it will be disliked.

And Allaah, Glorified and Exalted, has mentioned that all three of these groups will eventually enter Paradise. The ones who hasten to do good will enter Paradise without reckoning. Those who are muqtasid will have an easy reckoning. And those who wrong themselves will be those who argue during the Reckoning, and he is under the will of Allaah, Mighty and Majestic; if He so wills, then He forgives him, and if He so wills then he punishes him in regards to his sins, and then he enters Paradise after that." (From "Majaalis Shahr Ramadhaan al-Mubaarak wa Itihaaf ahl Eemaan bi Duroos Shahr Ramadhaan" Pages 94-95)

So strive, my sister, to be of those who will enter Paradise with no reckoning, and with Allaah is the success.

Family Time

The Story of the Prophet Muhammad, Part 4

No matter how much we write about the characteristics of our Prophet, may Allaah's praise and salutations be upon him, we cannot fulfill his rights. We could run the ink dry in our pens, and use up all of our paper, and we would not have finished writing about the wonderful character, the good manners, the beautiful attributes, and the generous actions of the Messenger of Allaah. He is Muhammad ibn Abdullah, and he was sent to all of creation as a mercy. Allaah chose this prophet and favored him over all other people. The Messenger of Allaah is the best of the children of Aadam. He is the one who will be allowed to intercede for his Ummah on the Day of Resurrection.

Some Characteristics of the Prophet

The Messenger of Allaah had the best of manners. His manners were the Qur'aan. There is not a single good thing mentioned in the Qur'aan except that he possessed it. He used to receive everyone with a smiling face, and he would speak gently to even the worst of people. He never shouted, and never responded to evil with evil. If someone said something bad to him, he would forgive them. He forbade the believers from cursing anyone. He never hit anyone, not a woman, a servant or an animal, except when he was fighting for the sake of Allaah. He never said "No" when he was asked for something. He would play with the children and kiss them.

He was the most courageous of people. One day, the people in Madinah were awakened at night by a huge noise. They all rushed out of their houses afraid. When they came out, they found that the Prophet had already gone all alone to see what was happening. He calmed them down, and said to them, "Don't worry, don't worry." The people used to seek his shelter on the battlefield because of his courage and fearlessness.

He was gentle and kind to the people. He, may Allaah's praise and salutations be upon him, said, *{Gentleness was never used in a matter except that it improved it, and it was never left out of anything without spoiling it.}*

He was very kind towards children. He used to take his children and kiss them. One day, he kissed his grandson al-Hasan. A man said to him, "I have ten children and I have never kissed any of them." The Messenger of Allaah looked at him and said, *{Whoever does not show mercy is not shown mercy himself.}* Sometimes, when he was praying, he would hear a baby crying, so he would shorten his prayer so that its mother could take it and soothe it.

He was also kind to his wives and family. He ordered the Muslims to treat their wives with kindness. When he would enter his house, he would help them with the housework. He was never above serving himself and others. He never complained about the food, even if he did not like it. If he wanted it, he ate it, and if he did not want it then he left it.

He was kind to all the weak people. He told the believers to treat their servants and slaves like their brothers. He told them to share their food with them and not to strike them. He said that anyone who hit his slave should free him to make up for it.

Even when the Messenger of Allaah was angry, he did not show it. He forgave all those who did evil to him. On the day of Uhud, the disbelievers cut his face and broke his tooth. He wiped off the blood that was running down his face, saying, *{Oh Allaah, forgive my people! Verily they do not know.}* One day, a Bedouin came and grabbed hold of the Messenger of Allaah's cloak. He pulled on it so hard that it left marks on the Prophet's neck, and said, "Oh Muhammad! Give me some of the money that Allaah has given you!" The Messenger of Allaah, may Allaah's praise and salutations be upon him, turned and smiled, and gave him what he asked for. He did not get upset with the man for hurting him and tugging on his clothes.

He was the most patient of people. He was patient through all of the hardships and trials that came to him from the Quraysh. He was patient through all of the time he was calling to Islaam, for twenty-three years. He never got tired or left off calling to Islaam.

He did not care for the things of this world. He and his family would sometimes go for two months without being able to eat anything but dates and water. Sometimes he would get so hungry that he would have to tie his stomach up with a rock to ease the pains. One day, he was laying on a rough mat that left marks on him where he had laid on it. Umar ibn Al-Khattab saw the marks and said, "Oh Prophet of Allaah, why don't you use a different bed than this?" The Messenger of Allaah replied, *{What do I have to do with this world?}*

The Messenger of Allaah was extremely shy and modest. He said, *{Modesty is part of Faith.}*

He was the most aware and afraid of his Lord. He would stand in prayer at night until his feet were swollen. He would cry while he was praying, and fast for many days at a time. He did all this even though Allaah had forgiven all of his sins. He, may Allaah's praise and salutations be upon him, said, {*Should I not be a grateful slave?*}

The Messenger of Allaah, may Allaah's praise and salutations be upon him, was the most handsome of people. He was neither tall nor short, but in between the two. His face was like the sun or the moon, and when he was happy, it would light up. He had hair that reached his ear lobes, dark eyes, and long eyelashes. He had a thick beard and thick eyebrows. He never talked without a good reason. He spoke clearly and precisely. He had all of the most beautiful qualities. This is because Allaah is the one who trained him, and said about him, ❴*Surely, you are on an exalted (standard) of conduct.*❵"-(Surat Al-Qalam, Ayaat 4)

The Mothers of the Believers:

He had eleven wives, and at the time of his death, he was married to nine of them.

1. Khadijah Bint Khuwaylid: She was his first wife. He did not marry any other wives while she was alive. He had six children from her: al-Qaasim, 'Abdullaah, Zaynab, Ruqayyah, Umm Kalthoum, and Fatimah.

2. Sawdah Bint Zam'ah: She was an early believer, and she made hijrah to Abyssinia along with her first husband, Sakraan. When they returned to Makkah, he died. The prophet married her so that her family could not take her and torment her for being a Muslim.

3. 'Aishah Bint Abi Bakr: She was the daughter of the Prophet's dearest friend, Abu Bakr. She was dear to the prophet, and she was very smart and knowledgeable.

4. Hafsah Bint 'Umar: She was the daughter of the second Khalifah, 'Umar ibn Khattaab. She had first been married to Khunays ibn Hudhaafah, but he died in from the wounds he received fighting in the battle of Uhud. She used to fast often and stand the night in prayers.

5. Zaynab Bint Khuzaymah: Two of her husbands were martyred, before the Prophet married her. She was known as the Mother of the Poor, because she was so kind and generous to them. She died eight months after the Prophet married her.

6. Umm Salamah: She was a very brave and courageous woman. She made hijrah to Abyssinia and then to Madinah with her husband, Abu Salamah. He died of the wounds he received while fighting at Uhud. Then the Messenger of Allaah married her and took care of her four children from Abu Salamah.

7. Juwayriyyah Bint Haarith: She was taken a prisoner in the battle of Mustaliq. The Prophet gave her the choice between returning her to her people, or freeing her and marrying her. She chose the Prophet. All of the Muslims set free their captives that were from her tribe, because they were now related to the Messenger of Allaah through marriage.

8. Zaynab Bint Jahsh: She was first married to Zayd ibn Haarithah, who was the Prophet's freed slave and adopted son before Allaah stopped adoption. After he divorced her, Allaah, from above the seven heavens, married her to the Messenger of Allaah.

9. Umm Habibah Bint Abu Sufyaan: She migrated with her husband, 'Ubaydullah ibn Jahsh, to Abyssinia. When they arrived, her husband turned Christian so she left him. She was married to the Prophet while she was still in Abyssinia. She had a daughter from her first husband named Habibah.

10. Safiyyah Bint Huyayy: She was taken prisoner when the Jews of Khaybar were defeated. She accepted Islaam, and the Messenger of Allaah bought her, freed her, and married her.

11. Maymunah Bint Haarith: She was fearful of Allaah, and the most charitable towards her relatives. When the Prophet's uncle, 'Abbaas, asked him to marry her, he accepted because of her good character.

12. The Messenger of Allaah also had a slave girl named Maariyah. He had a son from her named Ibraahim. He died before he was weaned.

The Children of the Prophet:

All of the Prophet's sons died as children. His daughters however, grew up to be married and have children. All of his daughters died before him except Faatimah.

1. His oldest daughter, Zaynab, was married to her cousin, Abul-Aas ibn Ar-Rabee'. She had a son, 'Ali, who died when he was a child, and a daughter, Umaamah. The Messenger of Allaah used to carry Umaamah while he was praying, and he said that she was the dearest of people to him.

2. Ruqayyah was married to 'Uthmaan Ibn Affaan, and she had 'Abdullaah, who died when he was six years old.

3. Umm Kalthoum was married to' Uthmaan after her sister died. 'Uthmaan was called Dhun-Nurayn, or the One with the Two Lights, because he was married to two of the Prophet's daughters.

4. Faatimah was married to 'Ali ibn Abi Taalib. She looked like the Prophet, and even walked like him. She had al-Hasan, al-Husayn, Zaynab, and Umm Kalthoum. The Messenger of Allaah used to love his grandchildren very much. He said that al-Hasan and al-Husayn would be the leaders of the youth in Paradise.

Hands on Learning

1. Make the page for Muhammad in your prophet book. Write the prophet's name with hollow letters and color them in as you like. Draw a little picture or write a verse from the Qur'aan from the story to remind you of who they were and what they did.

2. Show your pages to someone in your family, or to a friend, and tell them all that you can remember about the story of Muhammad.

3. Make a list of the characteristics of the Prophet Muhammad, may Allaah's praise and salutations be upon him. Look at how balanced he was- he was gentle and kind, but when he was in battle he was a courageous warrior. It is important in our lives to be balanced like this, and he is the best example for us concerning it. Think about the characteristics you wrote down, and try to work on these things within yourself, insh'Allaah.

4. Have you ever seen a family tree? A family tree is a diagram that shows how people are related to each other. Sometimes it has several generations in it, but sometimes it is only grandparents, parents, and the children. Ask your parents to help you make a family tree for the Messenger of Allaah, may Allaah's praise and salutations be upon him. Just go back to the first lesson about him in this series, and see who his grandfather was. Begin with his grandfather, then his parents, then him and his wives, and then his children, and then his grandchildren. If you enjoy doing this, try making one for your own family, insh'Allaah. You can find examples of family trees in books and on the internet, insh'Allaah- your parents can help you! If you like, why not try making a family tree for yourself, showing you and your own family!

Day 27:
The Letter و: وداع رمضان
(*Wadaa' Ramadhaan*)
(saying farewell to Ramadhaan)

When Ramadhaan begins to depart our minds are filled with grief and sadness and our eyes give forth tears of sadness and pain due to leaving the month of Ramadhaan.

This is because we do not know whether it is written for us to ever see Ramadhaan again, or whether this will be the final parting.

So I advise you, oh my beloved sister, to exert yourself in good works until the last minute in the month.

Remember that the pious predecessors would supplicate to Allaah for six months to bring them Ramadhaan, and then supplicate for another six months for their works to be accepted.

And from their supplications was "Oh Allaah, make me submit to Ramadhaan and make it peaceful for me, and accept it from me with approval."

So we ask Allaah that this month end with His forgiveness and our release from the Fire, and that He return it to us for many years and a lengthy time, and that the Muslim Ummah will become dressed in glory, dominion and victory.

Further Points of Benefit

The advent of Ramadhaan is a joyous occasion, as we look forward to this month of blessings. The leaving of the month should occasion in us the opposite- we should feel sad that this blessed month is leaving us, along with the specific benefits that we can only experience during Ramadhaan. But this should not be an occasion for us to feel as though we are off the hook and no longer need to perform good deeds and strive in our worship of Allaah, the Most High. Indeed, this should be a year-round endeavor; always we should be looking for ways to please our Lord and increase in worship and remembrance of Him. So often people are lazy or slack off during most of the year, and then when Ramadhaan comes they begin to increase in good deeds, read more Qur'aan, and fast. While it is good that they do this during Ramadhaan, they should see the month as a starting point- an opportunity to establish good deeds that benefit them in this life and the Hereafter when performed consistently. Indeed the consistent act is from the best of acts, alhamdulillah. May Allaah make us steadfast and consistent in striving for His pleasure.

Sheikh Saalih Fauzaan, may Allaah preserve him, says,

"Oh servants of Allaah: a short while ago you were greeting the blessed of Ramadhaan; and today you are bidding farewell to it. And it will bear witness to Allaah as to what your deeds were within it. So good tidings for he whom the month of Ramadhaan bears witness to Allaah with good concerning him, and intercedes for him for the good deeds he performed in it that he will enter Paradise and be released from the Fire. And woe to him of whom it complains to Allaah of his evil deeds, and complains of his laziness and wasting of time; so end this month with a good ending, for verily deeds are known by their end results. So whoever performed good deeds in this month, then he should finish it with good deeds; and whoever did evil deeds than he should hurry to repentance and do good deeds in what is left for him of Ramadhaan. So finish it with good, and continue on with the good deeds which you perform in the remainder of the month. As the Lord of the Months is One, and He knows what you are doing and witnesses all that you do. He has commanded you to perform good deeds and obey Him throughout all of your life. And so whoever worships the month of Ramadhaan, then it has finished and ended. And whoever worships Allaah, then Allaah is Eternally Living and will never die. So he should continue his worship at all times; unlike those who worship Allaah in Ramadhaan only. So they pay much attention to their prayers and attending the masjids and reciting Qur'aan and giving charity from their wealth- then when Ramadhaan finishes, they become tired of good deeds, and lazy, and sometimes do not even go to Juma'ah, not to mention the daily congregational prayer- so they destroy that which they have built and obliterate what they have done, and it is as if they believe that their good deeds in Ramadhaan make up for what they do in the rest of the year from evil deeds and terrible sins and abandoning obligations and doing that which is prohibited. And they do not know that the expiation of sins during Ramadhaan is only if they abandon major and destructive sins.

"If you avoid the great sins which you are forbidden to do, We shall expiate from you your (small) sins, and admit you to a Noble Entrance (i.e. Paradise)."-(Surat an-Nisaa', Ayat 31)

...and some of the Pious Predecessors were asked about people who exert themselves in good deeds during Ramadhaan, and then when it is finished they perform evil deeds and become as one who is lost. They replied, "How evil are people who do not know Allaah except during Ramadhaan!" Yes! Because whoever truly knows Allaah fears Him at all times." (From "Majaalis Shahr Ramadhaan al-Mubaarak wa Itihaaf ahl Eemaan bi Duroos Shahr Ramadhaan" Pages 211-212)

Family Time

Alhamdulillah, we hope and pray that in this blessed month of Ramadhaan you have learned more about those who were chosen by Allaah to be His prophets and messengers and to spread the message of tawheed across the earth. We were not able to tell you about all the prophets and messengers, nor were we able to tell you everything about each one, mash'Allaah. You should take it upon yourself to strive to learn more about them from the Qur'aan and other authentic sources, because they are the best examples for you to follow in your life, insh'Allaah.

Remember Ibraaheem and the sun, moon and stars? He first said to his people that he would worship those things- then as he saw that they all went away with time, he reaffirmed that he truly only worshipped Allaah, the Most High, and nothing else- as Allaah will never die and go away, alhamdulillah. He did not truly worship those other things, but he was trying to teach his people and show them how foolish they were.

Remember 'Umar, after the Messenger of Allaah, may Allaah's praise and salutations be upon him, died? He did not want to believe that he had truly died, he loved him so much. But what did Abu Bakr say? He said, ""Whoever worshipped Muhammad, then Muhammad is dead. And whoever worshipped Allaah, then Allaah is Alive. He does not die." Like the sun and the moon and the stars, people live on the earth for a certain time decreed by Allaah, and then they die.

Allaah was never born, and Allaah will never die. He is the Ever-Living, the Eternal. There is nothing that Allaah cannot do. He sent us the prophets and the messengers because He loves us and wants us to be guided to success in this life and the next. It is from His mercy that He sends Books, and He chooses righteous men to guide and lead us- the prophets and messengers, alhamdulillah.

So look at the prophets and messengers who you have learned about this month. Think of their patience- Nuh calling his people for hundreds of years, Ayoob with his illness, Ya'qub with thinking that he had lost his beloved Yusuf, Yusuf wrongly accused and put in prison, Muhammad calling to the people in Makkah and being persecuted by the Quraysh. Think of their bravery- Ibraaheem standing before the people after he had broken their idols, and being cast into a fire, Daawud fighting Jalut, who was much older and larger than him and more skilled in battle, Moosa and Haarun facing the magicians of Fir'awn. Think of their faith, their trust in Allaah, and their love for their people. Alhamdulillah, they are guides for us through what they taught us with their speech, as well as with their actions.

Insh'Allaah, look through your prophet book at least once a month, and remember the stories of each of these pious, good men. Tell other people about them and what they did. Tell them about Allaah, and about Islaam, and about being good. Do your best to learn more about Islaam, and to make Islaam a part of your life. Be brave, patient, strong, and good like these prophets and messengers were. Look to them, and to the stories of pious people other than them like the Companions of the Messenger of Allaah, may Allaah's praise and salutations be upon him, and remember that these were real people- they were born and died and loved and lived just like you and I- and do your best to model your character after theirs.

And always, always remember that Allaah, the Most High, is always there for you with His knowledge, and He is always ready to forgive our sins if we repent to Him, and He wants what is best for you, and will listen to you anytime you call on Him.

And Allaah knows best.

Day 28:

The Letter ي: يمن الحسنة

(*Yumn al-Hasana*)

(the blessings of good deeds)

Verily from the blessings of good deeds is that it is easy to repeat a good deed after one has performed it once.

Sheikh al-Islaam ibn Taymiyyah, may Allaah have mercy upon him, mentioned that the second good deed may increase the reward of the first good deed.

So do not, oh my sister, make the end of Ramadhaan the end of your good deeds and obedience to Allaah.

Hasten, may Allaah protect and watch over you, to fast the voluntary fasts outside of Ramadhaan, such as fasting the six days of Shawwal after making up any missed days. Also, take care to make the night prayer and recite the Noble Qur'aan and give charity and be pious and perform good deeds for the rest of your life.

In ending, I ask Allaah, Mighty and Majestic, that our last works and times be good.

May Allaah accept from me and you good deeds.

Further Points of Benefit

Sheikh Saalih Fauzaan, may Allaah preserve him, says,

"Oh people! Fear Allaah, the Most High, and contemplate the speed with which days and nights pass. And remember that you will soon leave on a journey from this world; so perform good deeds in order to provide for the journey. For the month of Ramadhaan has come with its good and blessings, and you lived through it; and now it has left and travelled quickly to bear witness to its Lord in favor of whoever knew its worth and benefitted from its good with obedience, and to testify against he who did not know its virtue and evilly wasted it. So each of us must take account of what he put forward in this month. So whoever put forward good should thank Allaah for it, and ask Him to accept it and allow him to continue on obedience for the rest of his life. And whoever was lazy during it should repent to Allaah and begin a new life and use his time wisely to make up for the life which he lost in heedlessness and evil deeds. So Allaah may expiate his former deeds, and enable him to do good for the rest of his life…

…and Jibreel told the Prophet, may Allaah's praise and salutations be upon him, { *"And whoever experienced Ramadhaan and was not forgiven, then he is far removed from Allaah. Say Ameen." So the Prophet, may Allaah's praise and salutations be upon him, said, "Ameen."*} (al-Bukhaari in "al-Adab al-Mufrad" (38), Muslim (1631) and other than them)" (From "Majaalis Shahr Ramadhaan al-Mubaarak wa Itihaaf ahl Eemaan bi Duroos Shahr Ramadhaan" Pages 219-221)

Family Time

Special Ramadhaan Meal Number Four

Last week we cooked and ate some food from Yemen. This week we are going to do something a little different. We are going to try dishes from a few different Muslim countries, instead of just choosing one country, since this is the last special Ramadhaan meal we are cooking. Again, remember that it is the Sunnah to break your fast with dates and water, so do that first, and then eat your meal later, insh'Allaah.

There are Muslims all over the world. If you can think of a country, there are most likely going to be Muslims in it, alhamdulillah. There are Muslims in the Middle East, like Saudi Arabia and Yemen. There are Muslims in Malaysia and Indonesia. There are Muslims in Africa and South America. There are Muslims in France, England and Germany. There are Muslims in Russia. There are Muslims in Australia. There are Muslims in China. There are Muslims in America. Islaam is the truth, and it is a complete way of life. Muslims can be any color, any race, and from any country. They can be male or female, young or old, short or tall, fat or thin, white or brown. Anyone can become Muslim- basically all they have to do is to believe in and worship Allaah alone, and affirm that Muhammad is His last and final Messenger, and to follow the religion of Islaam in their hearts, on their tongues, and with their limbs.

Try to find the countries that these foods are from on a map of the world, insh'Allaah. As you do it, think about there being Muslims in so many different places, all around the world, alhamdulilaah!

Piaju (Onion Lentil Snack- from Bangladesh)
Soak in cold water for one hour:

1 lb red lentils (or brown will work as well)

Drain them, and blend them in the blender

Add:

2 onions, finely chopped

1 tsp salt

½ tsp black pepper

1-2 hot peppers, seeds removed, finely chopped (optional)

1 tbsp of cilantro, finely diced, or 1 tsp ground coriander

Mix the ingredients well. Drop by the spoonful into heated oil. Fry until golden brown, and serve while still warm.

Tomatoes Vinaigrette (Tomatoes in an Oil and Vinegar Dressing- France)

Slice and place in an overlapping pattern on a pretty serving dish:

tomatoes

cucumbers

Combine in a small bowl: ½ cup chopped, fresh parsley

3 cloves of garlic, finely minced

3 tbsp olive oil (or sunflower)

3 tbsp apple cider vinegar

Salt and pepper to taste

Spoon the dressing over the vegetables and let stand for at least one hour. Make sure you spoon the dressing over the vegetables a few times to help blend the flavors. Chill in the fridge if you like, and serve.

Sukuma Wike (African greens- Kenya)

In a small amount of water, briefly cook, just until tender:

1 bunch of kale or spinach or other greens

1 finely chopped green pepper

Brown in a little oil:

1 large onion, thinly sliced

Add and fry until the oil separates:

2 Tbsp tomato paste

2 cloves of garlic, crushed

Add the cooked greens and mix thoroughly.

Maraq (Somali stew- Somalia)

In a large saucepan, sauté

1 ½ onions, finely chopped

Add and brown:

1 lb stewing or ground beef

Add:

3 large tomatoes, chopped

Cook for about ten minutes, stirring occasionally

Add:

1 cup squash, cubed (can be zucchini or winter squash)

¾ cup okra, sliced

3 carrots, sliced

½ cup tomato paste

1 cup water

Cook on high for 15 minutes

Add:

2 medium potatoes, cubed

1 large green pepper, chopped

1 tbsp salt

½ tsp black pepper

1 tbsp ground cumin (or curry powder)

3 cloves of garlic, minced or crushed

2 hot peppers, seeds removed, diced (optional)

1 cup of water (or enough to make it a thick stew consistency)

Simmer until the meat is done and the vegetables are tender.

Remove from heat and add:

½ cup cilantro, chopped finely (optional)

Serve with bread or rice.

Dessert:

Ka'kat at-Tamr (Date Cake- from Saudi Arabia)
Ingredients:

For the cake:

½ pound dried dates, pitted and coarsely chopped

7 tbsp softened butter, plus extra for the dish

1 cup white sugar

1 ¾ cup flour

1 tsp baking powder

1 tsp baking soda

1 tsp vanilla extract

1 beaten egg

For the topping:

¾ cup brown sugar

6 tbsp butter

5 tbsp heavy cream

1. Place the dates in a glass or metal bowl. Bring 1 cup of water to the boil, pour it over the dates, and set them aside until they are plumped up. Do not drain off the water.

2. Preheat the oven to 375 degrees. Grease a 7 by 11 inch baking pan with the extra butter

3. Cream the butter and sugar together thoroughly, until fluffy. You can use a hand held mixer for this or do it by hand. Sift the flour and baking powder together and set aside. Add the vanilla and baking soda to the bowl of dates and their soaking water and stir well.

4. Add the egg and a third of the flour/baking powder mixture to the creamed butter and sugar, and beat well for a couple of minutes. Add the remaining flour gradually, beating all the while, until it is all in the batter. Add the date mixture and beat until well blended.

5. Pour the batter into the baking dish and bake until the cake springs back up when touched lightly on the top, or when a toothpick inserted in the middle comes out clean. This should take about 30 minutes. Remove from the oven.

6. Preheat the broiler in the oven. Using a fork, poke holes all over the top of the cake.

7. Prepare the topping: Combine all the ingredients in a saucepan and cook over medium heat, stirring constantly, until it bubbles slightly- about 3 minutes or so. Pour this over the surface of the baked cake, then put the cake under the broiler for about 30 seconds, until the surface begins to bubble. Remove the dish from oven, let it cool a little, and cut into squares.

This is really good with ice cream, but that isn't the traditional way to eat it!

Day 29:

A Few Words Concerning the 'Eid from Sheikh Saalih Fauzaan, may Allaah preserve him

The Sheikh, may Allaah preserve him, said, "And from that which Allaah has legislated for you after this blessed month has ended is the Eid prayer, thanking Allaah for allowing you to fulfill the obligation of fasting. As Allaah, the Most High, has likewise legislated the prayer on Eid al-Adha in order to thank Allaah for allowing you to fulfill the obligation of Hajj. And these are the two Eids of the people of Islaam. It has been narrated in an authentic narration from the Prophet, may Allaah's praise and salutations be upon him, that when he came to Medina the people of Medina had two days in which they would play and celebrate. So he, may Allaah's praise and salutations be upon him, said, *{ Allaah has substituted for you other ones (Eids) which are better than these: Eid al-Adha and Eid al-Fitr. }* (Abu Daawud (1134) and other than him) So it is not permissible to have more holidays than these two Eids, such as birthdays and national holidays- because they are holidays of ignorance, whether they are called "holidays" or "remembrances" or days or weeks or years.

And the Eid of the people of Islaam was called "Eid" because it returns and is repeated every year with happiness and joy due to that which Allaah has made easy from fasting and Hajj- which are two pillars of the pillars of Islaam…

And the Prophet, may Allaah's praise and salutations be upon him, commanded everyone to attend the Eid prayer, including the women. So it is the Sunnah for the women to attend, without perfuming themselves or wearing decorative clothing, and without mixing with the men…

And going out to the Eid prayer is manifesting one's Islaam and is a sign from the outward signs (that one is a Muslim). So take care to attend it, may Allaah have mercy on you, as it is from that which prefects and completes this blessed month. Also take care to have khushoo (concentration) in your prayer, and to lower your gaze, and to not allow your clothing to drag on the ground (for the men). Also, make sure to keep your tongue away from evil or lying speech, and your hearing from listening to he said and he said, and music. Keep away from the parties of idle talk and entertainment and aimless amusement which some of the ignorant people hold.

For obedience to Allaah should be followed with obedience, instead of that which contradicts or opposes it. And this is the reason that the Prophet, may Allaah's praise and salutations be upon him, legislated following the fast of Ramadhaan with fasting six days of Shawwal. And Imaam Muslim narrated that the Prophet, may Allaah's praise and salutations be upon him, said *{Whoever fasted Ramadhaan and followed it with six days of Shawwal, then it is as if he has fasted forever. }* (Muslim (1164)) Meaning, in reward, because the reward for a good deed is multiplied ten times.

So Ramadhaan is as ten months, and the six days of Shawwal are as two months. And as this is the number of months in the year, it is as if the Muslim has fasted them all. So take care, may Allaah have mercy upon you, to fast these six days, so as to obtain this great reward.

(From "Majaalis Shahr Ramadhaan al-Mubaarak wa Itihaaf ahl Eemaan bi Duroos Shahr Ramadhaan" Pages 214-215)

The Nakhlah Educational Series: Mission and Methodology

Mission

The Purpose of the 'Nakhlah Educational Series' is to contribute to the present knowledge based efforts which enable Muslim individuals, families, and communities to understand and learn Islaam and then to develop within and truly live Islaam. Our commitment and goal is to contribute beneficial publications and works that:

Firstly, reflect the priority, message and methodology of all the prophets and messengers sent to humanity, meaning that single revealed message which embodies the very purpose of life, and of human creation. As Allaah the Most High has said,

⟨ *We sent a Messenger to every nation ordering them that they should worship Allaah alone, obey Him and make their worship purely for Him, and that they should avoid everything worshipped besides Allaah. So from them there were those whom Allaah guided to His religion, and there were those who were unbelievers for whom misguidance was ordained. So travel through the land and see the destruction that befell those who denied the Messengers and disbelieved.*⟩—(Surah an-Nahl: 36)

Sheikh Rabee'a ibn Haadee al-Madkhalee in his work entitled, '*The Methodology of the Prophets in Calling to Allaah, That is the Way of Wisdom and Intelligence.*' explains the essential, enduring message of all the prophets:

"*So what was the message which these noble, chosen men, may Allaah's praises and salutations of peace be upon them all, brought to their people? Indeed their mission encompassed every matter of good and distanced and restrained every matter of evil. They brought forth to mankind everything needed for their well-being and happiness in this world and the Hereafter. There is nothing good except that they guided the people towards it, and nothing evil except that they warned the people against it. …*

This was the message found with all of the Messengers; that they should guide to every good and warn against every evil. However where did they start, what did they begin with and what did they concentrate upon? There are a number of essentials, basic principles, and fundamentals which all their calls were founded upon, and which were the starting point for calling the people to Allaah. These fundamental points and principles are: 1. The worship of Allaah alone without any associates 2. The sending of prophets to guide creation 3. The belief in the resurrection and the life of the Hereafter

These three principles are the area of commonality and unity within their calls, and stand as the fundamental principles which they were established upon. These principles are given the greatest importance in the Qur'an and are fully explained in it. They are also its most important purpose upon which it centers and which it continually mentions. It further quotes intellectual and observable proofs for them in all its chapters as well as within most of its accounts of previous nations and given examples. This is known to those who have full understanding, and are able to consider carefully and comprehend well. All the Books revealed by Allaah have given great importance to these points and all of the various revealed laws of guidance are agreed upon them. And the most important and sublime of these three principles, and the most fundamental of them all is directing one's worship only towards Allaah alone, the Blessed and the Most High."

Today one finds that there are indeed many paths, groups, and organizations apparently presenting themselves as representing Islaam, which struggle to put forth an outwardly pleasing appearance to the general Muslims; but when their methods are placed upon the precise scale of conforming to priorities and methodology of the message of the prophets sent by Allaah, they can only be recognized as deficient paths- not simply in practice but in principle- leading not to success but rather only to inevitable failure. As Sheikh Saaleh al-Fauzaan, may Allaah preserve him, states in his introduction to the same above mentioned work on the methodology of all the prophets,

"So whichever call is not built upon these foundations, and whatever methodology is not from the methodology of the Messengers - then it will be frustrated and fail, and it will be effort and toil without any benefit. The clearest proofs of this are those present day groups and organizations which set out a methodology and program for themselves and their efforts of calling the people to Islaam which is different from the methodology of the Messengers. These groups have neglected the importance of the people having the correct belief and creed - except for a very few of them - and instead call for the correction of side-issues."

There can be no true success in any form for us as individuals, families, or larger communities without making the encompassing worship of Allaah alone, with no partners or associates, the very and only foundation of our lives. It is necessary that each individual knowingly choose to base his life upon that same foundation taught by all the prophets and messengers sent by the Lord of all the worlds, rather than simply delving into the assorted secondary concerns and issues invited to by the various numerous parties, innovated movements, and groups. Indeed Sheikh al-Albaanee, may Allaah have mercy upon him, stated:

"... We unreservedly combat against this way of having various different parties and groups. As this false way- of group or organizational allegiances - conforms to the statement of Allaah the Most High, ❧ ***But they have broken their religion among them into sects, each group rejoicing in what is with it as its beliefs. And every party is pleased with whatever they stand with.*** ❧*—(Surah al-Mu'minoon: 53) And in truth they are no separate groups and parties in Islaam itself. There is only one true party, as is stated in a verse in the Qur'an,* ❧ ***Verily, it is the party of Allaah that will be the successful.*** ❧*—(Surah al-Mujadilaah: 58). The party of Allaah are those people who stand with the Messenger of Allaah, may Allaah's praise and salutations be upon him, meaning that an individual proceeds upon the methodology of the Companions of the Messenger. Due to this we call for having sound knowledge of the Book and the Sunnah."*

(Knowledge Based Issues & Sharee'ah Rulings: The Rulings of The Guiding Scholar Sheikh Muhammad Naasiruddeen al-Albaanee Made in the City of Medina & In the Emirates – [Emiratee Fatwa no 114. P.30])

Two Essential Foundations

Secondly, building upon the above foundation, our commitment is to contributing publications and works which reflect the inherited message and methodology of the acknowledged scholars of the many various branches of Sharee'ah knowledge who stood upon the straight path of preserved guidance in every century and time since the time of our Messenger, may Allaah's praise and salutations be upon him. These people of knowledge, who are the inheritors of the Final Messenger, have always adhered closely to the two revealed sources of guidance: the Book of Allaah and the Sunnah of the Messenger of Allaah- may Allaah's praise and salutations be upon him, upon the united consensus, standing with the body of guided Muslims in every century - preserving and transmitting the true religion generation after generation. Indeed the Messenger of Allaah, may Allaah's praise and salutations be upon him, informed us that, *{ A group of people amongst my Ummah will remain obedient to Allaah's orders. They will not be harmed by those who leave them nor by those who oppose them, until Allaah's command for the Last Day comes upon them while they remain on the right path. }* (Authentically narrated in Saheeh al-Bukhaaree).

We live in an age in which the question frequently asked is, *"How do we make Islaam a reality?"* and perhaps the related and more fundamental question is, *"What is Islaam?"*, such that innumerable different voices quickly stand to offer countless different conflicting answers through books, lectures, and every available form of modern media. Yet the only true course of properly understanding this question and its answer- for ourselves and our families -is to return to the criterion given to us by our beloved Messenger, may Allaah's praise and salutations be upon him. Indeed the Messenger of Allaah, may Allaah's praise and salutations be upon him, indicated in an authentic narration, clarifying the matter beyond doubt, that the only "Islaam" which enables one to be truly successful and saved in this world and the next is as he said, *{...that which I am upon and my Companions are upon today.}* (authentically narrated in Jaam'ea at-Tirmidhee) referring to that Islaam which was stands upon unchanging revealed knowledge. While every other changed and altered form of Islaam, whether through some form of extremism or negligence, or through the addition or removal of something, regardless of whether that came from a good intention or an evil one- is not the religion that Allaah informed us about of when He revealed, ❧ *This day, those who disbelieved have given up all hope of your religion; so fear them not, but fear Me. This day, I have perfected your religion for you, completed My Favor upon you, and have chosen for you Islaam as your religion.*❧—(Surah al-Maa'edah: 3)

The guiding scholar Sheikh al-Albaanee, may have mercy upon him, said,

"...And specifically mentioning those among the callers who have taken upon themselves the guiding of the young Muslim generation upon Islaam, working to educate them with its education, and to socialize them with its culture. Yet they themselves have generally not attempted to unify their understanding of those matters about Islaam regarding which the people of Islaam today differ about so severely.

And the situation is certainly not as is falsely supposed by some individuals from among them who are heedless or negligent - that the differences that exist among them are only in secondary

matters without entering into or affecting the fundamental issues or principles of the religion; and the examples to prove that this is not true are numerous and recognized by those who have studied the books of the many differing groups and sects, or by the one who has knowledge of the various differing concepts and beliefs held by the Muslims today."(Mukhtasir al-'Uloo Lil'Alee al-Ghafaar, page 55)

Similarly he, may Allaah have mercy upon him, explained:

"Indeed, Islaam is the only solution, and this statement is something which the various different Islamic groups, organizations, and movements could never disagree about. And this is something which is from the blessings of Allaah upon the Muslims. However there are significant differences between the different Islamic groups, organizations, and movements that are present today regarding that domain which working within will bring about our rectification. What is that area of work to endeavor within, striving to restore a way of life truly reflecting Islaam, renewing that system of living which comes from Islaam, and in order to establish the Islamic government? The groups and movements significantly differ upon this issue or point. Yet we hold that it is required to begin with the matters of tasfeeyah –clarification, and tarbeeyah -education and cultivation, with both of them being undertaken together.

As if we were to start with the issue of governing and politics, then it has been seen that those who occupy themselves with this focus firstly posses beliefs which are clearly corrupted and ruined, and secondly that their personal behavior, from the aspect of conforming to Islaam, is very far from conforming to the actual guidance of the Sharee'ah. While those who first concern themselves with working just to unite the people and gather the masses together under a broad banner of the general term "Islaam", then it is seen that within the minds of those speakers who raise such calls -in reality there is fact no actual clear understanding of what Islaam is. Moreover, the understanding they have of Islaam has no significant impact in starting to change and reform their own lives. Due to this reason you find that many such individuals from here and there, who hold this perspective, are unable to truly realize or reflect Islaam even in areas of their own personal lives in matters which it is in fact easily possible for them to implement. As he holds that no one - regardless of whether it is because of his arrogance or pridefulness - can enter into directing him in an area of his personal life!

Yet at the same time these same individuals are raising their voices saying, "Judgment is only for Allaah!" and "It is required that judgment of affairs be according to what Allaah revealed." And this is indeed a true statement. But the one who does not possess something certainly cannot give or offer it to others. The majority of Muslims today have not established the judgment of Allaah fully upon themselves, yet they still seek from others to establish the judgment of Allaah within their governments...

...And I understand that this issue or subject is not immune from there being those who oppose our methodology of tasfeeyah and tarbeeyah. As there is the one who would say, "But establishing this tasfeeyah and tarbeeyah is a matter which requires many long years!" So, I respond by saying, this is not an important consideration in this matter, what is important is that we carry out what we have been commanded to do within our religion and by our Mighty Lord. What is important is that we begin by properly understanding our religion first and foremost. After this is accomplished then it will not be important whether the road itself is long or short.

And indeed I direct this statement of mine towards those men who are callers to the religion among the Muslims, and towards the scholars and those who direct our affairs. I call for them to stand upon complete knowledge of true Islaam, and to fight against every form of negligence and heedlessness regarding the religion, and against differing and disputes, as Allaah has said, *❮...and do not dispute with one another for fear that you lose courage and your strength departs ❯—(Surah Al-Anfaal: 46).*

(Quoted from the work, 'The Life of Sheikh al-Albaanee, His Influence in Present Day Fields of Sharee'ah Knowledge, & the Praise of the Scholars for Him.' volume 1 page 380-385)

The guiding scholar Sheikh Zayd al-Madkhalee, may Allaah protect him, stated in his writing, 'The Well Established Principles of the Way of the First Generations of Muslims: It's Enduring & Excellent Distinct Characteristics' that,

"From among these principles and characteristics is that the methodology of tasfeeyah -or clarification, and tarbeeyah -or education and cultivation- is clearly affirmed and established as a true way coming from the first three generations of Islaam, and is something well known to the people of true merit from among them, as is concluded by considering all the related evidence. What is intended by tasfeeyah, when referring to it generally, is clarifying that which is the truth from that which is falsehood, what is goodness from that which is harmful and corrupt, and when referring to its specific meanings it is distinguishing the noble Sunnah of the Prophet and the people of the Sunnah from those innovated matters brought into the religion and the people who are supporters of such innovations.

As for what is intended by tarbeeyah, it is calling all of the creation to take on the manners and embrace the excellent character invited to by that guidance revealed to them by their Lord through His worshiper and Messenger Muhammad, may Allaah's praise and salutations be upon him; so that they might have good character, manners, and behavior. As without this they cannot have a good life, nor can they put right their present condition or their final destination. And we seek refuge in Allaah from the evil of not being able to achieve that rectification."

Thus the methodology of the people of standing upon the Prophet's Sunnah, and proceeding upon the 'way of the believers' in every century is reflected in a focus and concern with these two essential matters: tasfeeyah or clarification of what is original, revealed message from the Lord of all the worlds, and tarbeeyah or education and raising of ourselves, our families, and our communities, and our lands upon what has been distinguished to be that true message and path.

Methodology:

The Roles of the Scholars & General Muslims In Raising the New Generation

The priority and focus of the 'Nakhlah Educational Series' is reflected within in the following statements of Sheikh al-Albaanee, may Allaah have mercy upon him:

"As for the other obligation, then I intend by this the education of the young generation upon

Islaam purified from all of those impurities we have mentioned, giving them a correct Islamic education from their very earliest years, without any influence of a foreign, disbelieving education."

(Silsilat al-Hadeeth ad-Da'eefah, Introduction page 2.)

"...And since the Messenger of Allaah, may Allaah's praise and salutations be upon him, has indicated that the only cure to remove this state of humiliation that we find ourselves entrenched within, is truly returning back to the religion. Then it is clearly obligatory upon us - through the people of knowledge- to correctly and properly understand the religion in a way that conforms to the sources of the Book of Allaah and the Sunnah, and that we educate and raise a new virtuous, righteous generation upon this."

(Clarification and Cultivation and the Need of the Muslims for Them)

It is essential in discussing our perspective upon this obligation of raising the new generation of Muslims, that we highlight and bring attention to a required pillar of these efforts as indicated by Sheikh al-Albaanee, may Allaah have mercy upon him, and others- in the golden words, *"through the people of knowledge"*. Since something we commonly experience today is that many people have various incorrect understandings of the role that the scholars should have in the life of a Muslim, failing to understand the way in which they fulfill their position as the inheritors of the Messenger of Allaah, may Allaah's praise and salutations be upon him, and stand as those who preserve and enable us to practice the guidance of Islaam. Indeed, the noble Imaam Sheikh as-Sa'dee, may Allaah have mercy upon him, in his work, *"A Definitive and Clear Explanation of the Work 'A Triumph for the Saved Sect'"* pages 237-240, has explained this crucial issue with an extraordinary explanation full of remarkable benefits:

"Section: Explaining the Conditions for These Two Source Texts to Suffice You -or the Finding of Sufficiency in these Two Sources of Revelation.

Overall the conditions needed to achieve this and bring it about return to two matters:

Firstly, the presence of the requirements necessary for achieving this; meaning a complete devotion to the Book and the Sunnah, and the putting forth of efforts both in seeking to understand their intended meanings, as well as in striving to be guided by them. What is required secondly is the pushing away of everything which prevents achieving this finding of sufficiency in them.

This is through having a firm determination to distance yourself from everything which contradicts these two source texts in what comes from the historical schools of jurisprudence, assorted various statements, differing principles and their resulting conclusions which the majority of people proceed upon. These matters which contradict the two sources of revelation include many affairs which, when the worshiper of Allaah repels them from himself and stands against them, the realm of his knowledge, understanding, and deeds then expands greatly. Through a devotion to them and a complete dedication towards these two sources of revelation, proceeding upon every path which assists one's understanding them, and receiving enlightenment from the light of the scholars and being guided by the guidance that they possess- you will achieve that complete sufficiency in them. And surely, in the positions they take towards the leading people of knowledge and the scholars, the people are three types of individuals:

The first of them is the one who goes to extremes in his attachment to the scholars. He makes their statements something which are infallible as if their words held the same position as those of the statements of the Messenger of Allaah, may Allaah's praise and salutations be upon him, as well as giving those scholars' statements precedence and predominance over the Book of Allaah and the Sunnah. This is despite the fact that every leading scholar who has been accepted by this Ummah was one who promoted and encouraged the following of the Book and the Sunnah, commanding the people not to follow their own statements nor their school of thought in anything which stood in opposition to the Book of Allaah and the Sunnah.

The second type is the one who generally rejects and invalidates the statements of the scholars and forbids the referring to the statements of the leading scholars of guidance and those people of knowledge who stand as brilliant lamps in the darkness. This type of person neither relies upon the light of discernment with the scholars, nor utilizes their stores of knowledge. Or even if perhaps they do so, they do not direct thanks towards them for this. And this manner and way prohibits them from tremendous good. Furthermore, that which motivates such individuals to proceed in this way is their falsely supposing that the obligation to follow the Messenger of Allaah, may Allaah's praise and salutations be upon him, and the giving of precedence to his statements over the statements of anyone else, requires that they do without any reliance upon the statements of the Companions, or those who followed them in goodness, or those leading scholars of guidance within the Ummah. And this is a glaring and extraordinary mistake.

As indeed the Companions and the people of knowledge are the means and the agency between the Messenger of Allaah, may Allaah's praise and salutations be upon him, and his Ummah- in the transmission and spreading his Sunnah in regard to both its wording and texts as well as its meanings and understanding. Therefore the one who follows them in what they convey in this is guided through their understandings, receives knowledge from the light they possess, benefits from the conclusions they have derived from these sources -of beneficial meanings and explanations, as well as in relation to subtle matters which scarcely occur to the minds of some of the other people of knowledge, or barely comes to be discerned by their minds. Consequently, from the blessing of Allaah upon this Ummah is that He has given them these guiding scholars who cultivate and educate them upon two clear types of excellent cultivation.

The first category is education from the direction of ones knowledge and understanding. They educate the Ummah upon the more essential and fundamental matters before the more complex affairs. They convey the meanings of the Book and the Sunnah to the minds and intellects of the people through efforts of teaching which rectifies, and through composing various beneficial books of knowledge which a worshiper doesn't even have the ability to adequately describe what is encompassed within them of aspects of knowledge and benefits. Works which reflect the presence of a clear white hand in deriving guidance from the Book of Allaah and the Sunnah, and through the arrangement, detailed clarification, division and explanation, through the gathering together of explanations, comparisons, conditions, pillars, and explanations about that which prevents the fulfillment of matters, as well as distinguishing between differing meanings and categorizing various knowledge based benefits.

The second category is education from the direction of ones conduct and actions. They cultivate the peoples characters encouraging them towards every praiseworthy aspect of good character, through explaining its ruling and high status, and what benefits comes to be realized from it, clarifying the reasons and paths which enable one to attain it, as well as those affairs which prevent, delay or hinder someone becoming one distinguished and characterized by it. Because they, in reality, are those who bring nourishment to the hearts and the souls; they are the doctors who treat the diseases of the heart and its defects. As such they educate the people through their statements, actions as well as their general guided way. Therefore the scholars have a tremendous right over this Ummah. The portion of love and esteem, respect and honor, and thanks due to them because their merits and their various good efforts stand above every other right after establishing the right of Allaah, and the right of His Messenger, may Allaah's praise and salutations be upon him.

Because of this, the third group of individuals in respect to the scholars are those who have been guided to understand their true role and position, and establish their rights, thanking them for their virtues and merits, benefiting by taking from the knowledge they have, while acknowledging their rank and status. They understand that the scholars are not infallible and that their statements must stand in conformance to the statements of the Messenger of Allaah, may Allaah's praise and salutations be upon him. And that each one from among them has that which is from guidance, knowledge, and correctness in his statements taken and benefited from, while turning away from whatever in mistaken within it.

Yet such a scholar is not to be belittled for his mistake, as he stands as one who strove to reach the truth; therefore his mistake will be forgiven, and he should be thanked for his efforts. One clarifies what was stated by of any one of these leaders from among men, when it is recognizes that it has some weakness or conflict to an evidence of the Sharee'ah, by explaining its weakness and the level of that weakness, without speaking evilly of the intention of those people of knowledge and religion, nor defaming them due to that error. Rather we say, as it is obligatory to say, "And those who came after them say: ❧ ***Our Lord! forgive us and our brethren who have preceded us in faith, and put not in our hearts any hatred against those who have believed. Our Lord! You are indeed full of kindness, Most Merciful.*** ❧ *-(Surah al-Hashr: 10).*

Accordingly, individuals of this third type are those who fulfill two different matters. They join together on one hand between giving precedence to the Book and the Sunnah over everything else, and, on the other hand, between comprehending the level and position of the scholars and the leading people of knowledge and guidance, and establishing this even if it is only done in regard to some of their rights upon us. So we ask Allaah to bless us to be from this type, and to make us from among the people of this third type, and to make us from those who love Him and love those who love Him, and those who love every action which brings us closer to everything He loves."

Upon this clarity regarding the proper understanding of our balanced position towards our guided Muslim scholars, consider the following words about the realm of work of the general people of faith, which explains our area of efforts and struggle as Muslim parents, found in the following statement by Sheikh Saaleh Fauzaan al-Fauzaan, may Allaah preserve him.

"*Question: Some people mistakenly believe that calling to Allaah is a matter not to be undertaken by anyone else other than the scholars without exception, and that it is not something required for other than the scholars according to that which they have knowledge of -to undertake any efforts of calling the people to Allaah. So what is your esteemed guidance regarding this?*" *The Sheikh responded by saying:*

"*This is not a misconception, but is in fact a reality. The call to Allaah cannot be established except through those who are scholars. And I state this. Yet, certainly there are clear issues which every person understands. As such, every individual should enjoin the good and forbid wrongdoing according to the level of his understanding. Such that he instructs and orders the members of his household to perform the ritual daily prayers and other matters that are clear and well known.*

*Undertaking this is something mandatory and required even upon the common people, such that they must command their children to perform their prayers in the masjid. The Messenger of Allaah, may Allaah praise and salutations be upon him, said, { **Command you children to pray at seven, and beat them due to its negligence at ten.**} (Authentic narration found in Sunan Abu Dawood). And the Messenger of Allaah, may Allaah praise and salutations be upon him, said, { **Each one of you is a guardian or a shepherd, and each of you is responsible for those under his guardianship....**} (Authentic narration found in Saheeh al-Bukhaaree). So this is called guardianship, and this is also called enjoining the good and forbidding wrongdoing. The Messenger of Allaah, may Allaah praise and salutations be upon him, said, { **The one from among you who sees a wrong should change it with his hand, and if he is unable to do so, then with his tongue, and if he is not able to do this, then with his heart.** } (Authentic narration found in Saheeh Muslim).*

So in relation to the common person, that which it is required from him to endeavor upon is that he commands the members of his household-as well as others -with the proper performance of the ritual prayers, the obligatory charity, with generally striving to obey Allaah, and to stay away from sins and transgressions, and that he purify and cleanse his home from disobedience, and that he educate and cultivate his children upon the obedience of Allaah's commands. This is what is required from him, even if he is a general person. As these types of matters are from that which is understood by every single person. This is something which is clear and apparent.

But as for the matters of putting forth rulings and judgments regarding matters in the religion, or entering into clarifying issues of what is permissible and what is forbidden, or explaining what is considered associating others in the worship due to Allaah and what is properly worshiping Him alone without any partner- then indeed these are matters which cannot be established except by the scholars"

(Beneficial Responses to Questions About Modern Methodologies, Question 15, page 22)

Similarly the guiding scholar Sheikh 'Abdul-'Azeez Ibn Baaz, may Allaah have mercy upon him, also emphasized this same overall responsibility:

"*...It is also upon a Muslim that he struggles diligently in that which will place his worldly affairs in a good state, just as he must also strive in the correcting of his religious affairs and the affairs of his own family. As the people of his household have a significant right over him that he strive diligently in rectifying their affair and guiding them towards goodness, due to the statement of Allaah, the*

Most Exalted, ❦ *Oh you who believe! Save yourselves and your families Hellfire whose fuel is men and stones* ❧ -(Surah at-Tahreem: 6)

So it is upon you to strive to correct the affairs of the members of your family. This includes your wife, your children- both male and female- and such as your own brothers. This concerns all of the people in your family, meaning you should strive to teach them the religion, guiding and directing them, and warning them from those matters Allaah has prohibited for us. Because you are the one who is responsible for them as shown in the statement of the Prophet, may Allaah's praise and salutations be upon him, *{ Every one of you is a guardian, and responsible for what is in his custody. The ruler is a guardian of his subjects and responsible for them; a husband is a guardian of his family and is responsible for it; a lady is a guardian of her husband's house and is responsible for it, and a servant is a guardian of his master's property and is responsible for it....}* Then the Messenger of Allaah, may Allaah's praise and salutations be upon him, continued to say, *{...so all of you are guardians and are responsible for those under your authority.}* (Authentically narrated in Saheeh al-Bukhaaree & Muslim)

It is upon us to strive diligently in correcting the affairs of the members of our families, from the aspect of purifying their sincerity of intention for Allaah's sake alone in all of their deeds, and ensuring that they truthfully believe in and follow the Messenger of Allaah, may Allaah's praise and salutations be upon him, their fulfilling the prayer and the other obligations which Allaah the Most Exalted has commanded for us, as well as from the direction of distancing them from everything which Allaah has prohibited.

It is upon every single man and women to give advice to their families about the fulfillment of what is obligatory upon them. Certainly, it is upon the woman as well as upon the man to perform this. In this way our homes become corrected and rectified in regard to the most important and essential matters. Allaah said to His Prophet, may Allaah's praise and salutations be upon him, ❦ *And enjoin the ritual prayers on your family...* ❧ (Surah Taha: 132) Similarly, Allaah the Most Exalted said to His prophet Ismaa'aeel, ❦ *And mention in the Book, Ismaa'aeel. Verily, he was true to what he promised, and he was a Messenger, and a Prophet. And he used to enjoin on his family and his people the ritual prayers and the obligatory charity, and his Lord was pleased with him.* ❧ -(Surah Maryam: 54-55)

As such, it is only proper that we model ourselves after the prophets and the best of people, and be concerned with the state of the members of our households. Do not be neglectful of them, oh worshipper of Allaah! Regardless of whether it is concerning your wife, your mother, father, grandfather, grandmother, your brothers, or your children; it is upon you to strive diligently in correcting their state and condition..."

(Collection of Various Rulings and Statements- Sheikh 'Abdul-'Azeez Ibn 'Abdullah Ibn Baaz, Vol. 6, page 47)

Content & Structure:

We hope to contribute works which enable every striving Muslim who acknowledges the proper position of the scholars, to fulfill the recognized duty and obligation which lays upon each one of us to bring the light of Islaam into our own lives as individuals as well as into our homes and among our families. Towards this goal we are committed to developing educational publications and comprehensive educational curriculums -through cooperation with and based upon the works of the scholars of Islaam and the students of knowledge. Works which, with the assistance of Allaah, the Most High, we can utilize to educate and instruct ourselves, our families and our communities upon Islaam in both principle and practice. The publications and works of the Nakhlah Educational Series are divided into the following categories:

Basic: Ages 4- 6

Elementary: Ages 6-11

Secondary: Ages 11-14

High School: Ages 14- Young Adult

General: Young Adult –Adult

Supplementary: All Ages

Publications and works within these stated levels will, with the permission of Allaah, encompass different beneficial areas and subjects, and will be offered in every permissible form of media and medium. As certainly, as the guiding scholar Sheikh Saaleh Fauzaan al-Fauzaan, may Allaah preserve him, has stated,

"Beneficial knowledge is itself divided into two categories. Firstly is that knowledge which is tremendous in its benefit, as it benefits in this world and continues to benefit in the Hereafter. This is religious Sharee'ah knowledge. And secondly, that which is limited and restricted to matters related to the life of this world, such as learning the processes of manufacturing various goods. This is a category of knowledge related specifically to worldly affairs.

…As for the learning of worldly knowledge, such as knowledge of manufacturing, then it is legislated upon us collectively to learn whatever the Muslims have a need for. Yet If they do not have a need for this knowledge, then learning it is a neutral matter upon the condition that it does not compete with or displace any areas of Sharee'ah knowledge…"

("Explanations of the Mistakes of Some Writers'", Pages 10-12)

So we strive always to remind ourselves and our brothers of this crucial point also indicated by Sheikh Sadeeq Ibn Hasan al-Qanoojee, may Allaah have mercy upon him, in: *'Abjad al-'Uloom'*, (page 89)

"…What is intended by knowledge in the mentioned hadeeth is knowledge of the religion and the distinctive Sharee'ah, knowledge of the Noble Book and the Pure Sunnah, of which there is no third along with them. But what is not meant in this narration are those invented areas of knowledge, whether they emerged in previous ages or today's world, which the people in these present times have devoted themselves to. They have specifically dedicated themselves to them in a manner

which prevents them from looking towards those areas of knowledge related to faith, and in a way which has preoccupied them from occupying themselves from what is actually wanted or desired by Allaah, the Most High, and His Messenger, who is the leader of men and Jinn. Such that the knowledge in the Qur'an has become something abandoned and the sciences of hadeeth have become obscure. While these new areas of knowledge related to manufacturing and production continually emerge from the nations of disbelief and apostasy, and they are called, "sciences", "arts", and "ideal development". And this sad state increases every day, indeed from Allaah we came and to Him shall we return....

...Additionally, although the various areas of beneficial knowledge all share some level of value, they all have differing importance and ranks. Among them is that which is to be considered according to its subject, such as medicine, and its subject is the human body. Or such as the sciences of 'tafseer' and its subject is the explanation of the words of Allaah, the Most Exalted and Most High, and the value of these two areas is not in any way unrecognized.

And from among the various areas there are those areas which are considered according to their objective, such as knowledge of upright character, and its goal is understanding the beneficial merits that an individual can come to possess. And from among them there are those areas which are considered according to the people's need for them, such as 'fiqh' which the need for it is urgent and essential. And from among them there are those areas which are considered according to their apparent strength, such as knowledge of physical sports and exercise, as it is something openly demonstrated.

And from the areas of knowledge are those areas which rise in their position of importance through their combining all these different matters within them, or the majority of them. Such as revealed religious knowledge, as its subject is indeed esteemed, its objective one of true merit, and its need is undeniably felt. Likewise one area of knowledge may be considered of superior rank than another in consideration of the results that it brings forth, or the strength of its outward manifestation, or due to the essentialness of its objective. Similarly the result that an area produces is certainly of higher estimation and significance in appraisal than the outward or apparent significance of some other areas of knowledge.

For that reason the highest ranking and most valuable area of knowledge is that of knowledge of Allaah the Most Perfect and the Most High, of His angels, and messengers, and all the particulars of these beliefs, as its result is that of eternal and continuing happiness."

We ask Allaah, the most High to bless us with success in contributing to the many efforts of our Muslim brothers and sisters committed to raising themselves as individuals and the next generation of our children upon that Islaam which Allaah has perfected and chosen for us, and which He has enabled the guided Muslims to proceed upon in each and every century. We ask him to forgive us, and forgive the Muslim men and the Muslim women, and to guide all the believers to everything He loves and is pleased with. The success is from Allaah, The Most High The Most Exalted, alone and all praise is due to Him.

Abu Sukhailah Khalil Ibn-Abelahyi
Taalib al-Ilm Educational Resources

GENERAL ANNOUNCEMENT:

Taalib al-Ilm Educational Publications is looking for
Distributors & Publication Contributors

Distributors:

We are working to make Taalib al-Ilm Education Resources publications available through distributors worldwide. As of 1433 h./2012 c.e. we offer local shipping from North America (United States), Europe & Africa (UK), & South East Asia (Australia), for soft cover, hardcover, as well as ebooks online. We offer quantity discounts worldwide including North and South America, Europe and U.K., Africa, and Asia, on all quantity printed purchases by individuals, masjids, Islamic centers, local study groups, Muslim homeschooling groups, conference vendors, and retail stores according to the following discount scale:

10% discount for order of	**USD**	**$100** or over
20% discount for order of	**USD**	**$200** or over
30% discount for order of	**USD**	**$500** or over
40% discount for order of	**USD**	**$1000** or over
50% discount for order of	**USD**	**$2000** or over

All new distributors receive an additional **10% discount** on any of the above discount levels for their **FIRST OR INITIAL ORDER ONLY**. For further information, please contact the sales department by e-mail: ***service@taalib.com***.

Publication Contributors:

Additionally, in an effort to further expand our publication library, we are seeking contributing authors, translators, and compilers with beneficial works of any area of Sharee'ah knowledge for submission of their works for potential publication by us. For details and all submission guidelines please email us at: ***service@taalib.com***

> **Referral bonus:** *Individuals who refer a new distributor or publication contributor to us can receive a **$25 PayPal payment**, upon a confirmed contract with a publication contributor or receipt of a newly referred distributor's initial order at the 40% discount level. Contact us for further information and conditions.*

Fundamentals of Arabic Class for Women Only

An Online Class for Muslim Women Taught by a Muslim Woman

Developed and Taught by Umm Mujaahid Khadijah Bint Lacina al-Amreekiyyah

[Available: **TBA**¦ Schedule: **Live Class Three times Weekly** ¦ price: **$60 Monthly** USD]
Course Includes All Materials In EBook Format

Course Features:

* Four Levels of Study & Supplementary Courses

* Limited class size

* Class meets online three times a week with the teacher

* Class moves at a moderate pace to ensure understanding of the concepts presented

* Begins with a short review of the Arabic alphabet, stressing correct pronunciation

* Grammar, morphology, and writing fundamentals

* Focus on understanding what is read and spoken

* Encompasses both speech and understanding

* Numerous exercises, both in class and out, to increase understanding and ability

* Practice in taking notes from Arabic lectures and simple translation

* Additional Out of class assignments and group projects

* Comprehensive reviews

* Periodic quizzes and tests

* End of class test will determine if one can advance to the next class

* Textbooks, dictionaries, and supplementary materials provided as ebooks

* Use of hadeeth texts and other Islamic material for reading,
understanding and translation exercises

* Class forum to make asking questions and doing group assignments easier

* The teacher will be available through email
to answer course questions and assist the students regularly

For more information about availability please visit
arabicforwomen.taalib.com

Please visit **study.taalib.com** *for information concerning other free and fee-based courses.*

BOOK PUBLICATION PREVIEW:

Al-Waajibaat: The Obligatory Matters
What it is Decreed that Every Male and Female Muslim Must Have Knowledge Of
-from the statements of Sheikh al-Islaam Muhammad ibn 'Abdul-Wahaab
(A Step By Step Course on The Fundamental Beliefs of Islaam- with Lesson Questions, Quizzes, & Exams)

Collected and Arranged by Umm Mujaahid Khadijah Bint Lacina al-Amreekiyyah

Available: **Now - Self Study/ Teachers Edition** pages: 250+ ¦ price: (S) **$17.50** (H) **$25**¦
Directed Study Edition pages: 190+ ¦ price: **$15** - **Exercise Workbook** pages: 100+ ¦ price: **$7**

Table of Contents:

BOOK PUBLICATION PREVIEW:

Statements of the Guiding Scholars of Our Age Regarding Books & their Advice to the Beginner Seeker of Knowledge

with Selections from the Following Scholars:

Sheikh 'Abdul-'Azeez ibn 'Abdullah ibn Baaz -Sheikh Muhammad ibn Saaleh al-'Utheimein - Sheikh Muhammad Naasiruddeen al-Albaanee - Sheikh Muqbil ibn Haadee al-Waada'ee - Sheikh 'Abdur-Rahman ibn Naaser as-Sa'adee - Sheikh Muhammad 'Amaan al-Jaamee - Sheikh Muhammad al-Ameen as-Shanqeetee - Sheikh Ahmad ibn Yahya an-Najmee

(May Allaah have mercy upon them.) &

Sheikh Saaleh al-Fauzaan ibn 'Abdullah al-Fauzaan - Sheikh Saaleh ibn 'Abdul-'Azeez Aal-Sheikh - Sheikh Muhammad ibn 'Abdul-Wahhab al-Wasaabee -Permanent Committee to Scholastic Research & Issuing Of Islamic Rulings

(May Allaah preserve them.)

With an introduction by: Sheikh Muhammad Ibn 'Abdullah al-Imaam
Collected and Translated by Abu Sukhailah Khalil Ibn-Abelahyi al-Amreekee

[Available: **Now** ¦ pages: 350+ ¦ price: (S) **$25** (H) **$32** ¦ eBook **$9.99**]

Summarized Table of Contents (A Selection of Some Questions)

Guidance and Direction for Every Male and Female Muslim

The revival of Islaam that we are witnessing: is it simply a reaction to the present corruption and far from Allaah's true way as some have portrayed it? Or is it founded and based upon that which will produce true results, if Allaah wills? * What is the correct and sound position to be adopted by the scholar, the student of knowledge, and the caller to Allaah in relation to the modern day groups, parties, and "Islamic" organizations? * Examine, may Allaah have mercy upon you, everything you hear from the people of your age. * Proceed with Caution, Oh caller to the 'Renewal' of the Religion! * Four questions regarding the terms 'Islamic thought' and 'freedom of thought' * Regarding Knowledge: Its Merits, and which Knowledge is Considered Obligatory * The Prophet Sought Refuge From Knowledge Which Does Not Benefit & Knowledge is of Two Types * The Categories of Knowledge and the Rulings Regarding them & The Ruling of Learning these Various Branches * Esteemed Sheikh please inform us about the concept of deriving rulings directly from the evidences, and the concept of blind following. What is meant by blind following and what is meant by a scholar independently deriving rulings? Was blind following present in the age of the Companions? and the next generation of the Successors to the Companions? Did some of them blindly follow others from among them in Sharee'ah rulings or not?' * What is the description of those scholars whom we should be guided by? * The Reasons for the Weakness of the Muslims in the Face of their Enemies & the Means to Cure This

Golden Advice that Benefits the Beginner Regarding Acquiring Knowledge

Should we begin with seeking knowledge or with calling to Allaah? * I want to seek Sharee'ah knowledge and begin studying; however, I don't know how to begin. What do you advise me in this regard? * For the beginning student of knowledge, for example in America, what is your advice regarding those books that he should begin with and then those to proceed to step-by-step? * With what do you advise the one who wants to seek Sharee'ah knowledge but he lives far away from the scholars, knowing, however, that he has a collection of books containing both complete books as well as summarized books? * With what do you advise the one who begins seeking knowledge when he is older in age? Additionally, if it is not easy for him to take knowledge from and sit often with a scholar, will he benefit from seeking knowledge without a scholar? * I have been seeking knowledge for some time; however I do not see its results upon myself or upon my family except to a small degree. So what is the reason for this, and what is the remedy for this situation? * What is best for the students of knowledge: to devote themselves completely to seeking knowledge, and then afterwards fully dedicate themselves to spreading knowledge among the people, inviting their neighbors and those around them to Allaah? Or is it better to seek knowledge for perhaps a month and then to stop studying, due to the need to engage in calling to Allaah and so proceed according to the limits of the knowledge one has acquired? * What are those matters within the methodology of the People of the Sunnah and the Jama'ah which it is permissible to differ in, while giving advice to each other remains; and which matters is it is not permissible for us to differ in? Is it permissible to differ in regards to the basic correct belief, or with the different issues of belief? In what source work can we find a simple clarification of this? * What is the proper way for the student of knowledge to act in situations where there is a difference of opinion in knowledge based issues, in order that unity is maintained between our hearts and conflicts are avoided? * What characteristics should be found within the one whom you wish to take knowledge from? * Are audio cassettes considered a method from the methods of acquiring knowledge? And what ways, for example, can we benefit from them? * The Ideological War: Its Characteristics, Methods & the Required Response to It * What is the Islamic ruling on reading daily newspapers and publications, or magazines, for the purpose of getting societal, Islamic, governmental, or cultural news in order to understand what is going on around us? * Is it permissible for someone to leave working in order to devote himself to seeking knowledge, while the responsibility of his family is upon his father and his brother? * If a student of knowledge receives discouragement regarding his efforts from his family, his wife, and some of his close relatives, what will assist him in shielding himself from this? * Is it permissible for the proficient student of knowledge to declare someone a person of innovation or to declare that someone has in reality abandoned Islaam, or is this a matter exclusively for the scholars? * Is it for the beginning student of knowledge to put forth criticism or praise regarding individuals, or to declare people to be innovators in the religion without relying upon evidence? * Oh Abu 'Abdur-Rahman, we need for you to inform us how you organize your time in seeking knowledge. When do you do your research, when do you teach your brothers, and how many lessons do you have during a day and a night? And we ask Allaah for sincerity of intention for you and for ourselves. * A Basic Summary of the Behavior and Manners of Scholars and Students * If Allaah grants someone success in their efforts of seeking beneficial knowledge and then they return to their land, how should they begin calling to Allaah?

Beneficial Guidance for Female Students of Sharee'ah Knowledge

What is the Sharee'ah knowledge that it is obligatory upon a woman to learn? * What do you say regarding women and calling to Allaah? * What is the Islamic ruling for a woman who fulfills all the conditions of seeking knowledge within her home, but despite this, she goes to the masjid to meet her sisters in faith or to convey to them knowledge that she has? * If a woman seeks knowledge in the masjid, when she returns home she needs to review what she has learned at the masjid and this takes considerable time. But she knows that work in her home waits for her as she assists her mother in the home. The affairs of her home take all of her time and seeking knowledge needs full dedication from her. So if she is occupied in her home, she is not able to acquire a great deal of knowledge. How can she reconcile between her commitment to her home and her dedication to seeking knowledge? * A woman studies within her home and she prefers to remain in her home- not even going out to the masjid. Is she better, or the woman who seeks knowledge outside and visits different masjids? * What is the ideal example of calling to Allaah by women?

Guidance from the Scholars Regarding Important Books to Acquire for Seeking Knowledge

Is it permissible to learn the religion solely from books without the scholars, specifically in the situation when it is difficult to learn from the hands of the scholars because of their scarcity? In addition, what is your view regarding the one who says, 'The one whose teacher is his book his errors are greater than that which he is correct in?' * We see that some people do not give importance to seeking knowledge from the hands of the scholars and are satisfied with studying books in their homes. They argue that Sheikh al-Albaanee (may Allaah the exalted preserve him) was able to reach the level of knowledge that he possesses solely by means of reading, not by means of taking from the scholars themselves. Is this correct and with what do you advise the one who says this? * We live in Britain and are from Ahlus-Sunnah wa al-Jama'ah. However, we do not have any scholars among us; also we only have a few translated books and these are not in the areas of fiqh or the explanation of the Qur'aan. So how should we study, using an acceptable methodology of study, upon the way of the people of the Sunnah and the Jama'ah? What do you advise us in regard to this? * We find that some of the common people and some of the students of knowledge make statements regarding Sharee'ah issues, while not being from the people possessing knowledge of these matters. Then these misguided statements spread among the general people and circulate among them. We need from you, our esteemed scholar, a clarification regarding this issue, so by Allaah what is your view of this? * It is commonly said among some of the people that the one who does not have a scholar, Shaytaan is his scholar. So what is your guidance for them, Esteemed Sheikh? * Which books do you advise us to read in the subject of correct beliefs, the explanation of the Qur'aan, hadeeth narrations and their related sciences, and in the subject of fiqh? * What are considered the most authentic books after the Noble Qur'aan? * Books of Guidance and Books of Misguidance. * What are those books a student of knowledge should begin with, and then those to proceed on to? * Oh Sheikh, we hope that you would name for us some of the books in conformance with the methodology of the first three generations of Islaam that it is proper for the youth upon that clear way to acquire and for him to place within his home library? * We require a good method for reading books. Is it enough to read them a single time or is it necessary to reread books? And if this is indeed necessary, how is this possible considering the large number of books? * Guidelines for Gathering and Maintaining a Beneficial Library * What are the most authentic books through which we know the transmitted accounts from the lives of the Successors of the Companions? * What is the ruling of the Sharee'ah regarding explanations of the Qur'aan known as scientific explanations? And what is the proper Sharee'ah guided relationship between verses of the Qur'aan and matters of scientific research, as there is much controversy regarding this issue? * Notes Regarding the Best Books taken from the Statements of Sheikh Muqbil * Beneficial Notes Regarding Books

The Warning of the Scholars from the Books of those who have Deviated & the Means and Ways of Going Astray

*What are the guidelines regarding reading the books of the innovators in the religion or listening to their tapes, if they contain benefit? Is it permissible for the common person to listen to the tapes of the preachers from among the innovators, or the people of division and group partisanship, or others similar to them? * As for those who previously were considered to be upon the correct methodology and then deviated from it, is it permissible for us to listen to their tapes or to read their books that they had written in the past, and similarly their recorded lectures? * We observe that some of those who associate themselves with the methodology of the first three generations occupy themselves with criticisms and warning from the astray groups and sects and neglect seeking knowledge, whereas others among them give priority to seeking knowledge and leave the matter of warnings and criticisms. This is such that it has reached the state where those of the second group say, 'Certainly, criticizing is not from the methodology of the people of the Sunnah at all.' So what is correct in this issue? * What is the difference between a statement of criticism and giving advice? * What are the reference books of the people of the Sunnah which are turned to in order to refute the people of innovation in the religion regarding those matters in which they have differed with the people of the Sunnah? * From where do we obtain beneficial knowledge?*

Clear Statements from the Scholars' Advice Regarding Memorizing Knowledge

*What is the correct way of seeking knowledge? Is it to memorize the texts of the different Sharee'ah sciences, or simply to understand them without memorization? We hope for your guidance regarding this, may Allaah the Exalted preserve you. * Which is better for the student of knowledge: to begin with the study of the explanations of the Noble Qur'aan, or the memorization of hadeeth texts or studying the correct understanding and fundamental principles of these two? * I am a young man who is almost thirty years old, and I have not completely memorized the Book of Allaah. But I have not ceased being consistent in my memorization, and I ask Allaah for success. Is it better in my efforts to seek knowledge, to memorize the book of Allaah completely, and after completing that to then seek general Sharee'ah knowledge, or to combine between seeking knowledge and memorizing the Qur'aan? * Please guide me to the way that will assist me in memorizing the Book of Allaah. * What is the ruling about the one who recites Qur'aan but makes mistakes in the pronunciation of short vowels? Will he be rewarded for such a recitation? * What is the correct way to memorize the Qur'aan and the ahaadeeth? * Which books explaining the meaning of the Qur'aan do you recommend that we read? Also, regarding memorization of the Qur'aan, if a person memorizes and then forgets is there any harm in that? So how can a person memorize and preserve what he has memorized? * What are the causes that assist the student of knowledge in memorization, may Allaah bless you with good? * Preserving Knowledge by Means of Writing it Down * Reviewing what you have Learned Preserves Knowledge*

Issues Related to the Verifiers of Books in our Age

Can we take from the book verifications of Shu'ayb al-Arnout and his brother? Along with the many people who verify the books from our righteous predecessors in this age; there are some verifiers who initially brought forth books in which are found beneficial points regarding general knowledge and correct belief. Then after they became well known among the ranks of youth, they began to bring forth strange statements and inconsistencies. How can the youth deal with this situation where there is little or no warning from the scholars regarding these shortcomings? From these verifiers, as an example, is the Sheikh 'Abdul-Qadir al-Arnaa'out and his verification of "Aqaawel at-Thiqaat" of Karemee. We benefit from his introduction in relation to issues of correct belief and his refutation the distortion of the source texts by Asha'ree sect.

However in contrast to this, in his comments within "Saheeh Ibn Hibbaan", he brings forth similar distortions as them of some attributes of Allaah and legitimizes it. So we hope for a warning from these errors, and that you clarify for us the condition and level of some of the authors and verifiers in our time.

BOOK PUBLICATION PREVIEW:

My Hijaab, My Path

A Comprehensive Knowledge Based Compilation on Muslim Women's Role & Dress

Collected and Translated by Umm Mujaahid Khadijah Bint Lacina al-Amreekiyyah

[Available: **Now**¦ pages: **190+** ¦ price: (S) **$17.50** (H) **$25**

Table of Contents:

My Home, My Path

A Comprehensive Source Book For Today's Muslim Woman Discussing Her Essential Role & Contribution To The Establishment of Islaam – Taken From The Words Of The People Of Knowledge

Collected and Translated by Umm Mujaahid Khadijah Bint Lacina al-Amreekiyyah

[Available: **Now**¦ pages: **380+** ¦ price: (S) **$22.50** (H) **$29.50** eBook **$9.99**]

Table of Contents:

BOOK PUBLICATION PREVIEW:

Thalaathatu al-Usool: The Three Fundamental Principles
A Step by Step Educational Course on Islaam
Based upon Commentaries of 'Thalaathatu al-Usool' of Sheikh Muhammad ibn 'Abdul Wahaab
(may Allaah have mercy upon him)

Collected and Arranged by Umm Mujaahid Khadijah Bint Lacina al-Amreekiyyah

[Available: **Now Self Study/ Teachers Edition** pages: 350+ ¦ price: (S) **$22.50** (H) **$29.50** ¦ eBook **$9.99**]
Directed Study Edition ¦ price: (S) **$17** - **Exercise Workbook** ¦ price: (S) **$10**]

Description:

*A complete course for the Believing men and women who want to learn their religion from the ground up, building a firm foundation upon which to base their actions. This is the **second** in our **Foundation Series** on Islamic beliefs and making them a reality in your life, which began with*
"al-Waajibaat: The Obligatory Matters".
The course utilizes various commentaries of Sheikh Muhammad ibn 'Abdul Wahaab's original text from the following scholars of our age:

Sheikh Muhammad ibn Saalih al-'Utheimeen
Sheikh Saaleh Ibn Sa'd as-Suhaaymee
Sheikh 'Abdul-'Azeez Ibn Baaz
Sheikh Saalih al-Fauzaan
Sheikh 'Abdullah ibn Saalih al-Fauzaan
Sheikh Muhammad 'Amaan al-Jaamee
Sheikh Saalih Aal-Sheikh (and others)

In addition to various statements of scholars of the Sunnah throughout the centuries

Course Features:

'Thalaathatu al-Usool' Arabic text and translation
Twenty-five lessons which discuss such vital topics as "Who is your Lord?"- "Who is your Prophet?"- "What is your religion?"- tawheed -shirk -the pillars of Islaam -the pillars of faith -having allegiance to the believers and how to deal with them, as well as the disbelievers -commanding the good and forbidding the evil -emigration to the lands of Islaam -and many many more. -advice and insight on how to make Islaam a reality in your life -how to put into practice all that you learn in this course Review questions and vocabulary after each chapter as well as quizzes and tests A compilation of points of benefit found throughout the book

(Support and discussion group for students at www.taalib.com)

The Cure, The Explanation, The Clear Affair, & The Brilliantly Distinct Signpost

A Step by Step Educational Course on Islaam
Based upon Commentaries of

'Usul as-Sunnah' of Imaam Ahmad
(may Allaah have mercy upon him)

Compiled and Translated by: Abu Sukhailah Khalil Ibn-Abelahyi

[Available: TBA ¦ price: TBA (Multi-volume) ¦ Size: **7.44"x9.69"** soft cover, hard cover, ebook]

A vital learning tool for striving, adult Muslims to learn their religion. The course is based upon various commentaries of Imaam Ahmad ibn Hanbal's original text, may Allaah have mercy upon him, from the following scholars of our age, may Allaah preserve them all:

- Sheikh Zayd Ibn Muhammad al-Madhlhalee
- Sheikh Saleeh Ibn Sa'd As-Suhaaymee
- Sheikh 'Abdul-'Azeez Ibn 'Abdullah ar-Raajeehee
- Sheikh 'Abdullah Al-Ghudayaan
- Sheikh Rabee'a Ibn Haadee al-Madhlhalee
- Sheikh Sa'd Ibn Naasir as-Shathree
- Sheikh 'Ubayd Ibn 'Abdullah al-Jabaaree
- Sheikh 'Abdullah Al-Bukharee
- Sheikh Hamaad Uthmaan
- Sheikh Falaah Ibn Ismaa'eel Mundaakir

In addition to various statements of scholars of the Sunnah throughout the centuries

Course Features:

Study of text divided into chapters formatted into multiple short lessons to facilitate learning . Each lesson has: evidence summary, lesson benefits, standard & review exercises 'Usul as-Sunnah' Arabic text & translation divided for easier memorization. A tool to understandings many of the most important beliefs of Islaam, as well as how to implement them and avoid common mistakes and misunderstandings.

BOOK PUBLICATION PREVIEW:

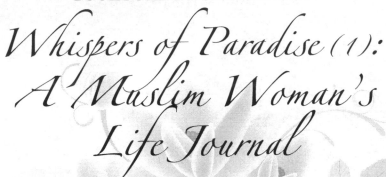

Whispers of Paradise (1): A Muslim Woman's Life Journal

An Islamic Daily Journal Which Encourages Reflection & Rectification

Collected and Edited by Taalib al-Ilm Educational Resources Development Staff

---

Abu Alee ath-Thaqafee said: Abu Hafs used to say:

"The one who does not each moment weigh his situation and condition against the scale of the Book of Allaah and the Sunnah, and does not question his very footsteps, then he is not to be considered worthy."

(Seyaar 'Alaam an-Nubala: vol. 12, page 512)

[Available: **Now** ¦ pages: **380+** ¦ price: (S) **$25** (H) **$32** ¦

[Elegantly designed edition is for the year 1434 / 2013]

Contents:

Publishers Introduction

12 Monthly calendar pages with beneficial quotations from Ibn Qayyim

Daily journal page based upon Islamic calendar (with corresponding C.E. dates)

Each daily journal page starts with one of the following:

-A Verse from the Noble Qur'an
-An Authentic Narration of the Messenger of Allaah
-An Authentic Supplication
-A Beneficial Point from a Biography of the Early Generations
-A Beneficial Statement from One of the Well Known Scholars, Past or Present

Additional Book Notes

Additional Book Notes

Additional Book Notes

Additional Book Notes